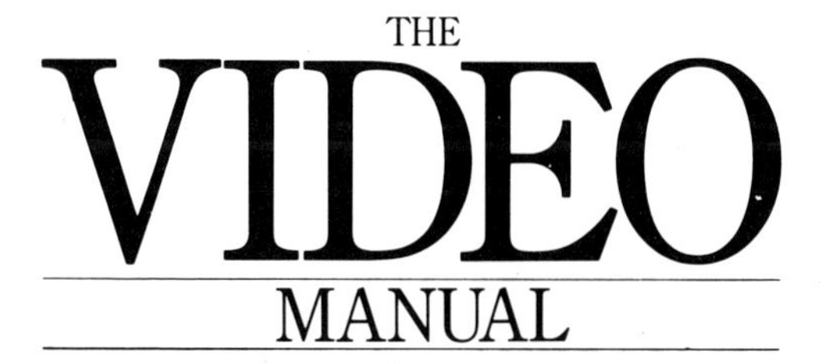
THE
VIDEO
MANUAL

THE

VIDEO

MANUAL

DAVID CHESHIRE

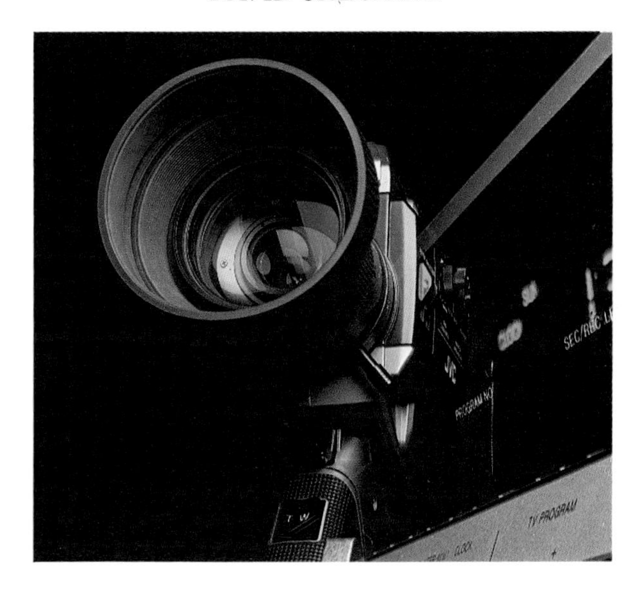

VNR VAN NOSTRAND REINHOLD COMPANY
NEW YORK CINCINNATI TORONTO LONDON MELBOURNE

An Adkinson Parrish Book

Library of Congress Catalog Card Number
81-22024
ISBN 0-442-21588-6 cloth
ISBN 0-442-21587-8 paper

Printed and bound in Great Britain
First published in the United States in 1982
by Van Nostrand Reinhold Company
135 West 50th Street
New York, N.Y. 10020, U.S.A.

Van Nostrand Reinhold Limited
1410 Birchmount Road
Scarborough, Ontario M1P 2E7, Canada

Designed and produced by
Adkinson Parrish Limited, London

Managing Editor
Clare Howell

Editor
Hilary Dickinson

Design Manager
Christopher White

Art Direction
Mike Rose and Robert Lamb
Rose & Lamb Design Partnership

Illustrators
Martin Atcherley Richard Blakeley
Philip Holmes Rob Shone Kim Whybrow

Camera-ready
Cedric Knight

16 15 14 13 12 11 10 9 8 7 6 5 4 3 2 1

Library of Congress Cataloging in Publication Data
Cheshire, David F.
The video manual
1. Home video systems. I. Title.
TK9961.C48 778.59'9 81-22024

ISBN 0-442-21588-6 AACR2
ISBN 0-442-21587-8 (pbk.)

Phototypeset by Carlinpoint Limited, London

Illustrations originated by East Anglian Engraving Ltd, Norwich

Printed by Hazell Watson & Viney Limited, Aylesbury, Bucks

Contents

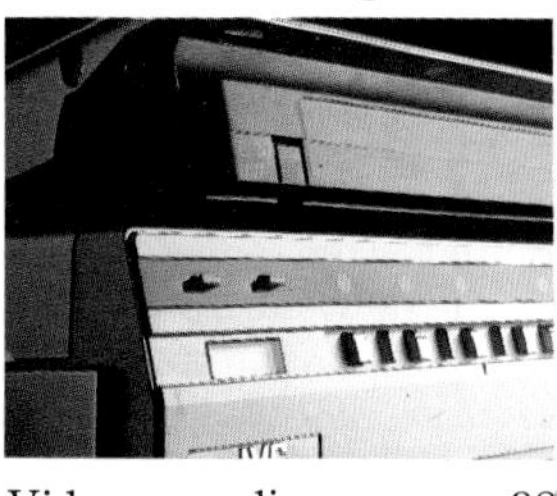

The camera

Making a video movie

Light and lighting

Sound

Expanding the image

Adding to your system

Practical information

Introduction

Ten years ago, the word 'video' would have meant, at best, some form of reference to broadcast television; a technical phrase heavy with professionalism and daunting with expertise. Now it evokes the most phenomenally popular explosion in domestic entertainment since the invention of television itself. In the USA, there are now nearly 4 million home video recorders. In Britain, where home ownership has *doubled* every year for the last three years, there are 1.4 million. As for Japan, it has been reported that one-third of the houses in Osaka with recorders do not yet have indoor lavatories — a startling indication of priorities indeed.

So what is it about video recorders, their cameras, and all their wondrous new gadgetry that so seizes the imagination of so many? This book is an attempt to offer some guidance to those who are venturing for the first time into that glittering new jungle, hung with alluring fruit; and also to open up new possibilities for the more seasoned user. There are exciting and astonishing avenues down which the newcomer could perhaps be persuaded to travel if he or she realized how easy the way has now become. Cameras; home tape movies; editing; documentaries; special effects; games and computers; lights; words and music: these are all made relatively simple by the new technology which, despite its forbidding appearance, is designed not to ensnare the video-buff in coils of tape, but to liberate him from the tyranny of broadcast schedules.

In the simplest, and most passive way, the liberation comes in the form of time-shift — you can watch the programme of your choice whenever *you* like, and if nothing is suitable you can watch a pre-

recorded film of *your* choice. But once the decision is made to buy a camera, the liberation is active and creative. The transition is soon made from the simplest, unedited domestic record to something more challenging, and from there perhaps to tapes designed for considered viewing by others — simple dramas, coaching tapes, demonstration or promotional tapes, sports reportage, instructional tapes. The cheapness of tape itself and the relatively indulgent nature of the technology makes these subjects accessible to many groups and individuals. What is more, copies can easily be made.

Further still up the ladder of video, more and more television is gradually becoming open to 'public access', and though slightly larger gauges of tape are needed at the present time — ¾-inch at least — small pressure groups and individuals with something to say are increasingly finding air-time. This development, which is long overdue, has been assisted by the explosive developments in broadcasting technology itself. With cable-TV and satellites combining to bring literally hundreds of channels into the home at any one time, something urgently needs to be done to cut through the mass of broadcast material. At the very least, those who in their wisdom must decide what is to fill all that air-time should be more inclined than ever before to look kindly on a cheap, well-made, and thoughtful programme from a fresh source.

This manual does not pretend to accompany the aspiring programme maker all the way into such semi-professional work; but it will attempt to provide signposts and, for the very beginner, the facts and the methods without which he cannot exploit the many possibilities.

tape inside
VHS
PULL ON / VOL
SUN
CLOCK
0:15
PROGRAM NO
SEC/REC LEN

The elements of video

Until quite recently, a TV receiver was all that an ordinary person could expect in his home in the way of 'video'. Suddenly, recorders have led to cameras, which in turn lead to lights, microphones, and editing, while the big screens and video discs offer other possibilities for the future. Fortunately, all these advances have generally speaking been accompanied by equivalent advances in the simplicity of operation, but nevertheless to get the best out of your expensive equipment it is important to understand at least the basic principles of video. At the very least, it will give you an insight into the almost miraculous technology that has suddenly been imported into our homes.

The video centre

The home TV set can be used to co-ordinate a very wide range of associated systems for both work and leisure. It can be connected to a video recorder and, for replay purposes only, to a video-disc player. A camera may be connected to the recorder or else to a separate portable recorder which can in turn be used to dub on to the main recorder, to provide you with fully edited tapes. The sound which you hear, both on broadcast programmes and from your own tapes and discs, can be fed through your domestic audio system for enhanced sound quality, and you can dub additional sound on to your tapes by the use of a tape recorder or microphone.

There is also a wide range of gadgets that can be plugged in to the basic TV receiver such as video games and home computers. The TV may even, in many countries, be used as a display screen for information from a central computer, either through broadcast channels or through the telephone. It is the receiver which lies at the heart of all this complexity and, as it were, makes the electronics visible.

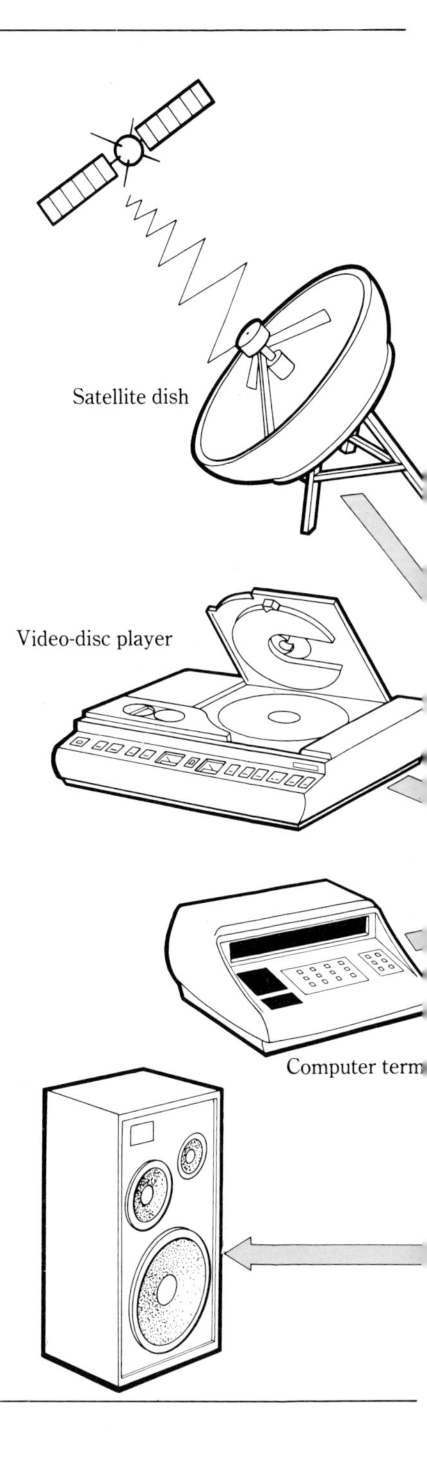

The most attractive aspect of the video centre, as a concept, is its flexibility. Once the basics of receiver and recorder have been established – though they, too, can easily be changed – the system may be upgraded to respond to the pace of technology, and to the growing sophistication of the video enthusiast.

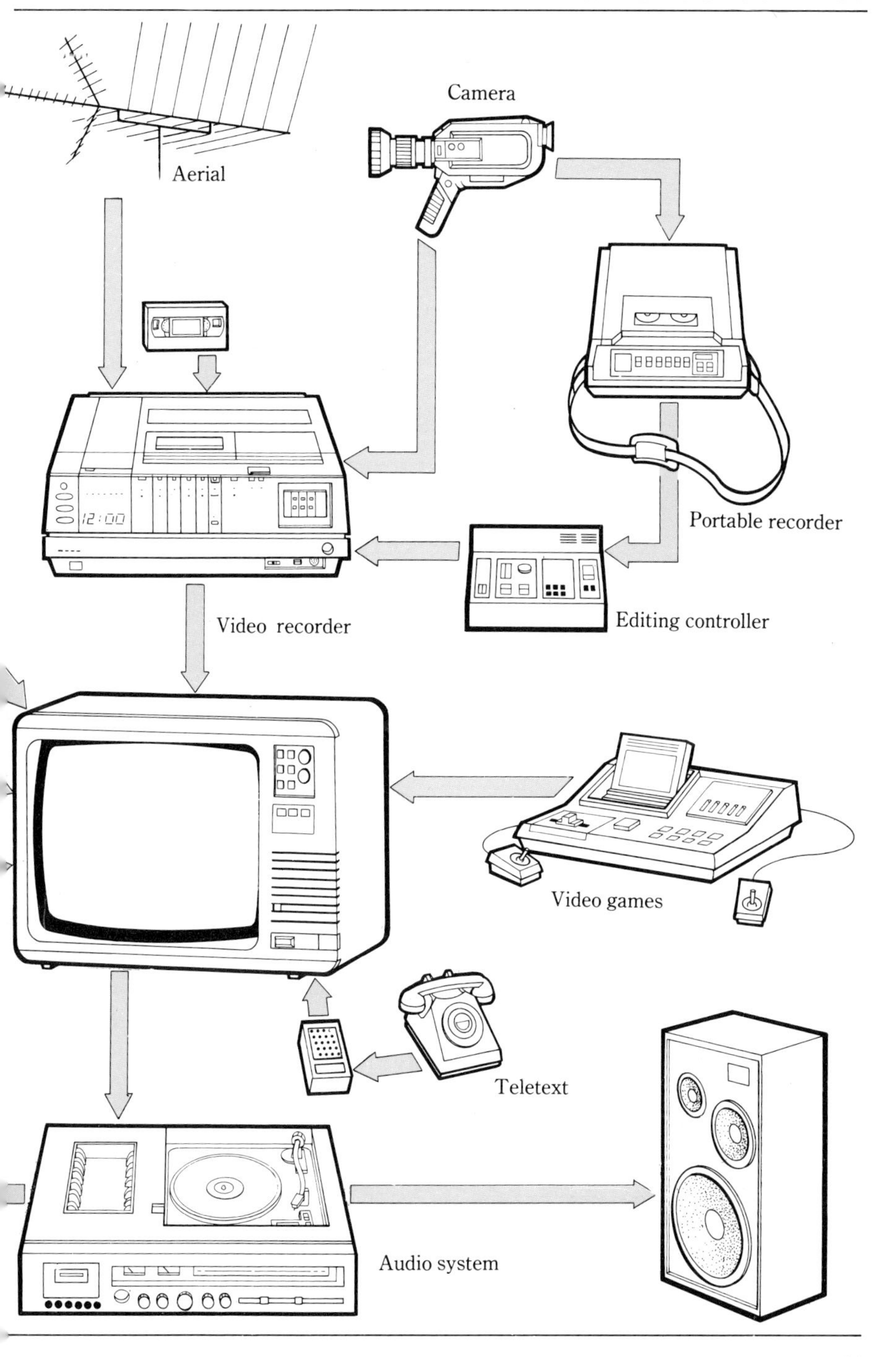
Camera
Aerial
Portable recorder
Video recorder
Editing controller
12:00
Video games
Teletext
Audio system

Choosing video equipment

The first essential for a good video system is a reliable receiver, and they vary considerably in quality. There is little point in buying a black and white TV in the 1980s, however attractive the price might seem to be. Virtually all TV programmes are made in colour, and in many cases this can actually make them incomprehensible in black and white. For example, most programmes on modern abstract art are simply a swirling mass of grey in monochrome.

When choosing a TV receiver, listen to the sound quality, compare the sharpness of the picture using a reference such as a test card, and be sure to buy a reputable brand. By the same token, take the question of servicing seriously. Ask yourself how large a set you need, and whether those extra facilities such as remote control are really necessary.

Any TV is only as good as the signal that is fed into it, and it is always worth investing in a proper external aerial, especially in areas of poor reception. If that fails, you should consider cable-vision (pp. 188-9) or one of the means of signal enhancement (pp.30-1). At all events, be sure that when the TV is installed it is correctly set up to

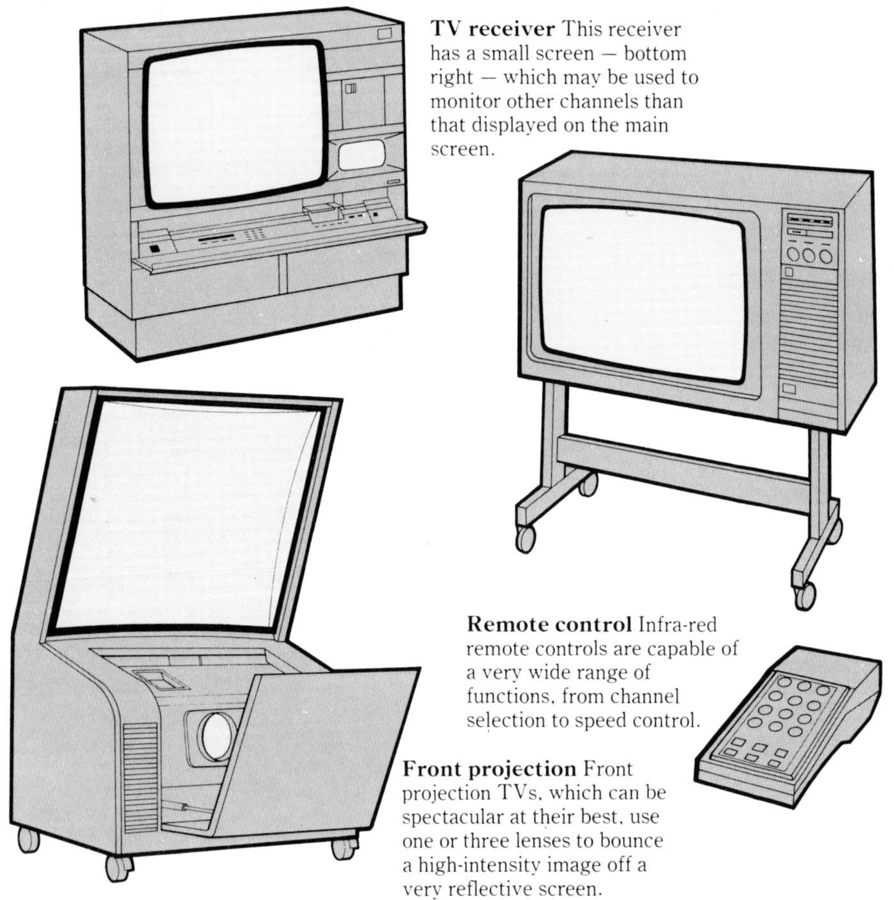

TV receiver This receiver has a small screen – bottom right – which may be used to monitor other channels than that displayed on the main screen.

Remote control Infra-red remote controls are capable of a very wide range of functions, from channel selection to speed control.

Front projection Front projection TVs, which can be spectacular at their best, use one or three lenses to bounce a high-intensity image off a very reflective screen.

your personal satisfaction. Look for natural skin tones, an absence of 'snowy' noise in shadow areas, a steady picture, a correct relation between height and width without undue 'cut-off', and good definition.

It is also highly desirable to have audio and video input and output sockets; this would make the receiver a true receiver/monitor (pp. 34-5). Next, consider sound quality: does the receiver have one speaker or two? tone controls? good frequency response? even provision for stereo broadcasts? When all this has been taken into consideration then it is time to worry about the actual appearance of the machine you are buying.

The next stage comes with your decision to acquire a video recorder or player. If you are only planning to use a tape recorder to replay pre-recorded tapes (say if reception is so bad in your area that nothing is worth taping anyway), opt for a video-disc player — both the discs and the hardware are cheaper and of higher quality than the equivalents on tape. But if you plan to tape programmes off air or to make your own video movies with a camera, you will need a recorder.

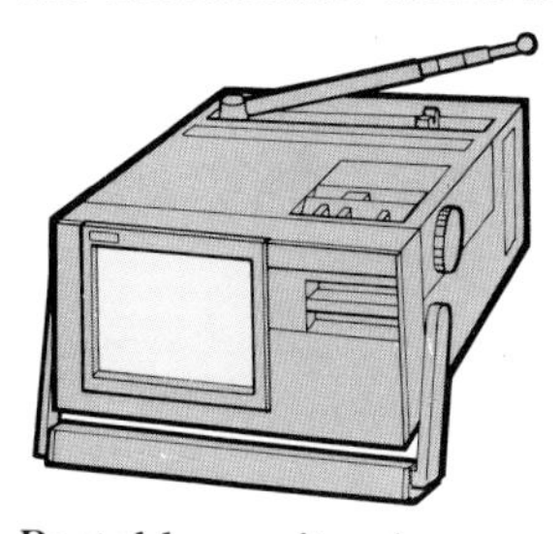

Portable monitor A portable monitor, which may or may not contain a tuner, runs off 12V DC (a car lighter socket, for instance), and can be used to check colour balance and quality.

Portable machines Small portables, such as this JVC model, can be operated off DC or AC. In this case, an FM/AM radio is included. The screen measures 6.35cm (2.5 in).

Back projection Back projection systems, though fainter than their front projection cousins, have the advantage of being one-piece units, and therefore arguably less prone to convergence problems.

There are essentially three domestic systems now available, and of these the two Japanese systems (Sony's Betamax and JVC's VHS) at present dominate the market, though Philips's Video 2000 has a foothold in Europe. Whichever you select, remember that you will be paying for all the extra facilities found on the more expensive models: freeze-frame, picture-search, multi-programming, roll-back editing, are very desirable features for some users, but you can save a lot of money if you forego them. Servicing and sales back-up are such a consideration that many users (particularly in the UK) rent or lease their sets. In any case, the video heads will wear out after several hundred hours of play, and they are not cheap to replace. This again makes rental attractive, though it is still unfamiliar in the USA and the rest of Europe.

Despite the arrival of very compact ¼-inch portable recorders such as the ¼-inch Technicolor or micro-video models (pp. 72-5), there is a powerful argument for keeping both your home and portable recorders in the same format. Your tapes will then be interchangeable, and a 'second-

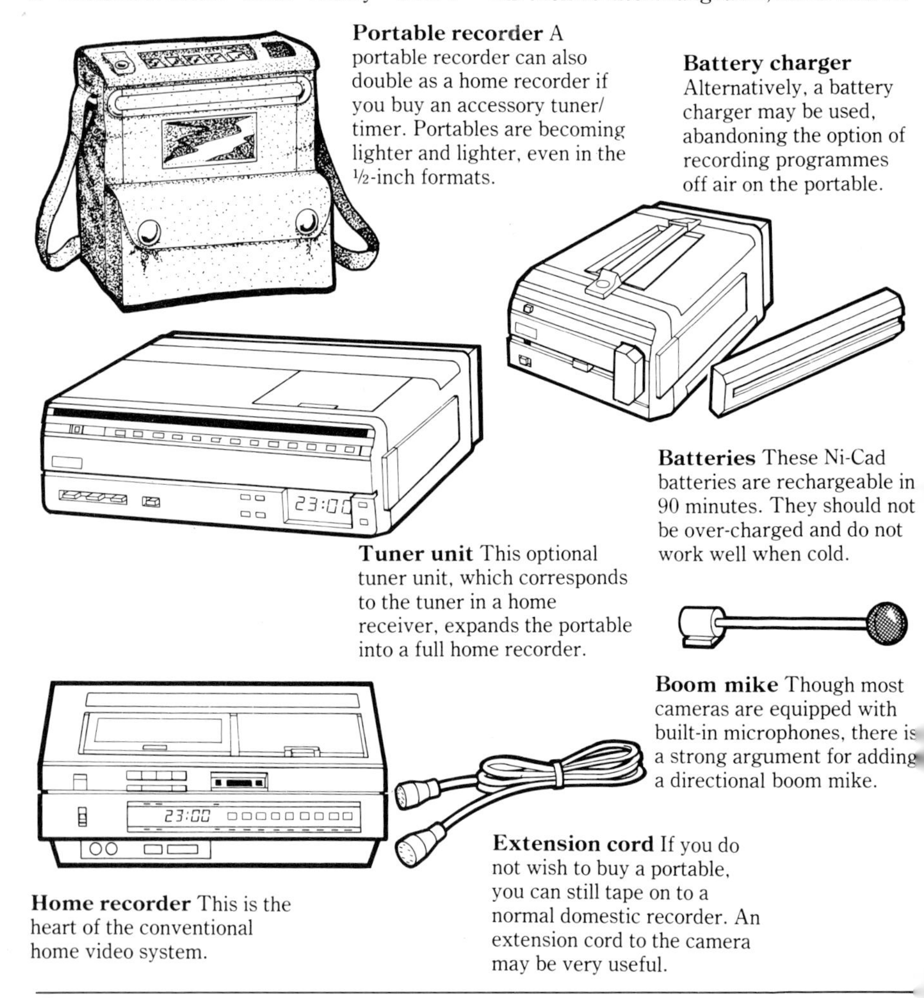

Portable recorder A portable recorder can also double as a home recorder if you buy an accessory tuner/timer. Portables are becoming lighter and lighter, even in the ½-inch formats.

Battery charger Alternatively, a battery charger may be used, abandoning the option of recording programmes off air on the portable.

Tuner unit This optional tuner unit, which corresponds to the tuner in a home receiver, expands the portable into a full home recorder.

Batteries These Ni-Cad batteries are rechargeable in 90 minutes. They should not be over-charged and do not work well when cold.

Boom mike Though most cameras are equipped with built-in microphones, there is a strong argument for adding a directional boom mike.

Home recorder This is the heart of the conventional home video system.

Extension cord If you do not wish to buy a portable, you can still tape on to a normal domestic recorder. An extension cord to the camera may be very useful.

generation' copy will not need to be made for replay on your basic recorder. However, with the new high-quality portables such as the JVC 2200 or Sony SL 2000, combined with a versatile tuner/timer, you can have the best of both worlds – a home video recorder which can be slung over the shoulder when you shoot outside. This does mean that you have only one machine in total, and so cannot edit your location material at all. This brings us to the last considerations in choosing a recorder. Do you intend to buy a camera or to edit from one machine to another? Will the recorder accept a remote-pause button from the camera? Will it then give you acceptably smooth cuts from one shot to the next? Will it give flash-free and roll-free edits when dubbing from a portable recorder on to the master tape? These must be borne in mind if you consider expanding your system.

Although there are no actual objections to mixing systems – say a JVC camera with a Sony recorder – the manufacturers have made it pretty difficult, and you will spend a great deal of time fiddling with plugs and adaptors. It may be easier to restrain your indignation and settle for one system.

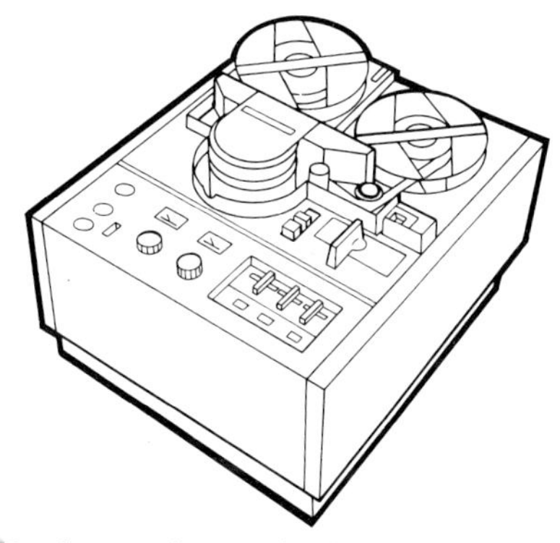

Reel-to-reel recorder In the late sixties and early seventies, portable amateur recording was usually done on ½-inch reel-to-reel recorders.

Video disc There are three video-disc replay systems on the market. They cannot be used for recording. It remains to be seen which of the three, if any, will triumph.

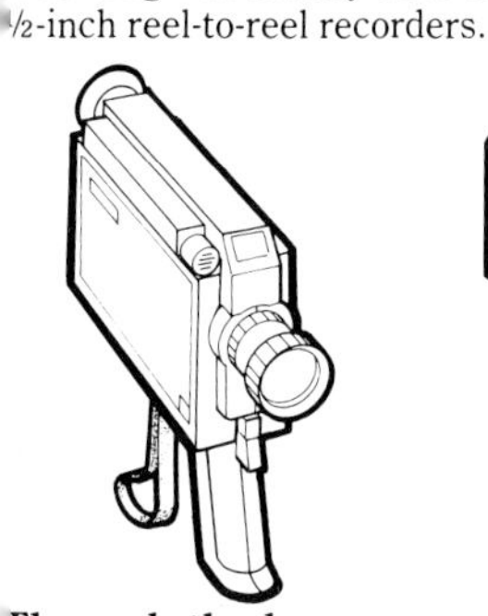

Through-the-lens viewfinder A through-the-lens viewfinder shows the image by means of an optical beamsplitter. As a result, some light is directed from the vidicon tube itself.

Electronic viewfinder Cameras such as this have electronic viewfinders – effectively small televisions which monitor the output of the camera when it is powered. They may also be used for replay on location.

CCD camera Some of the latest cameras have replaced the vidicon tube with a CCD microchip, with a reduction in size – here the recorder is also included in the camera.

How the image is formed

The central principle of all video equipment is that a focused image must be converted into an electrical signal which can be transmitted either by cable or by a radio frequency. When the signal is received, it can be reassembled on a screen as a visible image. All visible images may be thought of as variations of light and shade. In order that they can be converted into electrical signals, they must be broken down into a very large number of dots, ranging from black through grey to pure white, which are in turn arranged as a series of slightly slanted horizontal lines on the screen — 625 in Europe, and 525 in the USA and Japan.

In order to convey the effect of motion, each of these lined 'pictures' must last no more than 1/25 sec (1/30 sec in USA), but in practice even this very brief duration would appear to flicker when viewed, so each picture of action is scanned *twice* by the tube by a series of interlaced lines which, when combined, produce a complete picture. Thus the 'field frequency' of each system is double the picture frequency — i.e. 50 Hz in Europe and 60 Hz in the USA and Japan. (This corresponds to the frequency of the power supplies in those countries.)

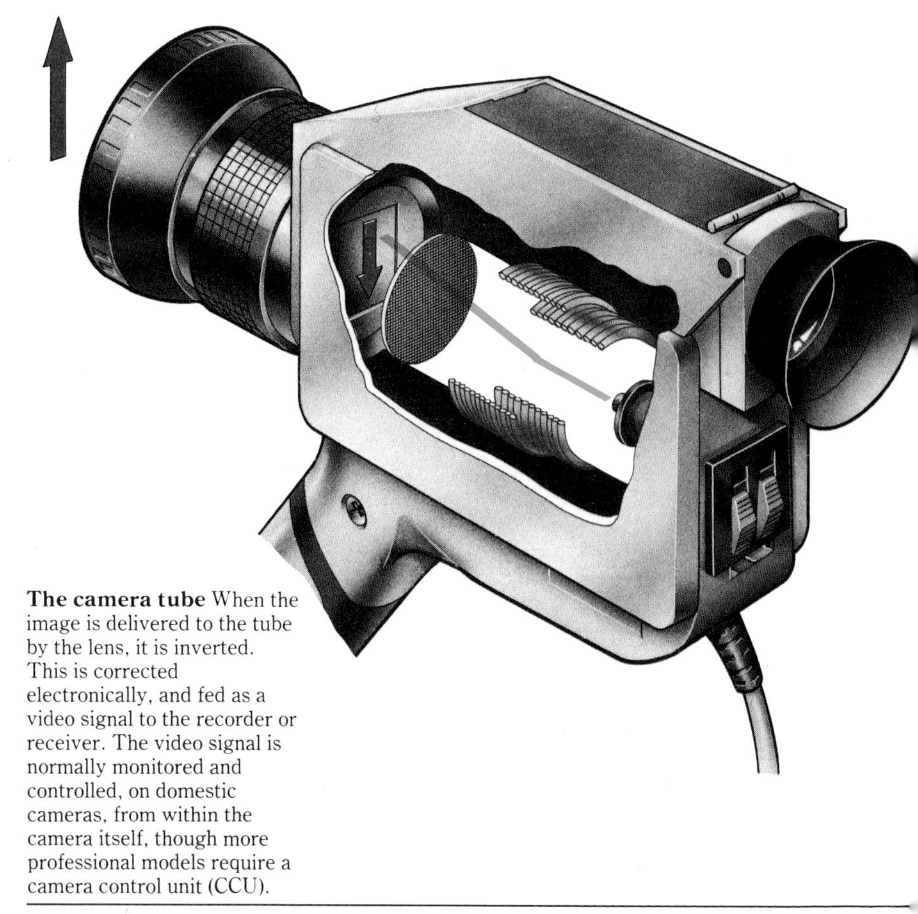

The camera tube When the image is delivered to the tube by the lens, it is inverted. This is corrected electronically, and fed as a video signal to the recorder or receiver. The video signal is normally monitored and controlled, on domestic cameras, from within the camera itself, though more professional models require a camera control unit (CCU).

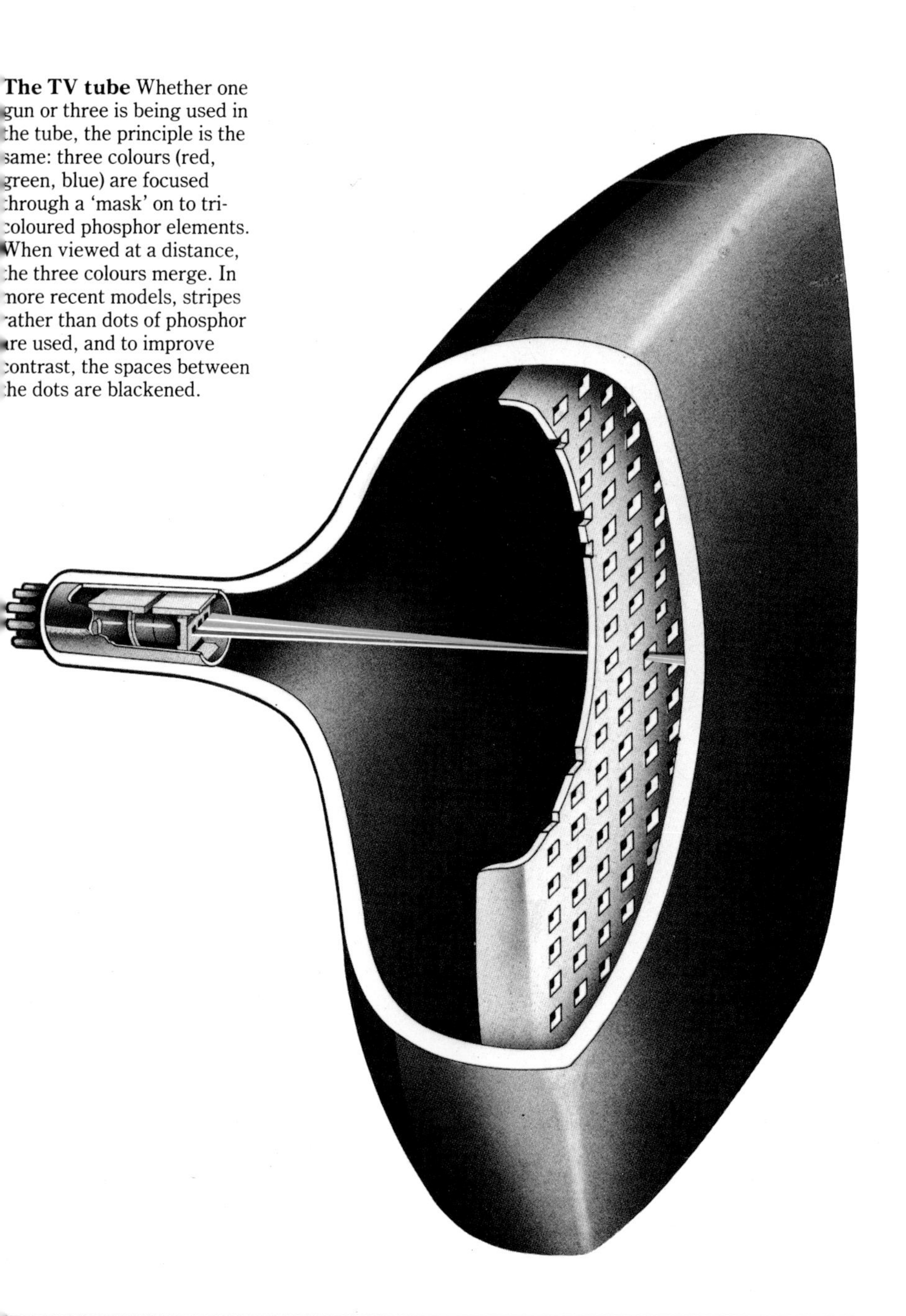

The TV tube Whether one gun or three is being used in the tube, the principle is the same: three colours (red, green, blue) are focused through a 'mask' on to tri-coloured phosphor elements. When viewed at a distance, the three colours merge. In more recent models, stripes rather than dots of phosphor are used, and to improve contrast, the spaces between the dots are blackened.

The camera tube

The most common form of tube in amateur and semi-professional work is the vidicon. The lens focuses the image on to a 'target' (normally either 17 mm (2/3 in) or 25 mm (1 in) in diameter). The target is coated on the side nearest the lens with conductive but transparent film such as tin oxide, and on the other side with a layer of photo-conductive material. The feature of the photoconductive material which makes possible a video signal is that it varies across its surface in electrical resistance according to how much light is falling on a given spot. All that is then needed is a method of sampling the mosaic of differing resistances across the target in an organized way that can later be duplicated on the TV screen.

This is done by a beam of electrons which are fired from a cathode at the back of the tube. When an electron hits the target, its charge, modified according to the resistance of that precise spot (and therefore according to the light falling on that spot), is passed through the outer conductive surface of the target as one tiny part of the video signal. To make up the whole picture-field, the fine stream of electrons begins in the top left-hand corner of the target and moves to the right and very

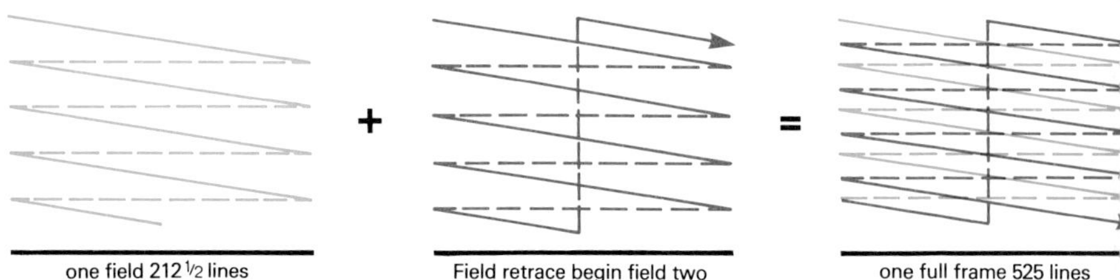

Field 1 The first scanning process only 'samples' half of the *field*, as though mowing half a lawn, in stripes, in preparation for a second run. It then returns to the top for a second 'field'.

Field 2 The second scanning, or *field*, takes care of the remaining alternate stripes in the next fraction of a second — 1/50 (UK), 1/60 (US).

The total frame Together they may be thought to have 'mown the lawn'; covered the entire ground, in 1/25 (UK) or 1/30 (US) of a second. The total *frame*, composed of two fields, is now complete, without visible flicker.

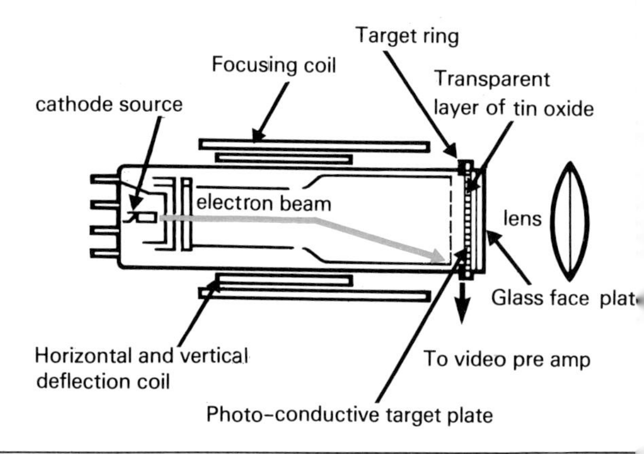

The vidicon tube It can be seen here how the electrons, emitted by the cathode, are swept to and fro across the target by magnetic deflection so that the beam scans the image on the target plate in a series of lines. As its resistance varies according to the light falling on a given spot, so does its resultant electrical output at any instant.

slightly down. When it gets to the right-hand edge, the spot flashes back to the left edge (a little lower this time) to sample the next line down, and so on to the bottom of the target. When it reaches the bottom, it must return instantly to the top left of the target for another field scan, which will be interlaced with the first to make a complete picture in 1/25 or 1/30 sec. This rapid return is known as flyback.

The direction of the beam is controlled by magnetic deflection coils that surround the tube, and the beam's movements are synchronized by a horizontal and a vertical sync pulse; these are known as the line sync and field sync, respectively. The line sync tells the beam when to return to the left to begin a new line, while the field sync contains the instruction to return to the top of the screen for the next field. The vertical pulse may be derived either from the mains (at 50 or 60 Hz), or from a crystal oscillator within the camera itself. The TV receiver will in turn monitor these pulses in the video signal to take its own cue to return to the top or the left of the screen. It is clear that only an accurate and regularly spaced sync pulse can produce coherent images. If the pulse is interrupted or irregular, the picture will roll or break up entirely.

Plumbicon and Saticon tubes
The Plumbicon tube, now quite common in professional use, is an improvement on the standard vidicon, in that it largely avoids the streaking to which the vidicon is subject when recording moving subjects at low light levels. The Saticon tube, which uses yet another chemical formulation for its photoconductive surface, is one of several new formulas designed to abate the problem.

CCD In the very latest one-piece camera/recorders, a charge-coupled device (CCD) is used in place of the conventional tube. It operates in a similar manner, except that it is solid-state. The very small 'chip' is scanned by a microscopic network of lines, both vertical and horizontal, etched on to its surface. This kind of solid-state technology is certain to replace tubes in the very near future.

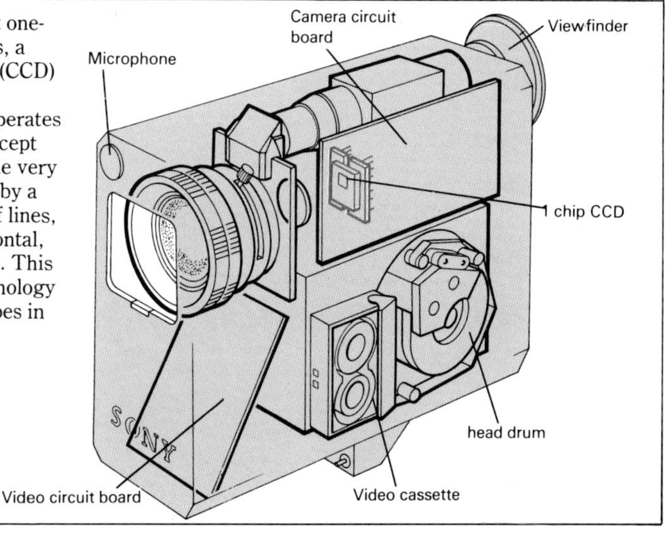

Colour and the eye

The information our eyes receive from the outside world is of two kinds: brightness and wavelength. The brightness of the object tells us how much light is falling upon it, whereas the wavelength of the light that we observe is conveyed to us as colour. Violet is the longest visible wavelength, and red the shortest, with all the other visible colours spaced out in between, as in a rainbow.

It is possible, however, to produce any of the colours in the spectrum by the combination of just three of its components, which are strategically placed midway and at either end of the rainbow: red, green, and blue (R,G,B). These are the primary colours, and if they are combined on projection they will form a perfect white at the centre, while around them will be found all the other colours that the eye can see. In video, the tint of a particular colour is referred to as a *hue,* and this hue is modified by its degree of brightness (or *luminance*) in the direction of either white or black. The luminance therefore also affects the degree to which the colour is light or deep, and this is known as the degree of *saturation* of that colour. In other words, red + green + blue give us hue. Hue + luminance give us the correctly saturated colour at the correct degree of brightness. This is all we need in order to see an object at the right colour.

In this blow-up of the eye of the girl in a standard UK television test chart, photographed from an actual receiver, you can see clearly that the subtle gradations of the colour of the eye are nothing more than red, green, and blue dots or bars of phosphor on the TV tube. Hold it at arm's length, and the colours will merge.

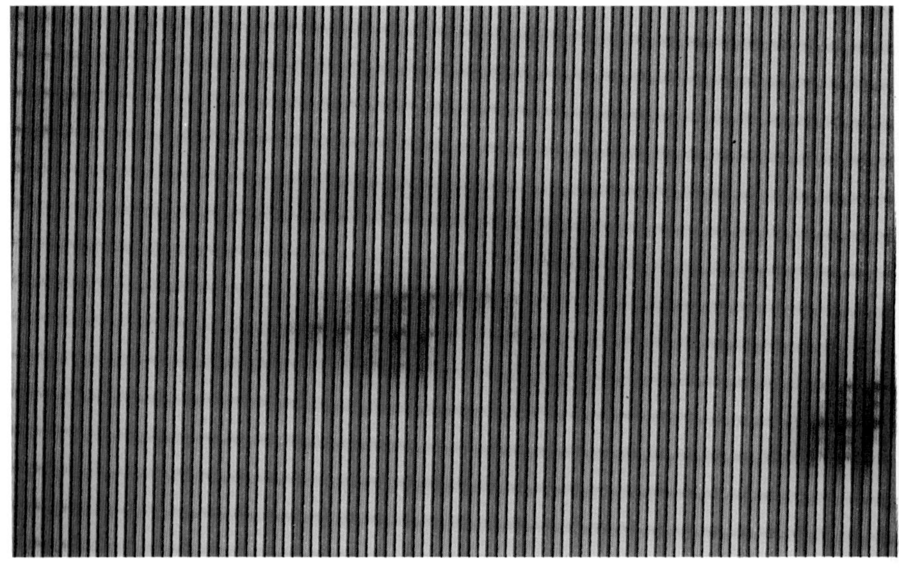

Colour addition Any colour in the spectrum can be created by combining red, green, and blue lights.

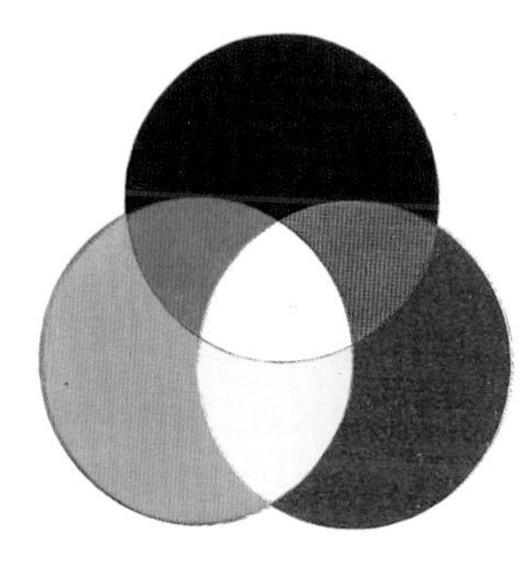

The colour TV screen is a mosaic of red, green, and blue dots or bars which, together, can create the impression of any given colour. This was, indeed, the principle behind one branch of Impressionist painting.

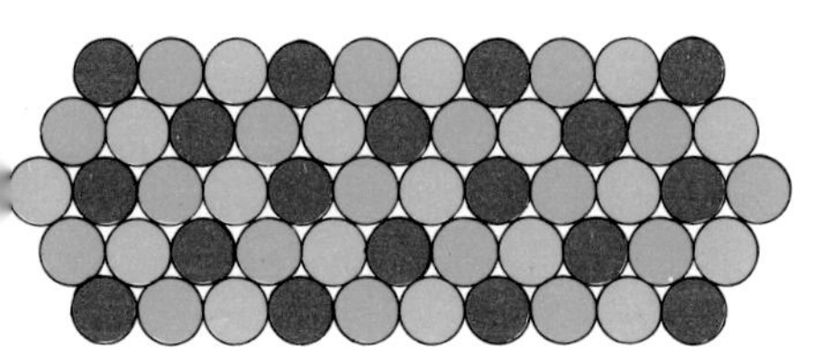

Hue, saturation, and luminance

Same hue, same luminance, different saturation

Same hue, same saturation, different luminance

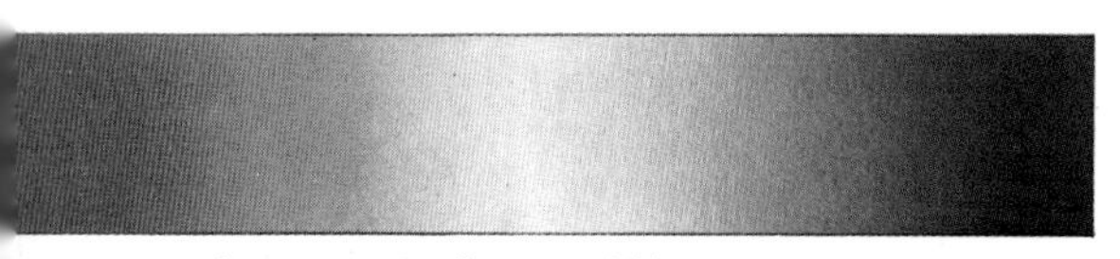

Same saturation, same luminance, different hue

The electromagnetic spectrum Visible light occupies a very small wavelength band.

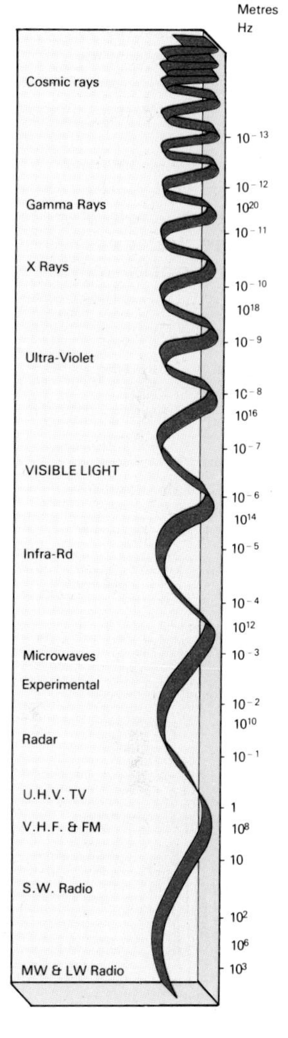

Colour and the video camera

A black and white camera need only concern itself with the luminance (known as Y) of the multitude of points that it scans across a given scene, whereas a colour camera has to analyse each point of the image not only for luminance, but also for hue – the colour, or *chroma*. This means *four* separate sources of information: R,G,B, and Y. In turn, the transmission system will have to communicate all this to the receiver, which will have to recombine it into an image.

As far as the camera is concerned, the simplest, but most cumbersome, way of approaching the problem is to provide four tubes with dichroic mirrors which act as colour filters to divert light to red, green, blue, and a luminance tube respectively. Alternatively, a three-tube camera can be used and the luminance can be derived simply by adding up the total output of the three tubes. These cameras are largely restricted to professional use.

It is now possible, however, to read both chroma *and* luminance from just one tube, which is surmounted by a *stripe filter* of three colours. These are scanned rapidly and alternately to give three colour outputs. The stripe filter tube may be supplemented by a separate vidicon for luminance, which makes it a two-tube camera, or (most commonly) the three outputs may be combined, giving a very compact one-tube camera, which is now almost universal among the small domestic equipment.

In addition to the facilities common on black and white cameras, colour cameras have adjustments for colour balance. This is often, perhaps confusingly, referred to as 'white balance'.

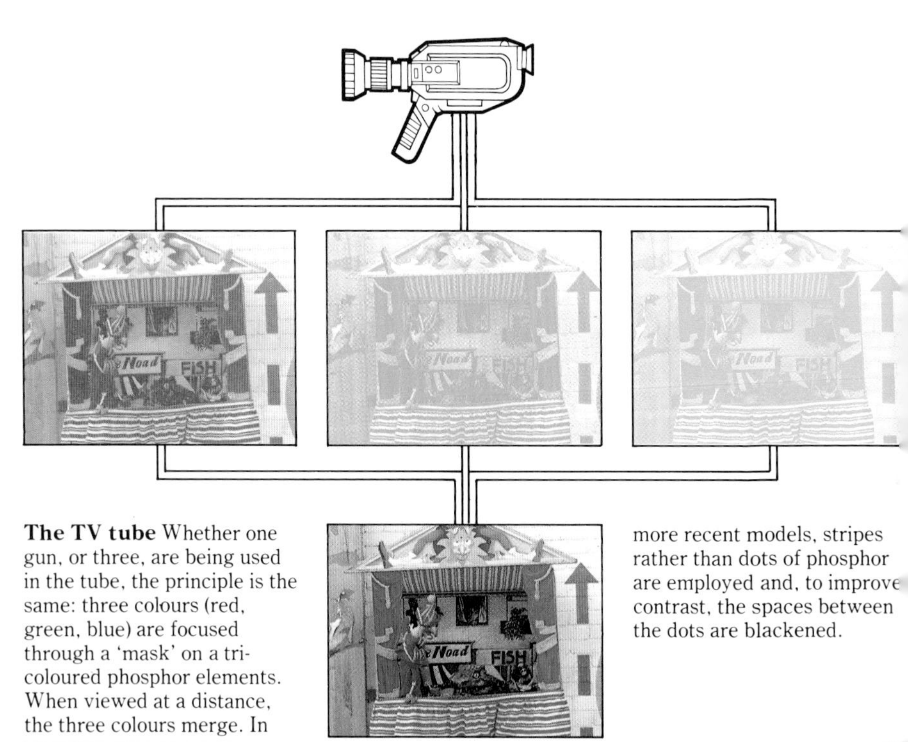

The TV tube Whether one gun, or three, are being used in the tube, the principle is the same: three colours (red, green, blue) are focused through a 'mask' on a tri-coloured phosphor elements. When viewed at a distance, the three colours merge. In more recent models, stripes rather than dots of phosphor are employed and, to improve contrast, the spaces between the dots are blackened.

Three-tube camera

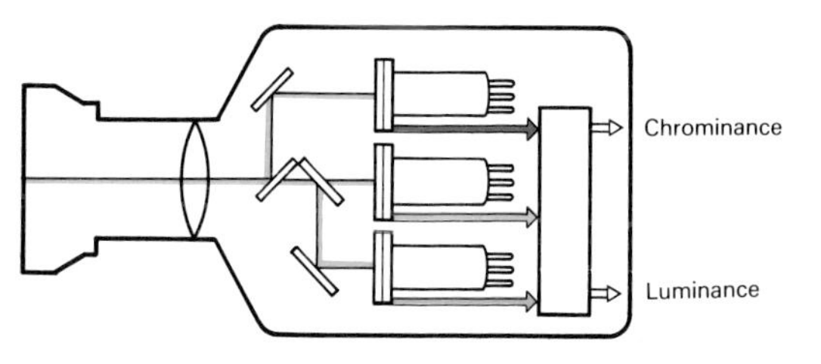

In this three-tube camera, the incoming light is split into its three component colours by a series of dichroic mirrors. Each tube monitors the luminance of its particular colour, and the three signals are recombined by the colour matrix to produce a video signal that contains full information on both brightness and colour.

Two-tube camera

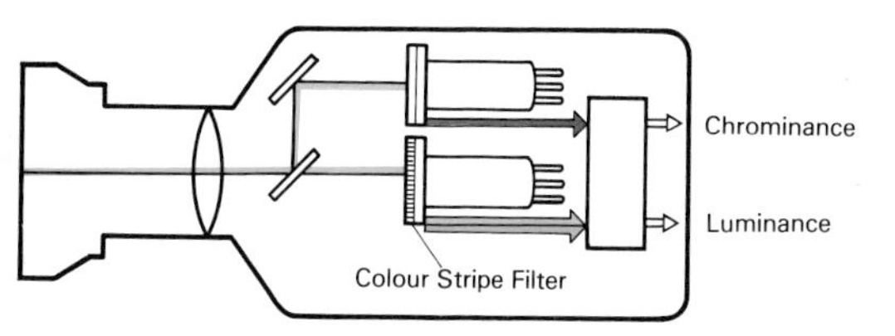

To save weight, a two-tube system can be used: here, one tube measures luminance, while the other samples red and blue. The value of green is derived by subtraction. All multi-tube cameras are prone to problems of registration, which can be resolved if one single tube is employed.

Single-tube camera

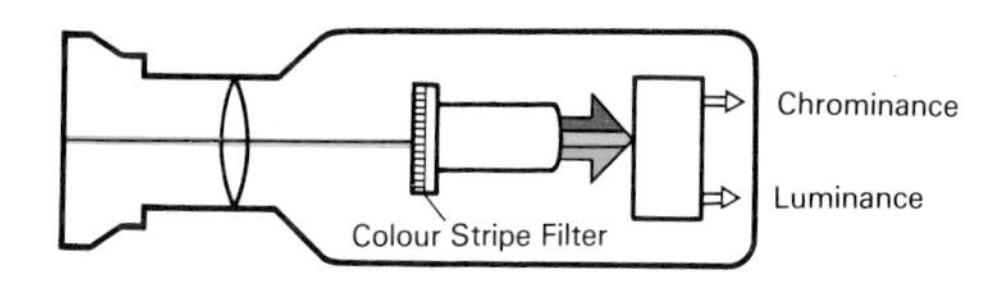

The single-tube camera is now the most common in the domestic field. There are no problems of registration, since the three colours and the luminance are derived from the same tube. The camera is very lightweight.

Stripe filter

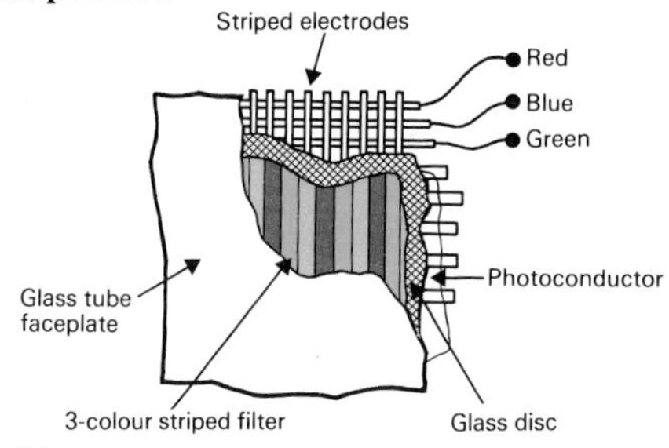

This is one of the two main systems for deriving a complete colour video signal from one vidicon. The face of the tube is striped in three colours which are 'read' by the corresponding striped electrodes on the target. Luminance is derived by adding together the three chroma outputs. This is called a tri-electrode vidicon.

CCD camera-recorder

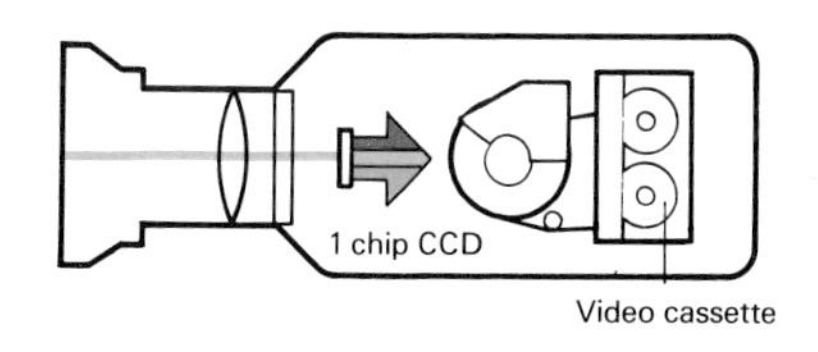

In this camera the entire 'tube' structure has been replaced by a single microchip, which is receptive to light (and colour) across its surface. It is certain to replace the conventional tube in due course, since it is lighter, less prone to 'lag', more sensitive, and much smaller.

The video signal

The video signal contains a number of pieces of information in addition to the straightforward 'picture': the receiver has to be told when to begin scanning a new line (the line sync pulse); it has to be told when to 'fly back' to the top of the screen (the field sync pulse); and it also has to be given a line-by-line reminder of the level of pure black, which will act as a reference for all the degrees of luminance in between. Lastly, in the case of a colour monitor, it will need a great deal more information about the hue, or chroma, of each particle of visual information (pp. 22-3).

The bandwidth and the lines

The range of frequencies that are encompassed by even a black and white video signal is very large, and it is directly related to the number of individual items of information that are to be transmitted in each second. It is expressed in *Hertz* (Hz). One Hertz, or unit of frequency, can contain two items of visual information, whereas the entire frame of a 625-line video signal will need no less than eleven million pieces of information per second — five and a half million Hertz (5.5 MHz). (Because of the difference in line standards, the bandwidth required in the USA is only 4 MHz — 20 per cent less than the European system, PAL.)

As each line in a signal carries many hundred elements of video detail, and each line is repeated 25 times per sec — 30 in the USA — it is only through this vast amount of electronic information that the definition of the image can be maintained, but this creates demands on technology that are unknown to sound radio. (The human ear, for instance, has at best a frequency 'bandwidth' of only 20,000 Hz.) Each line lasts only 64 microseconds, of which 51.5 are taken up with picture information. The rest of the time is devoted to line sync pulse, colour reference burst, and 'blanking level' which acts as a reference black against which the signal can be measured all the way up to 'peak white'.

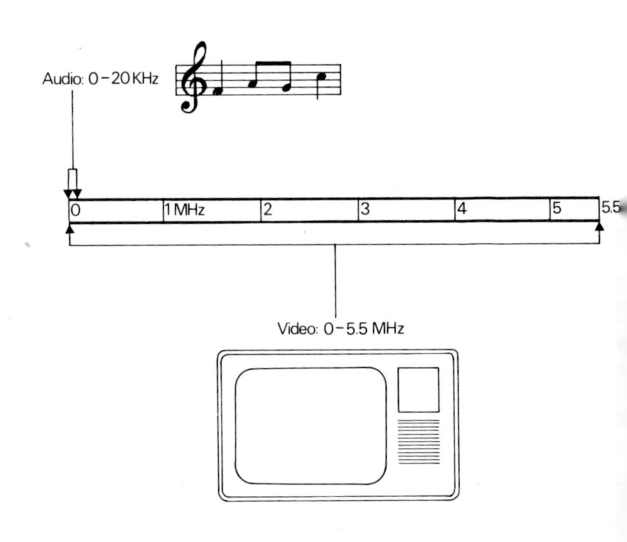

The bandwidth required for video is enormously larger than that required for even the very finest audio signal, since so many pieces of information must be transmitted every second. In practice, colour TV requires a bandwidth of 5.5 MHz (4 MHz in USA).

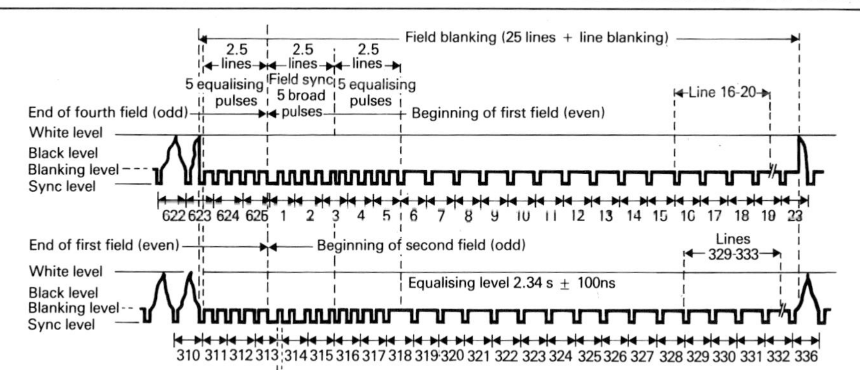

Broad pulse separation
4.7 ± 100ns

The above diagram shows just the tops of two successive fields, line by line, in a 625-line picture. The actual video image does not begin until lines 23 and 326, respectively. What is seen here is the field sync pulses, and the equalizing pulses (for establishing black level). The first video signal field will then run from lines 23 to 310, at which point the second field begins (line 311).

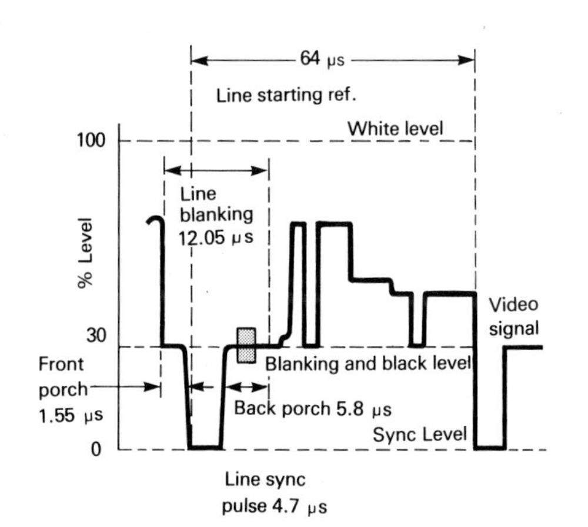

Here, diagrammatically, is *one* line of video, beginning with the line sync pulse, then the colour burst, and black level, followed by the video signal for that line, which in this case touches peak white at two points across the screen.

This is how *one single line* of video information would appear on an oscilloscope. Note how the video signal ranges from peak white to pure black — or 'blanking level' — in the line selected from the centre of the frame.

Encoding for colour

'Encoding' is the term used to describe the process by which the colour information in the camera (chroma) is added to the luminance information in such a way that it can subsequently be decoded and displayed on the receiver. If each of the four components (R,G,B,Y) were allotted the same amount of room in the available bandwidth, the bandwidth would have to be enormously large. However, the problem can be solved by a form of electronic 'algebra'. The luminance signal (Y) is subtracted from both the blue and the red signals, giving B-Y and R-Y. These two signals are modulated on to a subcarrier, which operates at a frequency of 4.43 MHz (Europe) or 3.58 MHz (USA).

Each line scan transmitted contains a very brief but very accurately phased 'burst' of the subcarrier, and this is placed immediately after the line sync pulse which has instructed the receiver to begin a new line scan. The algebra can now be decoded in such a way that green too can be derived: since we know the values of red, blue, and the total luminance, green must be the missing factor: $G = Y - (R + B)$.

The three international systems

The above is necessarily a very schematic description of a very sophisticated process. In practice, the three colour systems in use at the present time use different methods for encoding and decoding their colours. They are completely incompatible, though converters do exist, and certain manufacturers offer receivers and semi-professional recorders that are switchable

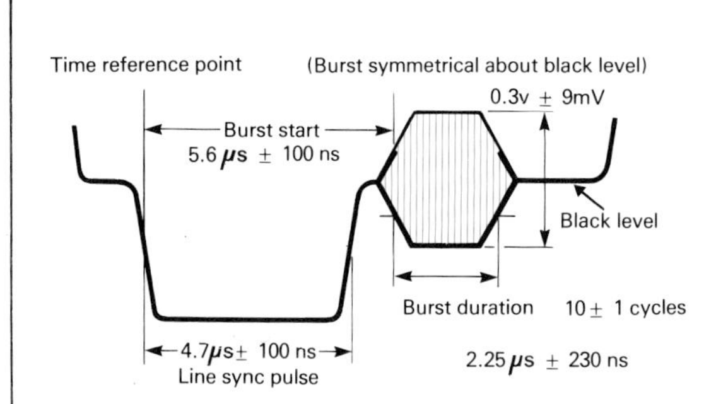

Colour burst This is the very brief portion of the begining of *one line* of one video field. The line sync pulse is followed by a very accurately phased 'colour burst'. Black level is then established, and the video signal for that given line will follow.

Green (G)

=

Luminance (Y)

−

between international standards for playback only.

The first system to be invented is still used in America, Japan, and some other countries. It is known as NTSC after the National Television Systems Committee of 1953. Unfortunately, the early system suffered — and still does — from a poor tolerance of phase distortion at every stage of the process, leading to the unkind nickname Never Twice Same Colour.

In the PAL system (Phase Alternation Line), which is the European standard (except for France), one of the two colour-difference signals is changed in phase every alternate line, while the other is not. By comparison of the phases in the receiver, any transmission distortions or errors can be cancelled out, and the hue of the colours accurately maintained. PAL is, however, only a minor variation — though a very significant improvement — on NTSC.

SECAM (Séquentiel Couleur à Mémoire), the French system also adopted by the Russians, is a far more radical departure. The R-Y signal is transmitted on one line, and the B-Y on the next. A memory circuit in the receiver compares the two, and the resulting colour stability enables total control of the colour at the point of transmission. The receivers are slightly more expensive than PAL or NTSC.

The three systems transmit on different line standards: NTSC, 525; PAL, 625; and SECAM, also, now, 625. All the systems can be viewed in monochrome on a black and white receiver.

Decoding the colour to derive a colour value for green, the combined red and blue signals are subtracted from the total luminance.

Red (R)

Blue (B)

Transmission

For transmission the video signal is made to modulate a carrier wave on a much higher frequency band: either Very High (VHF) or Ultra-High (UHF). VHF frequencies run from 30 to 300 MHz, and UHF from 300 to 3000 MHz. In Europe, each video channel requires an 8 MHz slice of this total available bandwidth, and there are altogether 68 channels, grouped into five 'Bands'. Band II is used for FM radio, which leaves two VHF bands, and two UHF, for video. In the USA, where the majority of broadcasts are in VHF, the band descriptions are different, and the channel width is only 6 MHz.

The different wavelengths of VHF and UHF confer different characteristics on to the respective transmissions. VHF is considerably less directional than UHF – it bends more easily around obstacles such as hills or buildings – but it is much more subject to electrical interference. On the other hand, VHF is somewhat less prone to the 'ghosting' that can afflict UHF when

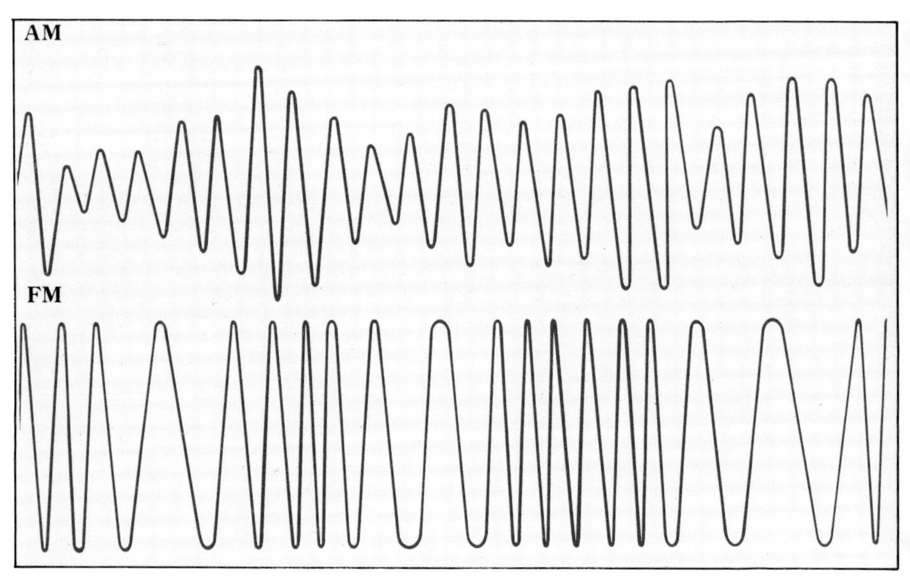

AM and FM AM (amplitude modulation) and FM (frequency modulation) may be thought of, purely metaphorically, in musical terms: in AM, the 'volume' is varied, in FM the 'pitch'. This difference is visible in these waveforms: in AM, the *amplitude* – visible as *height* – varies; in FM, the variation is in the *frequency* with which the waveform recurs – this is visible as the *distance between peaks* in the wave.

Transmission and reception The signal received by an antenna contains direct and reflected components, especially reflections from the ground and (less fortunately) high buildings. The more directional the antenna, the less critical these interferences will be. Satellite have no such problems.

spurious images are bounced off tall buildings, for example. The lower frequencies of VHF require a larger antenna (aerial) than the frequencies of UHF, since dimensions of antennas are directly related to wavelength.

With those differences, both the European UHF and American VHF/UHF frequencies employ amplitude modulation (AM) for the vision carrier signal and frequency modulation (FM) for the sound subcarrier. Transmitting antennas usually have an omni-directional radius — in other words, the signal is radiated equally on all sides — though there may be special circumstances when a directional pattern is adopted. The received power of the signal depends on the power of the transmitter and the distance from the receiver, but the electromagnetic radiation must of course be converted into a current by a receiving antenna which is of the correct type, positioned at the right height, and pointing in the right direction.

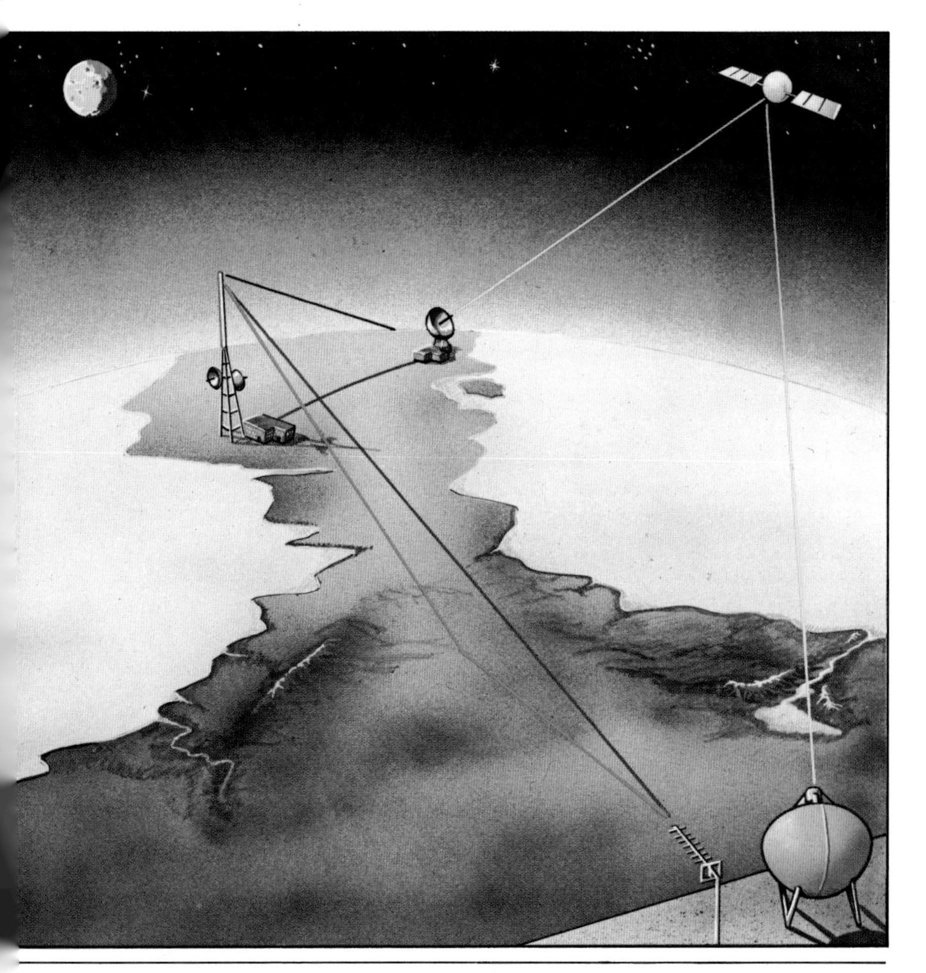

Reception

The simplest form of aerial is a *dipole*. When the dipole is placed in an electromagnetic field, it will generate a current which can then be fed to the receiver and amplified. The dimensions of the dipole must be carefully matched to the wavelength that is to be monitored. However, a simple dipole is inadequate except in the very highest field strengths, and in practice an *array* is used to give both greater directionality and greater gain. In all cases the dipole must be aligned at right angles to the transmitter.

The antenna

By adding extra dipoles (known as directors) at precise distances in front of the main dipole, and a reflector behind the dipole, very significant improvements are achieved in the voltage that the aerial will deliver, though it must be correctly aligned: a high-gain aerial will have a margin of error of only about 15° on either side of the line that runs towards the transmitter.

Positioning the aerial

Unless you have cable-vision, the type and position of the aerial will be absolutely crucial in determining the quality of the image on your screen. In most cases, an indoor aerial will *not* produce satisfactory results. It is too small, does not have a clear line of sight to the transmitter, and in any case does not benefit from the very

Dipole and wavelength
The length of the dipole is directly related to the wavelength which you wish to receive. A VHF aerial is therefore much bigger, horizontally, than a UHF aerial.

Positioning the aerial The longer the aerial array, the more heavily directional it becomes. The pattern of directivity is commonly described as an ellipse, pointing straight at the transmitter. It is clear that aerials *must* be accurately aligned.

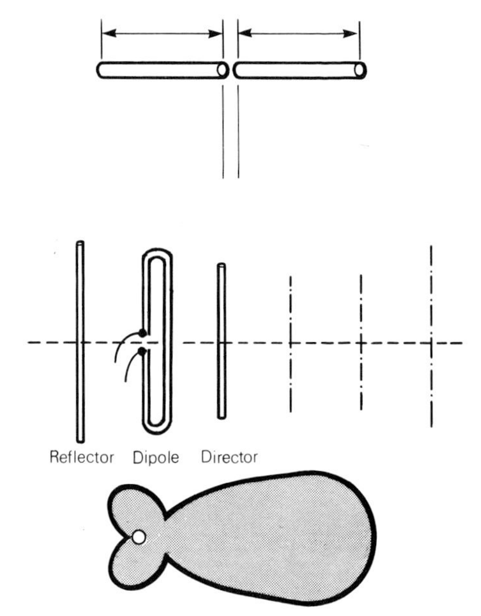

A typical yagi array

important signal that is bounced back from the surface of the earth itself. (This is less true for high-rise apartment dwellers, but they may well have a communal aerial.)

For an ordinary house, the aerial must be on the roof, at a good but not excessive height, and accurately aligned — an astonishing number of aerials face the wrong way. A good engineer should be able to determine the optimum position with a signal strength meter. Make sure that the aerial is not blown out of position by storms. If several stations are to be covered, it is possible to install a rotating aerial. The orientation will depend on the polarization of the transmitter (horizontal or vertical), and in some areas, particularly inner cities, you may well get best results by pointing the antenna slightly skywards.

Connecting the aerial

The feeder cable used to connect the aerial should have the lowest possible loss, and the 75-ohm coaxial cable used in Europe also exists in a low-loss version if you have a long cable-run from the aerial. This is more expensive, but worth it. In the USA, a 300-ohm twin feeder is commonly used for VHF.

Boosting reception

If you are in a weak-signal area, or if you have one or more extra sockets running off one aerial, you may need either a high-gain aerial or an amplifier close to the aerial.

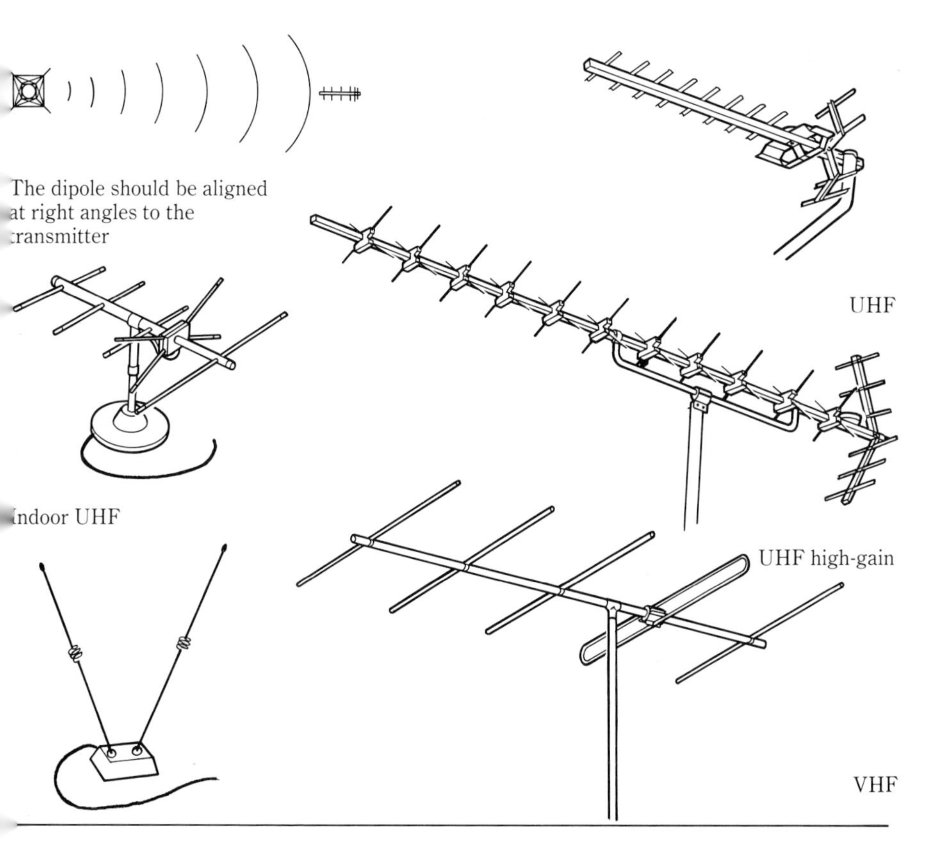

The dipole should be aligned at right angles to the transmitter

Indoor UHF

UHF

UHF high-gain

VHF

The TV receiver

The TV set in the home is different from the monitor used in the studio in that it must contain a tuner. The transmitter is sending out modulated signals in the VHF or UHF wavebands, and these are referred to as rf signals. The receiver has to convert these to signals which can in turn be broken into video and audio, and finally into red, green, blue, and luminance. When these are recombined on the screen (decoded), we have full colour video, and audio.

The key to a colour receiver, when all the above decoding has been achieved, is the tube itself. In a conventional tube there are three guns which correspond to the three colours. Each will deliver a stream of electrons which at any given moment corresponds in strength to the over-all brightness and hue of the exact point of the picture that is being scanned. The balance between the three guns determines the hue, and the sum of their power determines the brightness of that part of the screen. In fact, each gun will strike a different-coloured

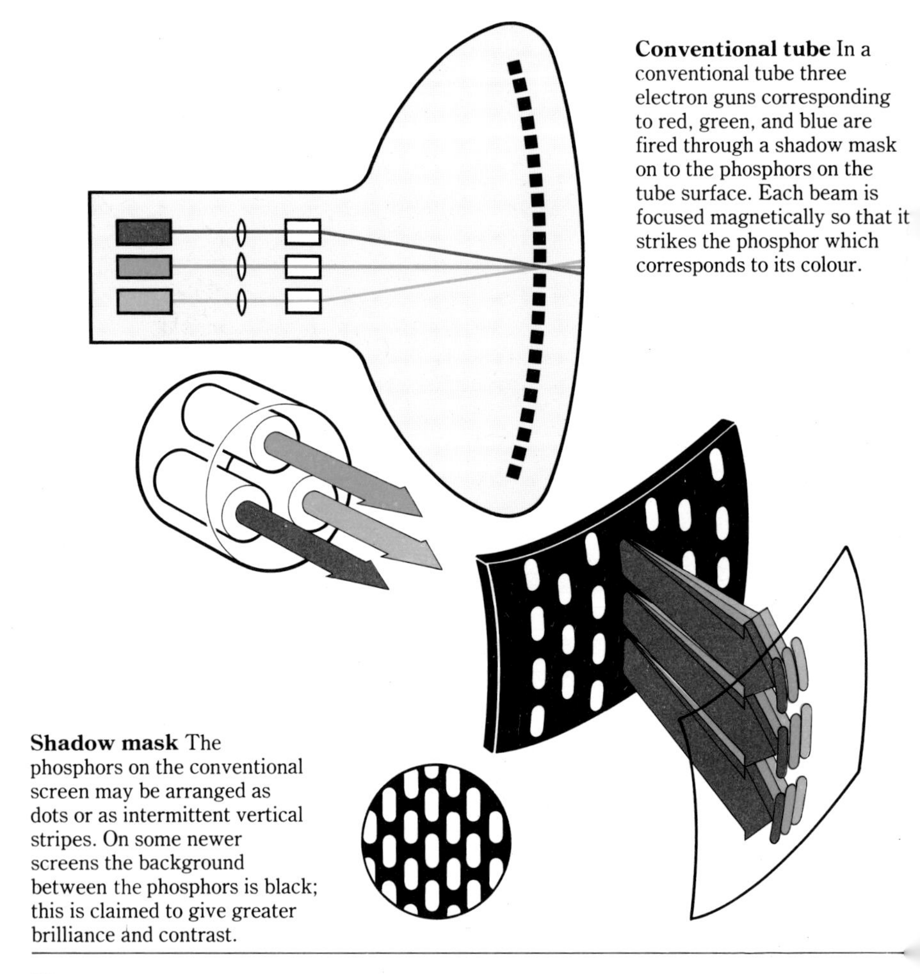

Conventional tube In a conventional tube three electron guns corresponding to red, green, and blue are fired through a shadow mask on to the phosphors on the tube surface. Each beam is focused magnetically so that it strikes the phosphor which corresponds to its colour.

Shadow mask The phosphors on the conventional screen may be arranged as dots or as intermittent vertical stripes. On some newer screens the background between the phosphors is black; this is claimed to give greater brilliance and contrast.

phosphor on the screen, after passing through what is known as a shadow mask. The phosphors were originally dots, but are now sometimes striped, and they are grouped in threes, known as triads, corresponding to the three electron guns. They are very small, and a typical TV set would have about one and a half million dots.

Choosing a TV receiver

The factors to look for in a good TV are in many cases obvious: good colour balance, sharpness, convergence, sound, and overall performance. Many people are now looking for remote control. Less common, but valuable, are: fine-tint control, which enables you to adjust the hue slightly to your own taste; a tone control on the sound; two speakers or even a stereo facility; an Audio Out socket at the rear for connection to an audio system; and, last but by no means least, audio and video inputs at the rear — with these, the receiver can also be used as a *monitor* (pp.34-5).

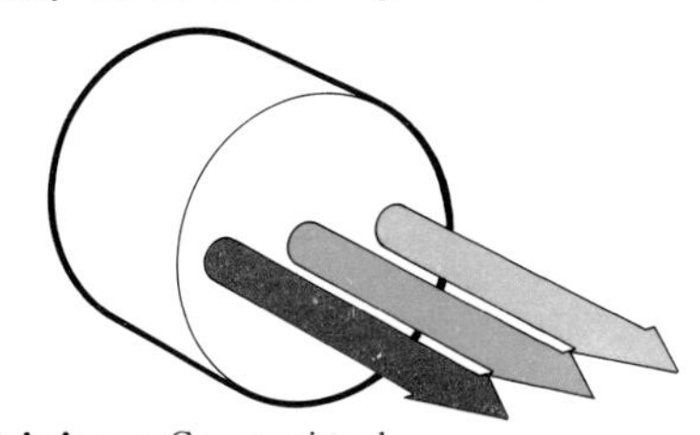

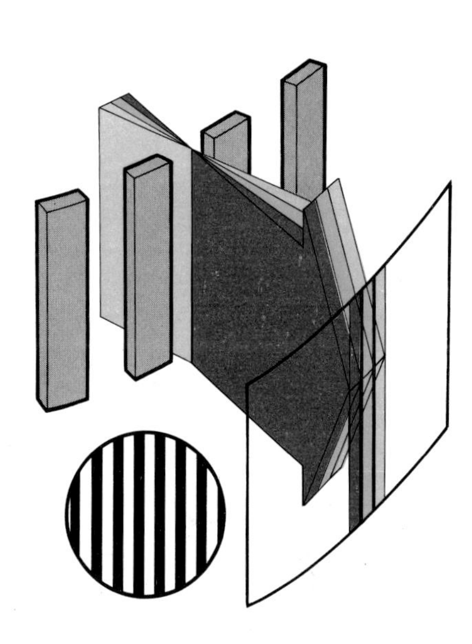

Trinitron Conventional ubes tend to develop a ecurrent fault: the onvergence of the beams, vhich is essential for sharply lefined images, tends to drift ver the course of time. In the Sony Trinitron system and dopted by other nanufacturers, one single gun s used, so that convergence is uaranteed. It fires through a ertical aperture grille on to ertically striped phosphors, nd gives an exceptionally right and sharp picture.

Cordless remote control

Remote controls are nowadays mostly cordless, and are operated either ultrasonically or in the infra-red wavelength. The former may startle your dog or cat (who can hear them), while infra-red models are capable of greater sophistication. However, if your video recorder has an infra-red control as well, there is a distinct danger of interference between the two controls. Both forms are fairly directional and powered by battery.

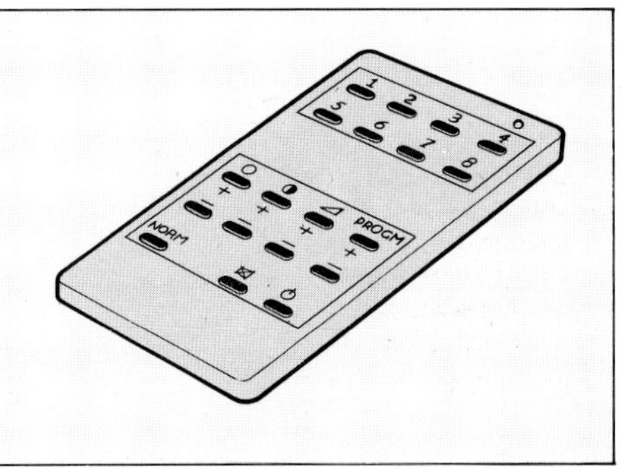

The TV monitor

Strictly speaking, a monitor will display picture only, the sound passing through a quite separate circuit. For most amateur and semi-professional purposes, one is talking about a monitor/receiver. This will not only replay sound if required but also contain a tuner for reception of rf signals from normal transmissions or from the rf output of a VCR. The difference between this and an ordinary receiver is that the monitor will have video and sound input and output sockets. This means that when you are hooking up a more complex video system of any kind, you do not have to go through the tedious process of converting the video signal of an rf signal and then reconverting through a tuner, which also affects the quality.

What to look for

A professional monitor will have very high definition, when fed with an excellent source, and it should be able to accept both 8-pin and UHF video cables (75-ohm). It should have a DC restoration circuit, sometimes known as black level clamp, which is also invaluable in a normal receiver — it maintains a true black, and thus ensures a full, rich range of tones all the way from pure black to peak white.

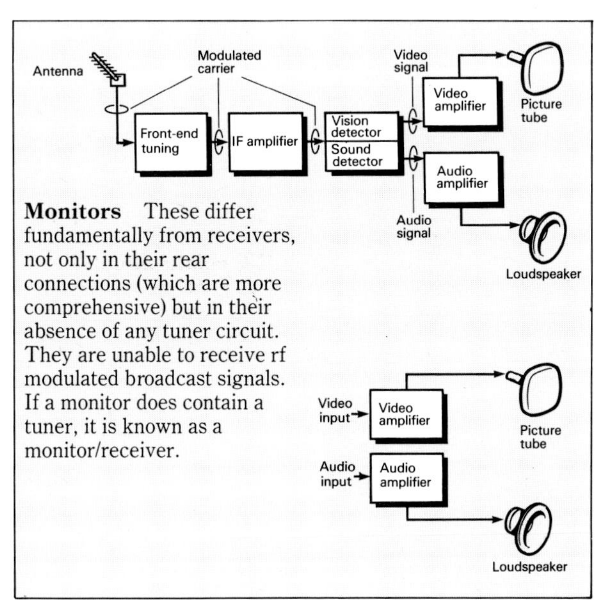

Monitors These differ fundamentally from receivers, not only in their rear connections (which are more comprehensive) but in their absence of any tuner circuit. They are unable to receive rf modulated broadcast signals. If a monitor does contain a tuner, it is known as a monitor/receiver.

1 Tint control
2 Colour control
3 Contrast control
4 Brightness control
5 Earphone jack
6 Power/Battery warning indicator
7 VTR input select switch
8 LINE input select switch
9 Power off/Volume control
10 Built-in speaker
11 Battery compartment
12 Mains power switch
13 AC input socket
14 DC input socket
15 Horizontal hold control
16 Vertical hold control
17 Height control
18 8-pin VTR input connector
19 75-ohm termination switch
20 Audio input/output DIN connector
21 Video input/output connector
22 Colour system select switch
23 Video line input connector
24 Audio input DIN connector
25 Output select switch
26 Audio output DIN connector
27 Video output connector

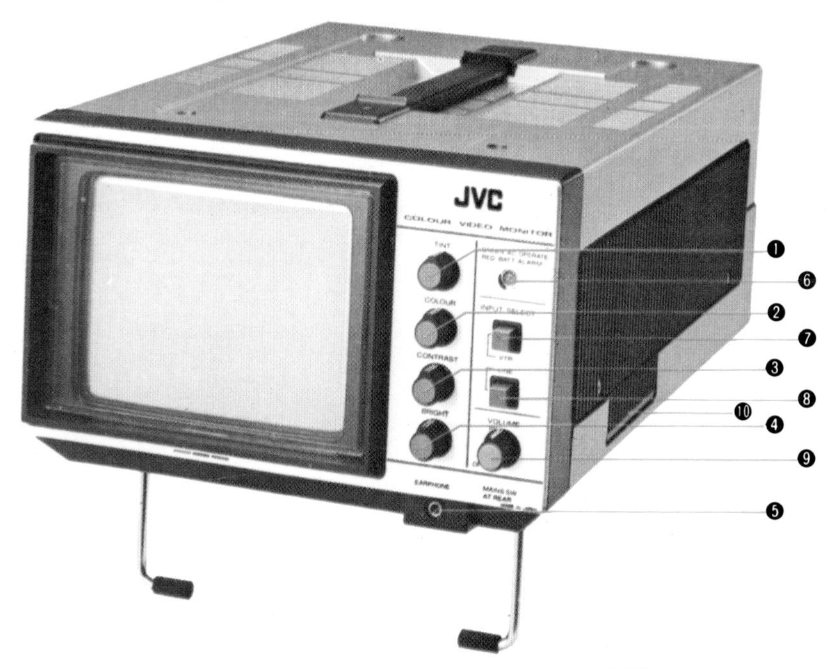

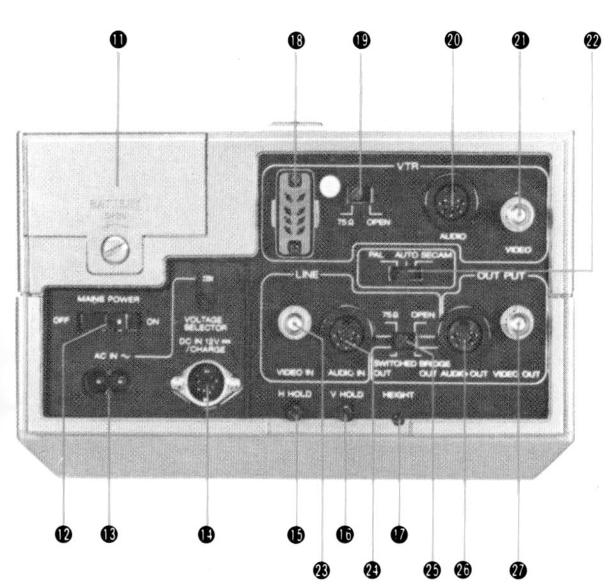

JVC colour monitor
This portable machine , which contains no tuner, is highly versatile; it can be run off DC (12V) or AC (110/120 V), and is suitable for PAL or SECAM. It is an ideal light monitor for location work.

JVC
REC LOCK

Video recording

With modern automatic machinery, it is extremely simple to undertake the basic tasks of video recording off air — time shift, recording on one channel while viewing another. In addition, modern machines offer sophisticated and attractive means of controlling the replay — picture-search, slow motion, cueing facilities, and so on. But this only begins to hint at what a video recorder can do. Once a camera is added, the possibilities are limitless. Where once the recorder was a mere passive instrument at the mercy of the whims of the programme controllers, it now becomes a truly creative tool whose uses are limited only by the imagination of the user.

Video recording

Tape is the recording medium used by both audio and video recorders. It is a very thin layer of polyester which is coated on one side with a layer of oxide that is capable of magnetization by the recording heads. The oxide is most commonly iron, though some newer types of tape include chromium dioxide, cobalt-doped, metal, and metal-evaporated tapes. These last types give considerably better frequency response, with a consequent improvement in picture quality and recording density.

The tape will also have a highly polished topcoat on the emulsion side to protect the heads and the emulsion, and to improve the head contact. There is also often a backing of carbon on the other side to reduce static as the tape passes across the head guides.

It was a considerable number of years after the invention of sound recording before the same principles could be applied to video. In sound, the frequencies that are required to be committed to the tape range from about 20 to 20,000 Hz, whereas in video, the range, or bandwidth, is nearer five and a half *million* Hertz (5.5 MHz). The amount of recorded information that can be packed on to tape depends on two primary factors: the speed of the tape across the record/replay heads; and the width of the tape head gap. The faster the effective 'writing speed' of the tape, and the finer the head gap, the more information can be absorbed for subsequent replay. In practice, this works out in home video to an effective writing speed of around 6 metres per second; more in professional machines.

Since it was clearly impractical to have the tape whistling past the heads at this speed, all the early efforts at video recording, and almost all of the subsequent developments, have been directed at achieving a high writing speed without excessive actual tape speed. This has

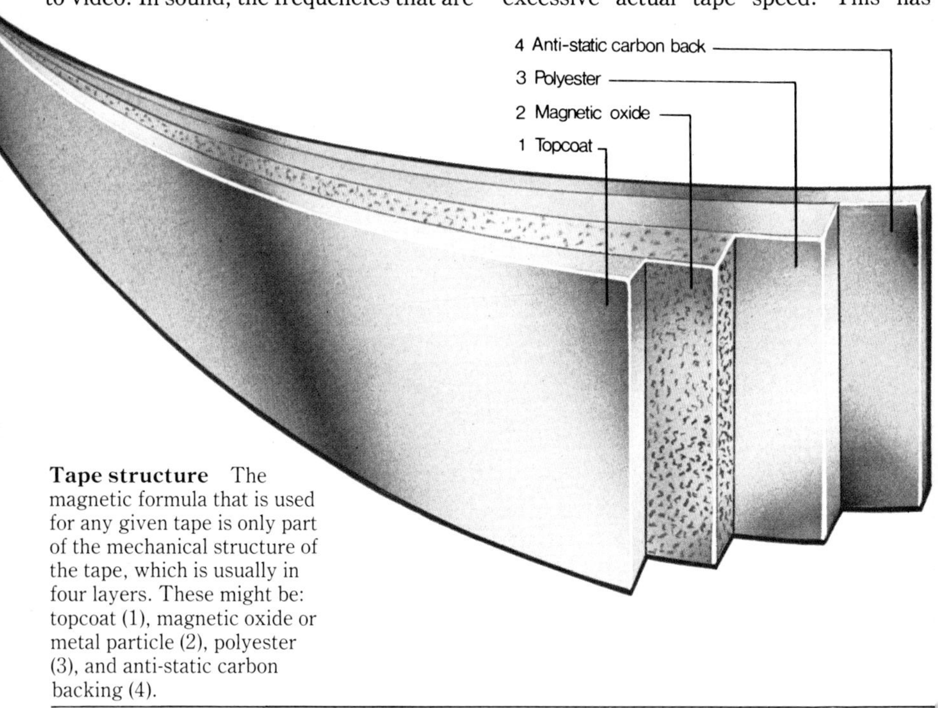

Tape structure The magnetic formula that is used for any given tape is only part of the mechanical structure of the tape, which is usually in four layers. These might be: topcoat (1), magnetic oxide or metal particle (2), polyester (3), and anti-static carbon backing (4).

meant that the tape heads themselves must move in relation to the tape. At the same time, technological advances have led to an ever-decreasing width in the tape itself (from 2-inch to ¼-inch).

The story of video recording

True video recording really began with the invention by Ampex of the Quadruplex recorder (Quad) in 1956. This used a 2-inch tape which travelled at 15 ips, and across which four recording heads spun at very high speeds. The video signal was thus laid down at a writing speed which was adequate for the bandwidth of black and white TV. An audio track ran longitudinally along the top of the tape, using a stationary record/replay head, while along the bottom was a cue and control track. Quad is still in use in studio work, but is being replaced by *helical scan* machines.

Helical scan is simply another way of moving the heads in relation to the tape movement. Instead of spinning the heads at right angles to the direction of travel of the tape, they spin in the same axis as the tape motion, though at a slight angle, with the result that the recorded tracks run at a very shallow angle. Each individual track is therefore much longer than in Quad recording, and in fact each contains one field (half a frame) of video.

At first, all these recorders were reel-to-reel, and black and white only. The tapes were either 1-inch or ½-inch. With colour came the first cassettes, and the first application of the machines to domestic use. Sony introduced its ¾-inch U-Matic cassette system in 1970, and this has now been refined to a very high professional standard. It is in fact the only cassette to have survived from the early years, which saw a proliferation of tape formats that were soon to become obsolete.

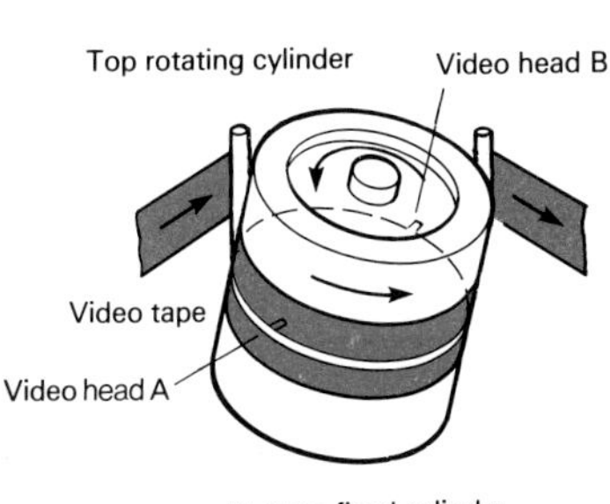

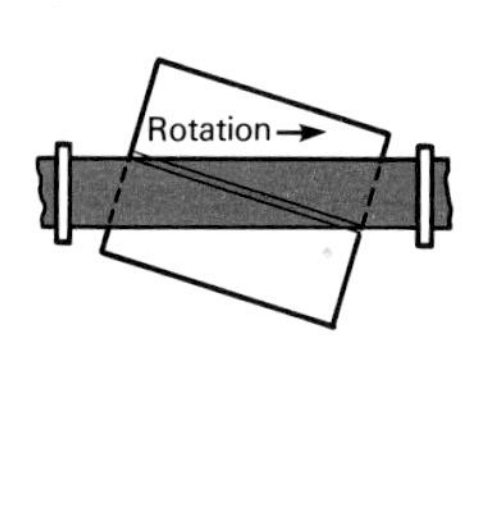

Helical scan In helical scan machines, which now are universal in the domestic market, and rapidly becoming so in the professional, the heads spin horizontally, but at a slight angle to the tape, creating a very long record path along the tape. Each pass of the record head creates one field.

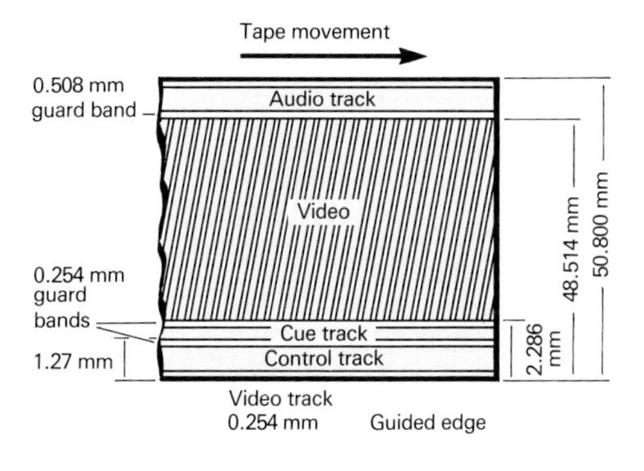

Quadruplex Quad recording, on 2-inch tape, is highly expensive and sophisticated. Each of the vertically rotating heads 'writes' just 16 lines of picture across the tape on each pass, and the tape moves horizontally at either 7½ or 15 ips. There is also space for a cue and control track, in addition to the audio track. Stereo too is a possible option.

The important innovations were the introduction of Sony's Betamax format in 1975, shortly followed by JVC's VHS system. Philips had beaten Sony to the start with its own ½-inch VCR system, but this has now been replaced with the very latest addition to the formats, the Philips/Grundig V2000 system. Here, although ½-inch tape is used, the cassette is two-sided, and only ¼ inch is used on each pass. Some of the newest, and smallest, portable recorders, such as the Technicolor and Funai systems, also use ¼-inch tape. Japanese manufacturers are attempting to standardize the planned ¼-inch one-piece camera/recorders, but the signs are not particularly hopeful that agreement will be reached without yet another costly and confusing war of the formats.

The story of video recording, then, is one of smaller and smaller tapes, at slower speeds, with longer playing times and vastly improved quality. The next logical step is purely solid-state recorder memory, with no moving parts at all, but the introduction of such a remarkable system is still some years away.

Guard bands and azimuth

In the earliest video recording systems, each track of video was separated from its neighbour, and from the audio and control tracks, by a 'guard band'. This empty patch of tape was designed to ensure that there was no interference between one track and the next; but it took up a good deal of the available space on the tape. It was found that by slightly tilting each alternate record/replay head at a slightly different angle (or azimuth) to the tape, the guard bands could be dispensed with, giving greater density and more economic use of tape and longer playing times.

The control track

The video image is controlled by two sync pulses: line sync and field sync. In a helical scan machine, the line sync is contained within the video information on the tape, but the recorder and the receiver need a separate field sync pulse which is laid along a control track at the edge of the tape. A separate stationary record/replay head is used for this track. It monitors the pulses on the tape and adjusts the speed accordingly. If the pulses are irregularly spaced (as in a 'crash edit' — pp. 168—9) the result will be a break-up of the picture, or a frame-roll, until the recorder has found its new rhythm again. The new Philips system has found an ingenious way of dispensing with the control track entirely, leaving a spare track for stereo or an extra language in pre-recorded tapes (pp. 54—5).

Head drum The diameter of the head drum is different for all the major helical scan video systems. They spin at a constant speed, according to country, but it is their diameter, related to the linear tape speed, which determines the eventual writing speed of the video heads across the tape.

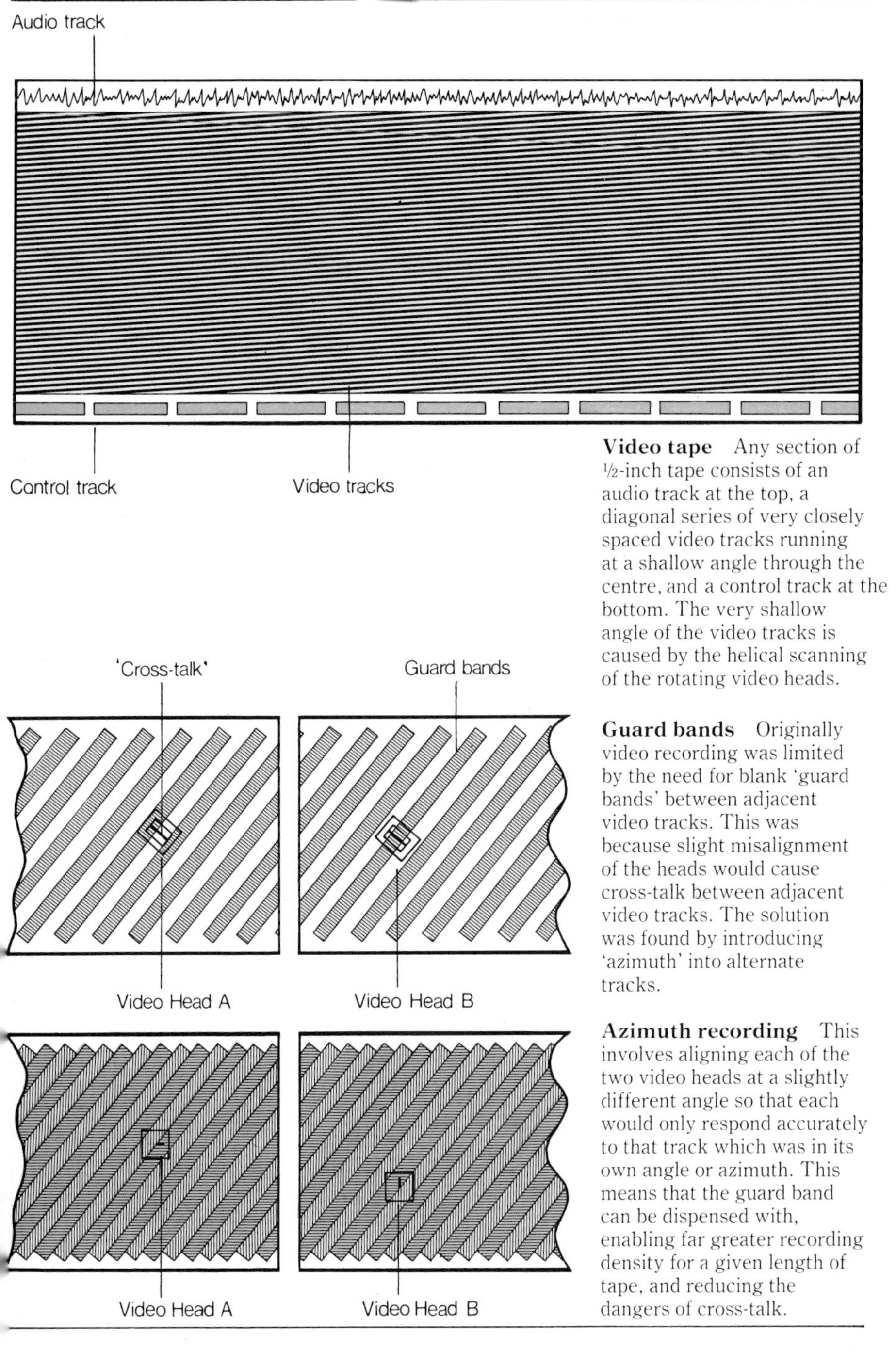

Video tape Any section of ½-inch tape consists of an audio track at the top, a diagonal series of very closely spaced video tracks running at a shallow angle through the centre, and a control track at the bottom. The very shallow angle of the video tracks is caused by the helical scanning of the rotating video heads.

Guard bands Originally video recording was limited by the need for blank 'guard bands' between adjacent video tracks. This was because slight misalignment of the heads would cause cross-talk between adjacent video tracks. The solution was found by introducing 'azimuth' into alternate tracks.

Azimuth recording This involves aligning each of the two video heads at a slightly different angle so that each would only respond accurately to that track which was in its own angle or azimuth. This means that the guard band can be dispensed with, enabling far greater recording density for a given length of tape, and reducing the dangers of cross-talk.

Using a video recorder

Recording from TV

All home video recorders are capable of recording from a VHF or, in Europe, a UHF aerial input, because they are equipped with tuners that de-modulate the rf signal that has been transmitted into a video signal that can be directly recorded. On replay, the video signal is re-modulated on to a new rf frequency, usually higher up the waveband. This is in turn de-modulated by the tuner in the home receiver, and presented on the screen. The quality of the recorded image will always be inferior, however, to the original signal, and you must therefore make sure that you are getting the very best reception you can if you wish to get good-quality pictures off air (pp. 30—1). You should also be sure that your receiver is correctly tuned to the VCR output, and that the VCR itself is accurately tuned to the stations selected on the tuner — these will usually incorporate some form of Automatic Frequency Control (AFC).

Time shift

The most simple, and most common, use of the VCR is to record a programme for replay at a time which is more convenient: for example, you may wish to watch one programme while recording another, or you may be in the middle of a meal just as your favourite serial is starting. In these circumstances, you simply begin the recording by pressing the record and play buttons simultaneously, and switch off at the end of the programme. The VCR is entirely independent of the TV receiver: it receives the rf signal direct from the aerial, passes it on to the receiver in rf form, and meanwhile gets on with its own recording irrespective of whichever programme you have selected on the TV. It can also produce an unmodulated video output for display on a monitor or monitor/ receiver.

Recording while you are out

A more sophisticated version of time-shift recording is now available, with varying degrees of complexity, on all the current domestic machines. A timer will enable you to select precise 'On' and 'Off' points for a given *time, day,* and *channel* — in some cases, many times, and many channels, and up to ninety-nine days may be punched into the micro-processor memory. On more simple machines, only one programe can be selected for recording. You must be certain that there is enough tape on the cassette to accommodate the programme, and you should *always* check the 'Out' setting on the timer. Do remember that programmes often change from published times so allow a degree of leeway. There is nothing more frustrating than to return home only to find that the machine has turned itself off at the climax of a coveted movie.

The multi-programme, multi-day feature is by no means a gimmick and is well worth considering when choosing a VCR. Furthermore, if you are away for very long periods, you might even consider the Sony system of stacking cassettes (see over for extended recording and, presumably, extended replay.

Counter The counter of any VCR is not a true footage counter, and for instance '100' at the beginning of the tape does not correspond in *duration* to '100' at the end of the tape. On this particular machine the time remaining on the tape may be read off from the row of dots in the upper right-hand corner. V2000 machines are unique in having a more precise read-out of elapsed recording time.

Clock The clock on a VCR usually has a diode display, which may be varied in brightness. It is also usually a 24-hour clock. It should be accurately set by reference either to a speaking clock on the telephone or a time reference on the radio. A useful feature of many VCRs is a rechargeable back-up battery which takes over if there is an interruption in the power supply. In this case a quartz oscillator would take over the function otherwise governed by the mains supply.

'rogramming To ›rogramme any VCR for ecording it is important to be ighly methodical. You must elect the programme, the day n which you wish the ecording to begin, the hour ı.m. or p.m.), the duration of ıe recording, and finally the hannel. It may be possible to re-select more than a dozen onsecutive recordings for up ɔ 99 days on some machines. 'he limitation is more likely ɔ be the total duration of the vailable tape.

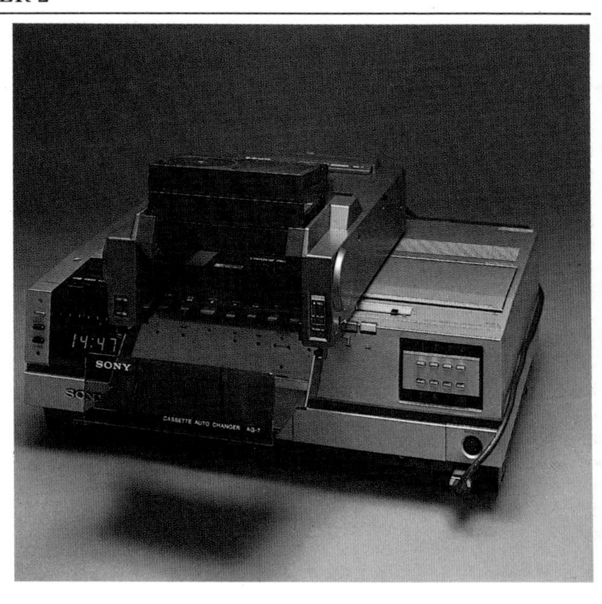

Sony C7 Betastack This cassette stacking system makes it possible for up to four separate tapes to be changed automatically, giving 13 hours of unattended recording or playback.

The Pause control

Leaving aside the value of the Pause control when making your own video tapes, this feature is very useful when you are taping a programme that is peppered with commercial breaks. If you are prepared to monitor the programme during the recording, you can press the Pause button as the commercial begins, and disengage it at the end. A remote control, either wired or cordless, will be particularly valuable, especially in the USA, where commercials are both longer and more frequent. In the pause mode the tape does not disengage from the drum, and there is thus no delay when you press the Pause button to re-start the recording at the end of the commercial. The control should not be used for longer than a few minutes, since it will cause excessive wear to both the heads and the stationary part of the tape against which they are rotating. The 'edit' which you have thus effected should not cause the picture to roll or to break up. On replay, the Pause control can be used for short periods to halt a programme – if the telephone rings, for example – without disengaging the tape. This means that you can pick up precisely where you left off.

Making your own home video tapes

With a suitable camera and connections, any modern VCR can be used to make home video tapes. If you have only a standard domestic VCR, you will be limited to shooting in one room (unless you want to move the recorder or else use a long extension cable to the camera), but with a portable VCR the possibilities are endless. Also, when combined with a tuner/timer and an AC adaptor unit, the portable VCR will function perfectly well as a normal domestic cassette recorder off the AC power supply (pp. 68–9). Modern VCRs are easier to connect than their predecessors, by means of a multi-pin plug on the front.

Pre-recorded tapes

Pre-recorded tapes are available in both the two main formats (VHS and Betamax), and they are now coming on to the market in the Philips V2000 and Funai ¼-inch formats as well, but the format must match your replay machine. You should also check the duration of the tape against the price to be sure that you are getting value for money. Pre-recorded tapes are still very expensive when compared to video discs, and are

Tracking control One problem when playing pre-recorded tapes, or tapes recorded by friends on another machine, is that the heads may not accurately track the previously recorded signal. The result is a horizontal noise-bar. This can be corrected by use of the tracking control. This adjusts the relative speed of the heads so that they accurately follow the movement of the recorded video tracks. Some machines have separate tracking controls for the slow motion and freeze-frame function, as opposed to normal play. After you have adjusted the control for a 'foreign' tape, return it to the automatic position.

likely to remain so, since discs can be stamped out whereas tapes must be laboriously recorded on a bank of slave machines. (There are, however, reports of a new high-speed tape copying process.) Furthermore, many tapes are pirated and therefore of poor quality, generations away from the stolen original. Nevertheless, in areas of poor reception, or where the movies are untempting, video tapes are the only solution — even at exorbitant prices. Rental is an attractive alternative.

Tracking
With pre-recorded cassettes, as with borrowed cassettes, you will probably need to adjust the tracking control. If a tape has not been recorded on your own machine, it will need some fine adjustment to obtain a stable picture. Turn the tracking control knob until you have obtained the optimum streak-free image. Do remember to return the tracking control to Normal or Auto after each replay session with a new tape.

Copying tapes
Any VCR can copy a tape from any other VCR if the correct audio and video connections are provided. The connections should be through the audio and video sockets rather than the rf socket, since the latter will introduce two quite unnecessary stages into the process. If you have the right plugs, you can copy a tape from one VCR on to another, but the quality loss will be noticeable on domestic ½-inch machines. On Sony U-Matic ¾-inch hi-band machines, by contrast, it is barely visible. With professional machines, an oscilloscope is needed to spot the difference between the copy and the original.

Adding sound
It is possible on most domestic machines to replace the original sound with a new soundtrack of your own — music, commentary, or effects; or a pre-mixed combination of all three. But on current equipment this involves the complete erasure of the original. This situation will change before long, and the same restrictions do not apply to professional equipment.

Slide to tape and film to tape
Both home movies and slides can be transferred on to tape relatively cheaply by a specialized video house, or you can do it yourself (pp. 176–7).

Additional features

Slow motion

This facility is now quite common on domestic recorders, though it is perhaps doubtful how often it is used in practice. The tape moves slowly, and very frequently at a variable speed, past the heads, which scan the image as it passes. This often leads to mistracking, which is visible as a thick row of dotted lines across one segment of the screen. It can be corrected on Betamax or VHS sets by the tracking control, which in some cases will be separate from the 'normal' tracking control. Some of the newer machines have a separate set of heads for the slow motion and freeze-frame facility, giving improved tracking. The V2000 system does not have this problem, since its dynamic track following array automatically aligns the heads with the tracks, whatever the speed of the tape, giving very good image stability. In slow motion, there is no sound replay in any system.

Freeze-frame

In freeze-frame mode, only one interlaced field is displayed, in all its graininess, and here too the tracking problems all too often become evident on both Betamax and VHS machines. The question again arises of how often this impressive effect will actually be used in practice — for sport, perhaps, or in the replay of assassinations? Freeze-frames should in any case not be held too long, since they cause wear on the heads and on the portion of the tape which they are scrutinizing.

Picture-search

This is the feature (sometimes referred to as 'shuttle-search') which allows you to

Slow motion Sports are one of the areas in which the slow-motion effect can be most useful. It can also be invaluable as an aid to coaching. In particular it is useful to have a variable-speed facility on the recorder control.

Freeze-frame In slow motion and freeze-frame it is normal to have some form of noise-bars visible on even well-adjusted machines. These can be largely removed by using the tracking control.

scan the image, without sound, at many times the normal speed. In Betamax and V2000 this can be very fast indeed, but the VHS system is at present somewhat restricted in the speeds offered. It is probably the single most valuable 'luxury' feature on a video recorder, since it enables you to find the exact place you want on the tape without the need for a precise tape-counter reference. It is unfortunately accompanied, on both VHS and Betamax systems currently available, by five or six thin noise-bars across the screen. V2000 has proved better in this respect. There is no sound replay in this mode, since it would be unintelligible.

X2 replay

A few machines, for example the JVC 7700, offer replay at twice the speed, with the sound electronically reduced in pitch so that it can be comprehended. The device cannot be too highly recommended to those who are easily bored.

Remote control

The remote control of the recorder will be separate from that of the TV, and in most cases will be vastly more complex. Since, if you have one, you will probably have both, be sure that they do not interfere with each other. There is a good deal to be said for opting for one corded control and one infra-red, for instance, so that the TV channel changer does not accidentally switch off the recorder in mid-film. In all cases, remember that infra-red and ultrasonic remote controls are highly directional; some more than others. Very few work at all round corners. In such rooms, it is advisable to stay with the cumbersome old cord.

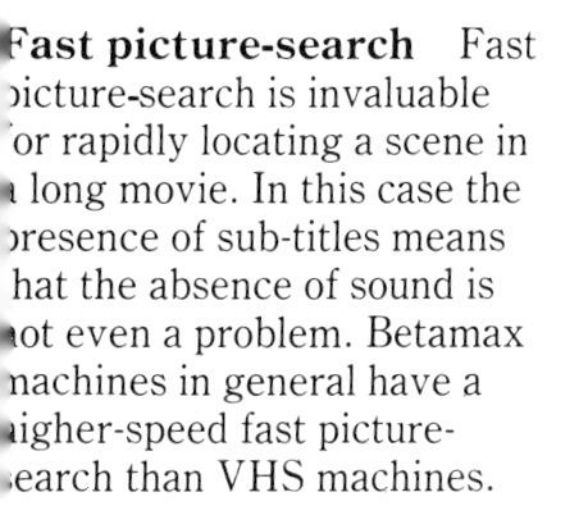

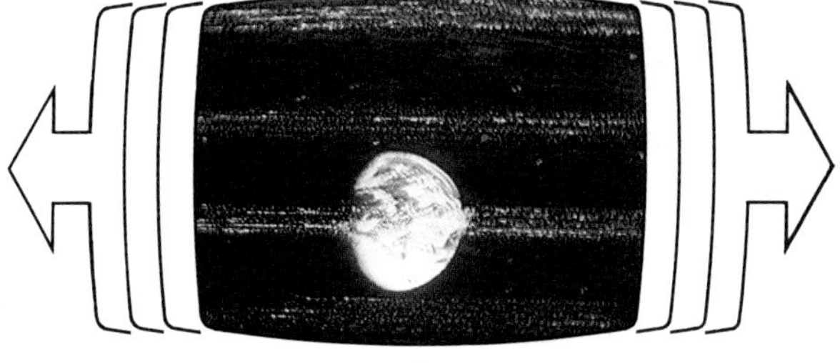

Fast picture-search Fast picture-search is invaluable for rapidly locating a scene in a long movie. In this case the presence of sub-titles means that the absence of sound is not even a problem. Betamax machines in general have a higher-speed fast picture-search than VHS machines.

Remote control Remote controls can be highly sophisticated. This infra-red model contains all the controls that are needed for programming the recorder as well as freeze-frame, slow motion, picture-search, and X2 playback. Provided there is a direct line of view to the recorder, the user need never leave his seat at all except to insert or remove a cassette.

Choosing a VCR system

At the present state of the art, the logical choice for a home recorder must be one of the three ½-inch cassette systems – VHS, Betamax, or V2000. The end-results are very similar, but the formats are quite incompatible; so how do you decide?

Which format?

Running time Running times are different in Europe and the USA for the various systems, since both Sony and VHS machines use variable speeds on their models for the US market, whereas in Europe the speeds are constant while the tape length is varied. The total running times available are given in the table.

It is important for users in the USA to remember that the slower speeds on VHS and Betamax entail a noticeable loss of quality. Also remember that the 8 hours' play on the Philips/Grundig V2000 machines is really 2 x 4, since the tape has to be turned over half-way through. However, this is still the most economical in terms of tape per minute. If very long runs are required, you may consider the Sony stacking system, which gives up to 14 hours 33 minutes of recording, unattended.

Quality Good picture quality is a combination of low visual noise, high definition, and picture stability. At their normal speeds, all three systems will resolve at least 250 lines, and this represents a bandwidth of about 3 MHz. Betamax enthusiasts claim that its writing speed of 6.6 m/sec gives it an edge over VHS (4.85 m/sec) and V2000 (5.08 m/sec), but the head gap and other features are quite as important as this difference. There is, however, a substantial difference between different machines *within* the different formats. You should test before buying. The quality of the tape you buy will of course have a very dramatic effect on the image. *It is worth spending the extra money if you want first-class results.*

Features The features that are now being crammed into video recorders are astonishing, though they add very considerably to the bill. They include: freeze-frame, picture-search, frame-by-frame advance, double-speed with sound artificially lowered, Dolby noise reduction, remote control (infra-red or cordless), multi-day, multi-progamme timers, memory, and so on. At the top of the line, both VHS and Betamax also offer a very valuable feature which becomes essential if you wish to edit from a portable recorder on to your home-based machine: a roll-back editing system which means that the incoming shot will not cause frame-roll on replay. It is well worth enquiring about this if you ever intend to edit. Otherwise, the only differences between the formats are minor: the Betamax offers somewhat faster picture-search speeds (40X – 40 times), and the V2000 should theoretically be capable of a number of tricks that have not yet been exploited by other manufacturers. In all these cases, ask yourself whether the extra expense is really justified: for instance, while picture-search is certainly useful, the freeze-frame that goes with it is rarely used in practice, however glamorous a novelty it may at first seem. *Match the hardware to your real needs (and your pocket).*

Will it become obsolete?

This is a very real worry, as anyone who bought one of the two earlier Philips VCRs will tell you. The investment in tapes alone can easily be very expensive, and you also want to be certain that enough of your friends will share the format to be able to exchange tapes. At the moment, VHS is fairly well ahead of Betamax in both Europe and the USA, though Philips/Grundig are making small inroads in Europe after a very shaky and belated start. Certainly, the amount of money spent so far on the two major systems should guarantee that both will survive until the next technological break-through. However, despite its technical brilliance, the V2000 format is still being treated with a certain caution by those who perhaps feel that even two formats is one too many.

To rent or to buy?

The combination of uncertainty over the formats and the complexity of the machinery involved has led many people, particularly in the UK, to rent their video recorders rather than buy them. This trend is now spreading to the USA in a small way. It is worth bearing in mind as an option, since the heads will certainly wear out after a time, and even routine maintenance can be quite expensive. What is more, you are guaranteed the most up-to-date technology in rental, since you can trade in the old model for a new one as it comes along. It is still crucial, however, to make the right decision about the format, since you will soon amass a tape library that you will not want to part with.

Times and speeds

VHS

Europe One speed only (2.34 cm/ sec, 0.92 ips). Duration according to the length of tape: up to 3 hours normally, though a 4-hour tape has recently been introduced.

USA/Japan Three speeds: SP, LP, and SLP. This gives 2, 4, and 6 hours' play respectively.

Betamax

Europe One speed only (1.873 cm/ sec, 0.74 ips). This gives up to 3¼ hours' play.

USA/Japan X1, X2, X3. X1 virtually extinct. X2, which corresponds to SP on VHS, gives 3 hours 20 minutes, and X3 gives 5 hours.

V2000

Europe One speed only (2.44 cm/ sec, 0.96 ips). Duration 2 x 4 hours per tape.

USA Not yet launched.

Track Widths (μm) VHS 49, Betamax 33, V2000 23.

VHS

The VHS, or Video Home System, was developed in Japan by JVC in 1976. In Europe it is now perhaps the most popular of all the domestic formats, while in the USA it shares pride of place with the Sony Betamax system (pp. 52-3). Like Betamax, the cassette is of the reel-to-reel variety, using a helical scanning drum of either two or sometimes four record/replay heads. The tape speed in Europe is 2.339 cm/sec (0.92 ips), and this gives very good definition because of the spinning heads. These rotate across the tape at 1500 rpm (1800 rpm in USA) so that nearly five *metres* (16½ ft) of oxide tape are effectively flowing under the video heads every second. The sound is recorded on a separate track through a stationary audio recording head. Some of the newer machines have Dolby noise reduction units to improve the reproduction.

The standard European speed gives up to 4 hours' recording/replay, but in the USA and Japan three speeds are available: Standard Play (SP) at 3.335 cm/sec (1.31 ips), Long Play (LP) at 1.667 cm/sec (0.66 ips), and Extended Play, or Super Long Play (EP/SLP) at 1.11 cm/sec (0.44 ips). These give 2, 4, and 6 hours' play respectively, though of course the quality is markedly lower at the more extended plays because of the slower tape speeds being

JVC HR-7700 This recorder features automatic front-loading and a wide range of functions which may be controlled remotely through an infra-red keyboard. The display panel can be programmed to show either time or a tape counter, or one of eight programmes stretching over 14 days that has been punched into the micro-processor memory. Other features include replay at double speed, Dolby noise reduction, frame-advance, and tape memory.

used. To compensate for the different requirements of slow-speed recording some manufacturers now incorporate a separate pair of video heads, with a finer head gap, which operate at the lower speeds. Other facilities universally offered include the usual multi-day, multi-channel programming (pp. 48-9), infra-red and corded remote control (p. 47), freeze-frame,fast and slow motion, with rapid search at up to ten times normal speed (p. 47), and many other refinements. However, unlike Betamax, VHS tapes cannot be scanned visually during the rapid-rewind phase, since the tape is disengaged from the heads in that mode. This has the advantage that wear is reduced on both the tapes and the heads, and a relatively fast picture-search (10X) is frequently offered instead. The disengagement of the tape also means that editing, dubbing, and re-recording require slightly different techniques from the Betamax system, in which the tape remains in contact with the heads during rapid rewind. (For these techniques, see pp. 170-5.)

There is a huge, and growing, selection of accessories from cameras to portable recorders, timer units, special effects, telecine units. It is a fine system that is here to stay until a new generation of video equipment arrives.

Recording parameters
The VHS system requires a control track, which leaves room for only one audio track on current machines. Here the angle of the video tracks has been greatly exaggerated — the very long sweeps of the video head are actually almost horizontal.

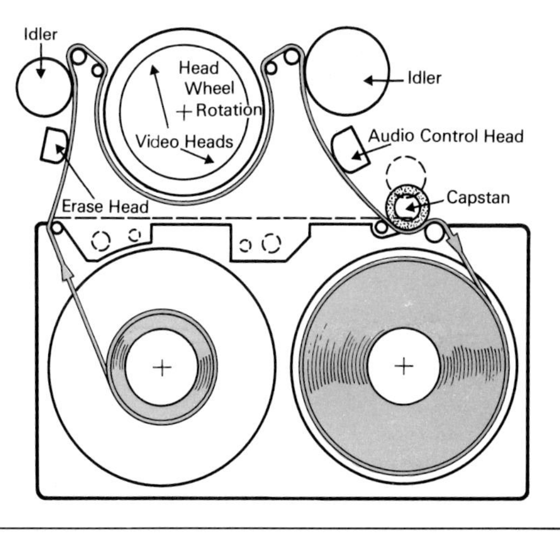

VHS cassette system The tape path is known as an M-wrap. The two loading poles remove the tape from the cassette in a fairly brief movement which enables comparatively rapid loading for record/replay; the tape is retracted into the cassette for rapid rewind.

Betamax

Sony first introduced the Beta format in the shape of the Betamax recorder, which played for one hour. This has since been developed for home use into the Beta 2 format which offers up to 3¼ hours' play in Europe, where it is simply known as Betamax. Japanese and US machines, on the other hand, have up to three speeds — X1, X2, and X3 — which give up to 5 hours' play per tape, with corresponding loss of quality at the slower speeds. (X1 is now virtually obsolete in home machines.)

Like VHS and V2000, Beta tapes are ½-inch, and the cassette size falls between the two rivals. The linear tape speed in Europe is slower than VHS (1.873 cm/sec, 0.74 ips, compared to 2.34 cm/sec, 0.92 ips), but thanks to a larger drum the actual writing speed is slightly higher (6.6 m/sec compared to 4.85 m/sec). The tape path is radically different from the so-called M-loading system used in the VHS machines. The B-load that is used in the Betamax is claimed to place considerably less strain on the tape than the VHS M-load, and the tape remains in place during rapid rewind. In fact, the complexity of the B-load is such that it cannot be retracted from the

Betamax cassette format In the Betamax cassette about 60 cm (2 ft) of tape are extracted during playing, recording, and fast picture-search. The complexity of this so-called B-wrap means that much more time is required to retract the tape into the cassette than in the rival VHS or V2000 systems. However, as less strain is placed on the tape in the Betamax systems, very fast picture-search is therefore possible.

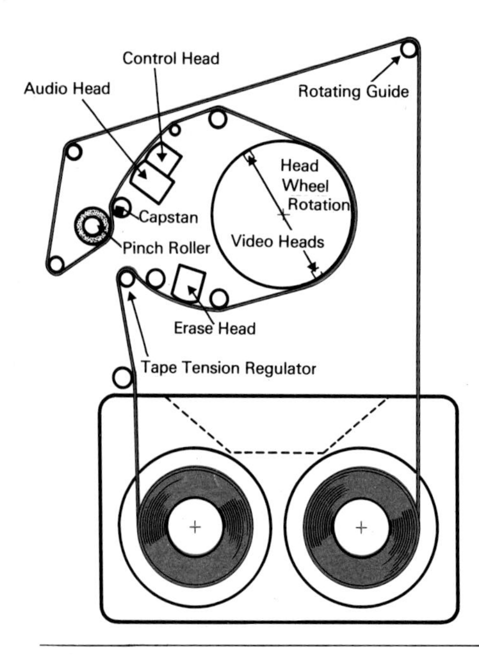

Sony C7 This recorder is at the top of the Sony range. Its full logic touch controls make it possible to go straight from rewind to play without pressing Stop; there is also an infra-red remote control. Seven forms of viewing are offered: normal, slow motion, still frame, frame-by-frame advance, triple speed, picture-search. Other features include an automatic programme search, a tape-end alarm, automatic rewind, and a digital tape counter.

drum into the cassette at anything like the speed of the VHS machines. One result of this is the very fast picture-search which is offered on some Betamax machines — 40X in one case.

The features available at the top end of the range are otherwise very similar to those on VHS, the only significant exception being the stacking arrangement which Sony have made for their C7: up to four tapes can be loaded, giving 13 hours of recording. This matches the four-programme, 14-day timer on the same machine so that, for example, four full-length features could easily be put on to tape while you were away on holiday. This machine also incorporates a very good Phase Edit control to reduce or eliminate frame-roll on edits. Other manufacturers include Sanyo, Toshiba, and Zenith.

Audio quality

Since the audio head is static, the audio quality is a direct reflection of the linear tape speed (see pp. 48-9). The speed of a standard audio casette is 4.76 cm/sec (1.87 ips). Noise reduction systems are therefore highly desirable.

V2000

The cassette

The V2000 is the latest, and in many ways the most innovative, of the three major systems on the market. It also represents a rather dramatic advance in the efficiency with which the area of available tape is employed, so that it can record 8 hours on to an area of tape that in the VHS system would only record 4 hours. What is more, it can take stereo sound, and the tapes are completely interchangeable between machines within the V2000 system *without* tracking adjustments.

The heart of the system is a cassette of paperback size, fitted with standard ½-inch tape. The cassette has tabs which tell the machine whether it is loaded with chromium dioxide or metal-evaporated tape, and, since two sides of the tape will be used for recording (as in a conventional audio cassette), there are *two* recording tabs (rather than the usual one) to prevent a programme being accidentally wiped. On each pass of the tape, only half (¼-inch) of it is used for recording or playback. At the end of each run, the cassette is flipped to employ the other half of the tape.

Dynamic track following

On the face of it, the compression of so much video information into such a small space of tape could only lead to a degraded image, though in fact the V2000 picture is at least as good as either of the other two systems. This has been achieved by a very sophisticated combination of techniques. To compress the tracks closer together, their width was reduced. Then, to ensure that the heads could follow these very narrow bands of video information accurately, they were equipped with 'dynamic track-following' systems: these

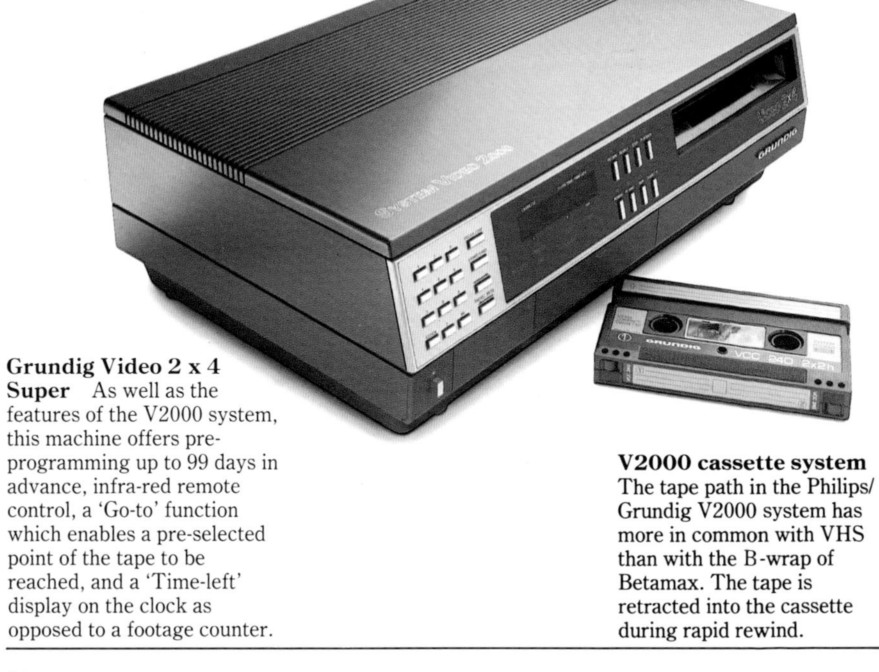

Grundig Video 2 x 4 Super As well as the features of the V2000 system, this machine offers pre-programming up to 99 days in advance, infra-red remote control, a 'Go-to' function which enables a pre-selected point of the tape to be reached, and a 'Time-left' display on the clock as opposed to a footage counter.

V2000 cassette system The tape path in the Philips/Grundig V2000 system has more in common with VHS than with the B-wrap of Betamax. The tape is retracted into the cassette during rapid rewind.

are small, piezo-electric ceramic plates which physically move the hcads in response to a sensing mechanism in the heads themselves. The track therefore did not need to be as wide, which saved a great deal of space, and as a bonus the control track could be dropped, since control was now automatic. This also meant that any V2000 recorded on one machine, or pre-recorded, could be played without adjustment on any other V2000.

The system offers very stable freeze-frame and picture-search modes, not to mention stereo sound and a host of possible features on the spare cue/control tracks that run unused (at present) down the centre of the tape. These might include not only additional commentaries, perhaps in another language, but also digital information such as a time code for computer editing. It is envisaged that some future machines will employ auto-reverse, so that 8 hours' recording will be possible without flipping the tape manually.

Will it last?

Philips were first in the European field with their N1500 and N1700 recorders in the early 1970s, but these machines failed in the face of Japanese competition, leaving a number of unhappy customers who had paid the price for leading the pack. The present V2000 format is technically brilliant, but the quality record so far has been discouraging, as has the initial failure to co-ordinate the position of the sound head between supposedly 'twin' Grundig and Philips machines. This has now been rectified, and it is only to be hoped that the apparent absurdity of introducing yet another format on to an already competitive market will be justified.

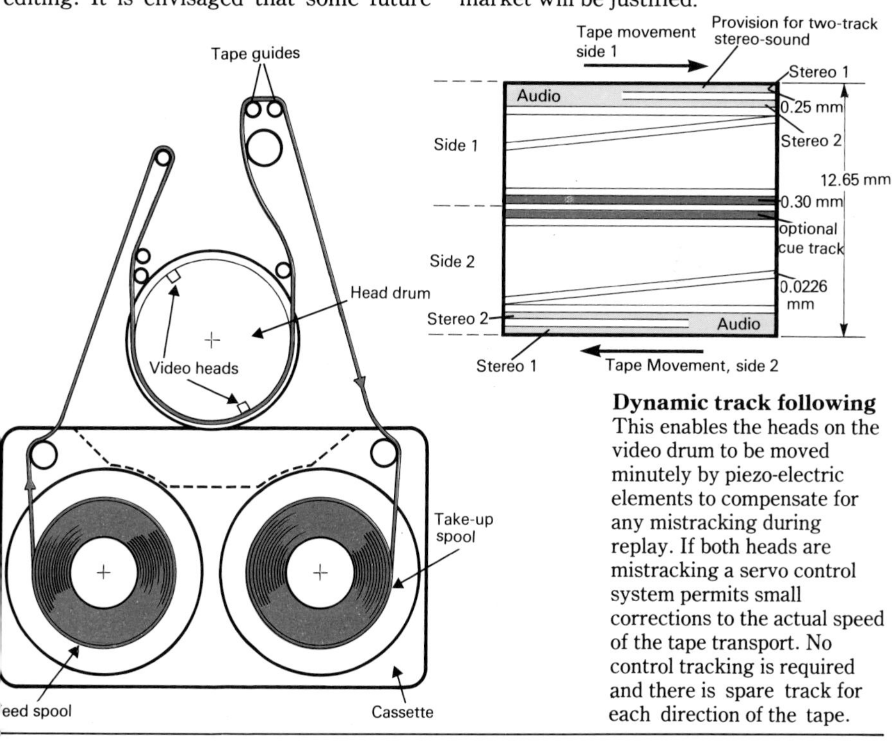

Dynamic track following
This enables the heads on the video drum to be moved minutely by piezo-electric elements to compensate for any mistracking during replay. If both heads are mistracking a servo control system permits small corrections to the actual speed of the tape transport. No control tracking is required and there is spare track for each direction of the tape.

Connecting and installing the VCR

It is always best to have your VCR installed professionally, and although this will certainly be done if you are renting the machine, it is a good idea to understand the principles involved.

Basically, the VCR contains a tuner like that in a TV. The antenna on the roof feeds directly to the VCR, which tunes into the various channels as though it were a TV. Next it effectively re-transmits those signals as radio waves through a cable to the TV *on a discrete channel of its own*. In Europe (UHF), this is normally Channel 36; in the USA, Channel 3 or 4 (VHF). To receive the signal put out by the VCR, the TV is tuned to the appropriate channel. In Europe, this is usually located on the sixth button, sometimes marked AV for Audio-visual. In the USA, it is simply CH3 or CH4. Thus the antenna is plugged into the VCR, and the other connecting cable runs from the RF Out socket on the VCR to the aerial socket on the TV.

The TV is capable of receiving the output of the VCR on the channel allocated to it, and all the other channels as well, since the aerial input has been split inside the VCR, passing half to the TV and half to the tuner of the VCR. This means that you can watch one programme while recording another.

The mode switch

The mode switch has three positions: TV; Video; and Timer. In TV mode, the VCR is effectively dormant, passing on signals to the TV without transmitting on its own channel. On Video, the TV can still receive all the channels, but it will also be receiving the output of the VCR if you select that channel on the TV. This will be either: silence, if no controls are engaged on the VCR; or tape replay output; or, if you are recording (or if you have depressed the Record button *alone* with a cassette inside the machine), you will see the channel that has been selected on the VCR. The Timer is for recording during your absence.

Adjusting the tuners

Most video recorders have a built-in test signal so that the video channel on your receiver may be accurately tuned to the

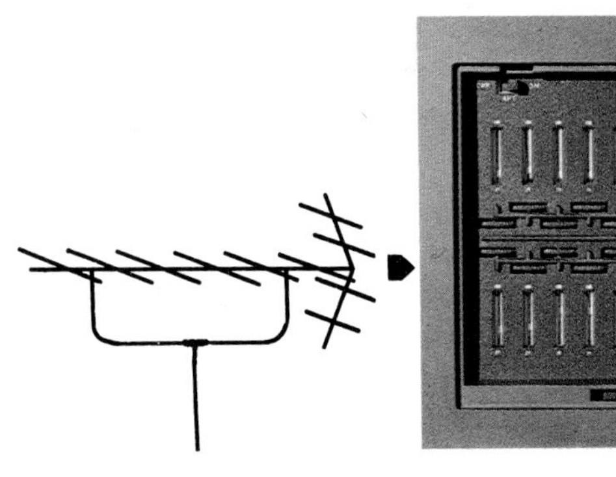

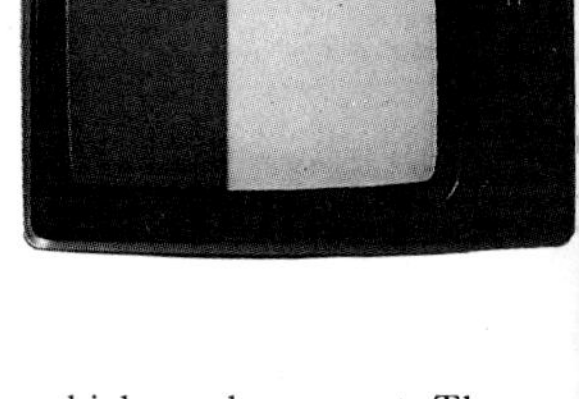

Adjusting the tuners The rf signal received by the antenna is first passed to the tuner on a VCR. This will contain several channels, each of which can be pre-set. The receiver must be tuned to the test signal emitted by the VCR just as though the VCR output were itself a broadcast station.

appropriate wavelength of the recorder's output. This is activated by the Set-up switch on the rear of the VCR, which should subsequently be returned to the Normal position to tune the various push-button channels on the recorder. Set the mode switch to Video, and the TV receiver to the channel allocated to the VCR. Load a cassette with the safety tab intact, and press the Record key. Any programme received by the tuner in the recorder will now be visible on the TV screen.

You can tune in each of the channels on the tuner panel. When each channel has been tuned to your satisfaction, the Automatic Frequency Control (AFC) will take over. In the USA, because of the proliferation of channels and because you have both VHF and UHF, not all the channels will be pre-set by push-buttons in this way, though the twelve principal VHF channels usually can be.

Note: in all the above setting-up operations, the TV/Camera switch should be set to TV. On newer models, the tuning process is entirely electronic which in combination with the AFC makes the whole process more or less foolproof.

How to set up your TV receiver

Let the set warm up in normal subdued room lighting. Turn the Colour or Chrominance control as far down as it will go, and reduce the Contrast until the picture is just visible. Dip the Brightness until the darkest parts of the picture become pure black, and then raise the Contrast until you have a picture with the full range from deep black to peak white, with detail in both the shadow areas and the highlights. Edge up the Colour until you just have satisfactory skin tones. The picture should now be correct for all well-graded transmissions.

In the USA, this procedure is made more tricky by the great colour variations between stations at any given time, and for the best results you may also need to adjust hue (tint) for each programme. This option is very rare on non-NTSC receivers, since it should be unnecessary on PAL or SECAM if the receiver is correctly set up.

A normal test card

Too much colour saturation

Too little colour

Too little contrast

Excessive contrast

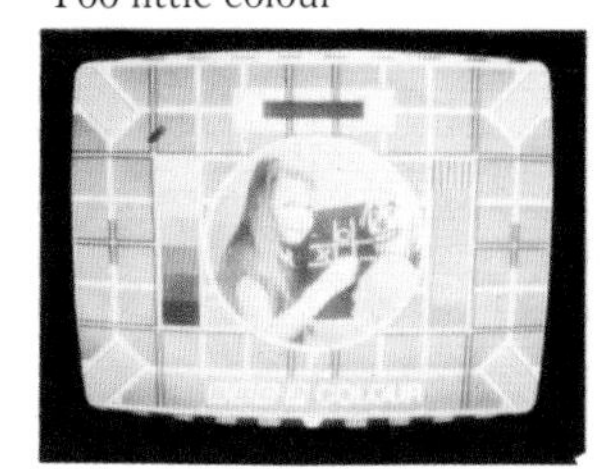

Too much brightness

Video disc 1

Video discs are a relatively new branch of video technology, and they differ from video tape recorders in several basic ways. Firstly, they are purely a replay system : they cannot be used to record programmes off air, nor can they be used in conjunction with a camera. Secondly, they are not based on magnetic tape and therefore offer 'random access' to any point on the recording at high speed. Lastly, they are much cheaper to produce than a pre-recorded tape, and the simplicity of manufacture (once the initial disc has been 'mastered') has obvious advantages.

However, as with tape, there are a number of totally incompatible systems on the market, and there is by no means any degree of certainty which will emerge as the dominant one. In each case, the disc containing the recording is required to revolve at high speeds, since video contains so much more information than a simple sound recording, and the accuracy required from the tracking system is vastly greater than that of even the most sophisticated hi-fi. There are three systems now on the market : the Philips/MCA laser optical system, known variously as LaserVision (UK) and Laserdisc (by Pioneer in the USA); the VHD, or Very High Density, system developed by JVC, which is a grooveless capacitance device; and the RCA Selectavision disc which is a grooved capacitance system.

Video disc systems

Laser Vision	*CED*
Philips/MCA	RCA Selectavision
Pioneer	Zenith
Grundig	CBS
Sanyo	
Hitachi	*VHD*
IBM	JVC
Sony	Matsushita
Mitsubishi	Panasonic
20th Century Fox	General Electric
Paramount	Thorn/EMI

Philips/MCA LaserVision

This is the most sophisticated, not to say exotic, video machine ever designed for home use. The disc is the same size as a conventional audio disc, but is smooth and reflective. The audio and video information is submerged (and protected) beneath a transparent outer layer, and consists of a minute series of pits in the plastic arranged in a spiral, like a conventional record. These tiny pits of electronic information are scanned by a very finely focused laser beam as the disc revolves at high speed: 1500 rpm in Europe, 1800 rpm in the USA and Japan. Each revolution corresponds to one frame for video, and the result is extremely high quality in picture, with stereo sound (or possibly mono sound in two languages!). The discs are designed to play for either 36 minutes per side, in which mode you can have slow motion, freeze-frame, and rapid access; or for one hour per side, which gives equal quality without all the additional facilities. They are known as Active Play and Long Play versions, though the Long Play discs are sometimes referred to as CLV or Constant Linear Velocity discs.

The advantages of this system are remarkable. Firstly, the laser does not ever make physical contact with the disc, which means that there is no wear. Then, because the actual surface of the disc is defocused by the laser, blemishes such as dust or finger-marks do not appear as noise on the signal. Best of all, the quality of reproduction far exceeds that of any domestic tape system, with stereo sound that can pass through your hi-fi. However, the Philips/MCA player and discs are almost certain to be the most expensive of the three rival systems.

Philips/MCA LaserVision The reflective disc can be handled freely, since, unlike a gramophone record, minor scratches and dirt do not appear on the recording. Once the lid is firmly closed, the disc is rotated at 1500 or 1800 rpm (according to country) and a safety lock prevents accidental opening.

In the Active Play mode, the disc permits rapid scanning of the entire side in just under thirty seconds. This represents 54 000 frames of video material, each of which can be frozen on the screen indefinitely, without wear.

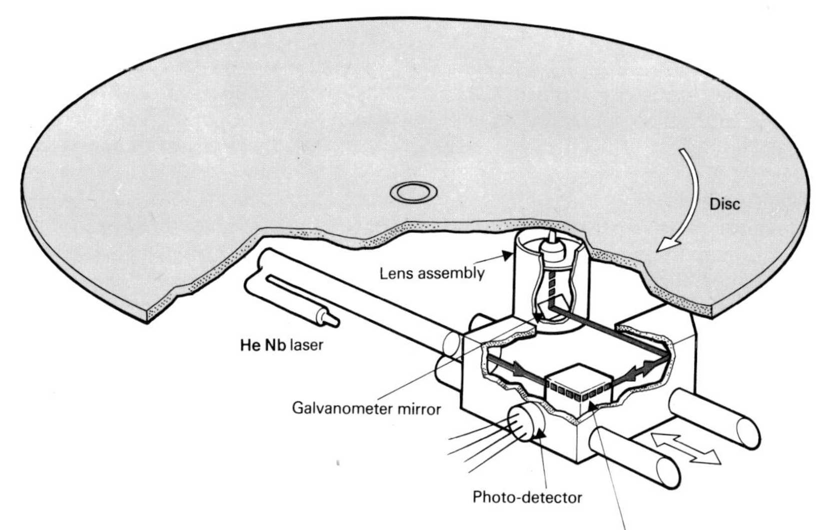

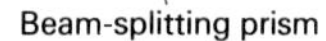

The Helium-Niobium laser tracks inwards across the rotating disc, and a photo-detector senses the fluctuations of the reflected light which is bounced back from the minute pits in the disc surface. The precision required is phenomenal, since the pitch, or separation, between tracks is only 1.66 *micrometers!* In collaboration with the film industry, a wide selection of movies will soon be available in the Long Play mode, while the possibilities for the Active Play mode range from the arts to sports, technical, and educational fields.

RCA Selectavision

Whereas the Philips/MCA system uses very advanced technology to achieve high-quality results, RCA's CED disc-player represents an attempt to use comparatively familiar means to attain a quality that is still superior to pre-recorded tapes, at a price that is about half that of a comparable video recorder. The disc-player uses a grooved capacitance system, and the electrode in the stylus senses the changes in capacitance as it passes along the groove at 450 rpm (US) or 500 rpm (Europe). Each revolution contains four frames, therefore, and the 'still-frame' facility is in fact the repetition of four frames.

As this is an electro-mechanical system, with the stylus actually in contact with the surface of the disc, it is highly vulnerable to accidental damage, and the disc is therefore shielded inside a caddy from which it can only be removed after it has been inserted into the player. This vulnerability is hardly surprising as each groove is only 1/38 the size of the standard LP groove, but it does mean that the disc is inherently more prone to wear than the laser system, which is immune to all except very violent handling.

The system is characterized by extreme simplicity of operation. With the control lever on Load, the caddy is inserted, the disc is loaded, the caddy removed, and the lever switched from Load to Play. The display panel will then indicate '0' for the beginning of the side you have selected. At the end of the side, the screen flashes 'E'. There is also a rapid-access mode which takes less than 30 seconds to reach any given point on a side, and an on-screen visual search mode which works at sixteen times the normal speed, without the severe picture break-up that is common on tape during picture-search. Playing time is one hour per side.

The sound was initially monophonic, but stereo is promised for future releases. Since RCA has joined with CBS to market this system, and since the capital cost of player and software is likely to be highly competitive, it must be reckoned as a contender despite its limitations.

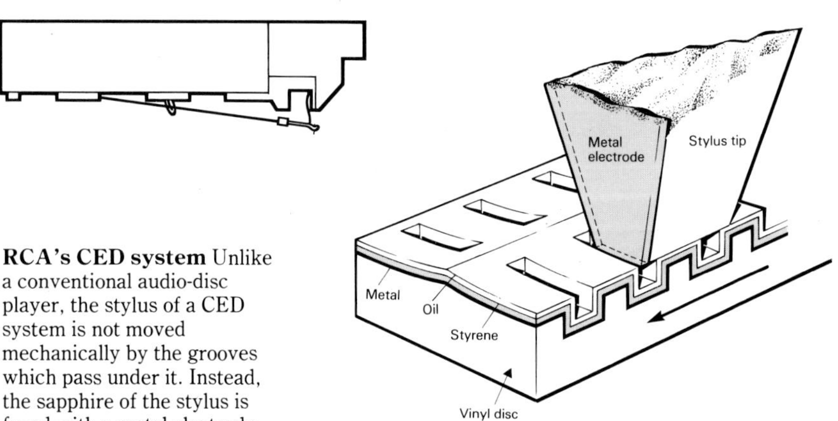

RCA's CED system Unlike a conventional audio-disc player, the stylus of a CED system is not moved mechanically by the grooves which pass under it. Instead, the sapphire of the stylus is faced with a metal electrode which senses the change in the capacitance of the metal components of the disc. The grooves appear smooth but are in fact pitted along their under-surface so that changes in electrical capacity can be generated between the disc surface and the stylus electrode. Since there is physical contact between stylus and disc some wear may be expected, although a life for the stylus of 1000 hours is claimed. The actual discs are reportedly more subject to wear than their VHD rivals.

JVC — Very High Density Disc

This is the third of the current disc-playing systems to have been introduced, and it resembles the RCA system in some ways. It, too, uses a sapphire stylus with a metal electrode to sense the capacitance charge in the pits in a disc surface, but the tracking controls are regulated not by grooves in the disc surface but by a servo system. Superimposed on to the spiral of programme pits is a companion spiral of tracking pits which are monitored by the servo system to guide the electrode.

The 10-in (25-cm) disc rotates at 900 rpm (US; 750 rpm for Europe), with a playing time of one hour per side, and two frames per revolution. The information area is about ten times greater than on the RCA system, so that mechanical wear is less of a problem, and the absence of grooves means that the stylus can move rapidly from side to side in the random-access mode. In addition to freeze-frame, this disc-player can also offer stereo sound, reverse play, slow and fast motion, and frame-by-frame advance.

This is the latest contender in the video disc race, and it combines some of the technical sophistication of the laser system with the relative economy of RCA Selectavision. However, it still uses a caddy to protect the disc, and the discs are subject to wear, as is the stylus. In the end, the battle between the rival systems may well be decided not by technical merit but by the market forces that lie behind the software offered in each system.

JVC disc-player Both CED and VHD disc-playing systems protect their discs in a caddy which is inserted in the front of the machine.

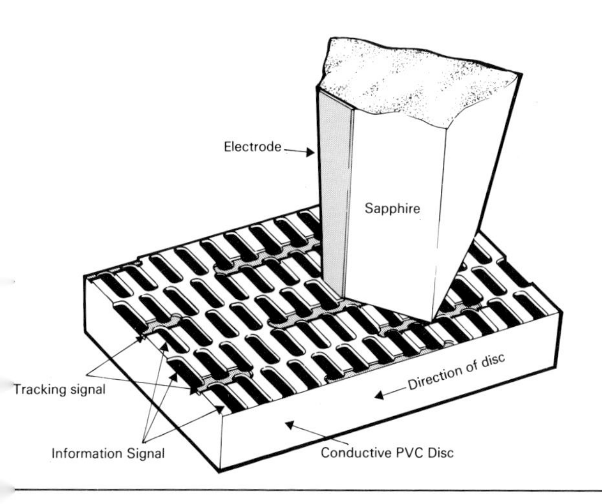

The VHD discs, unlike the CED system, have no grooves. Instead, the position of the stylus on the disc is regulated by a servo mechanism, guided by a series of pits in the disc which control the tracking. The absence of grooves would seem to indicate a longer playing life for the discs than the CED system. As stereo video discs become more common the lack of a stereo facility in the CED system may prove conclusive in the battle of the formats.

U-Matic ¾-inch cassettes

Sony's U-Matic ¾-inch cassette system was introduced in the USA in 1969 and in Europe in 1973, and has now become the unquestioned standard for high-quality semi-professional and professional use. The cassette is larger than a ½-inch cassette, and the tape speed higher at 3¾ ips. One hour of play is available per tape. The scanning is helical, and there are two audio tracks in addition to the control track: these may be selected independently during recording, and they are linked on most machines to VU meters (as is the video level).

Some ¾-inch machines are specifically designed as editing machines: they may be linked to a standard record/replay machine through an editing controller, to provide the extremely valuable function of giving perfect edits to the exact frame (pp. 172–3). These machines usually incorporate so-called 'flying erase heads' in the drum, which enable the machine to erase one field at a time. Both insert *and* assembly edits are possible, in audio and/or video. Other controls not usually found on a ½-inch VCR include Skew, a tension control which corrects a distortion usually found at the top of the frame on replay. The Tracking control, as with other cassette machines, is also principally used to compensate for mistracking caused by

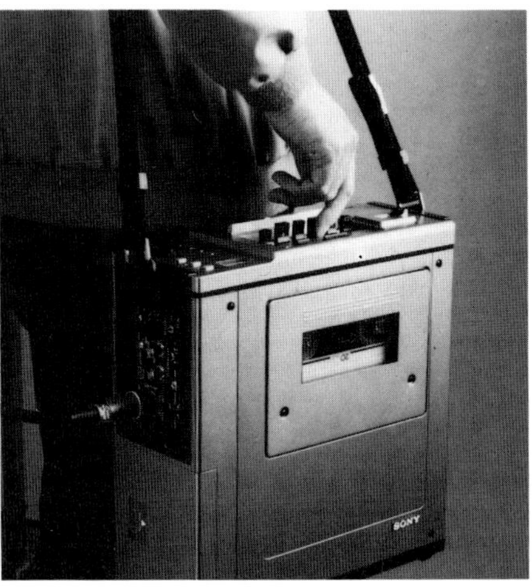

Sony U-Matic ¾-inch portable This machine gives highly professional results on location, and though it is a miracle of compression it still places a very heavy load on the operator when worn over the shoulder.

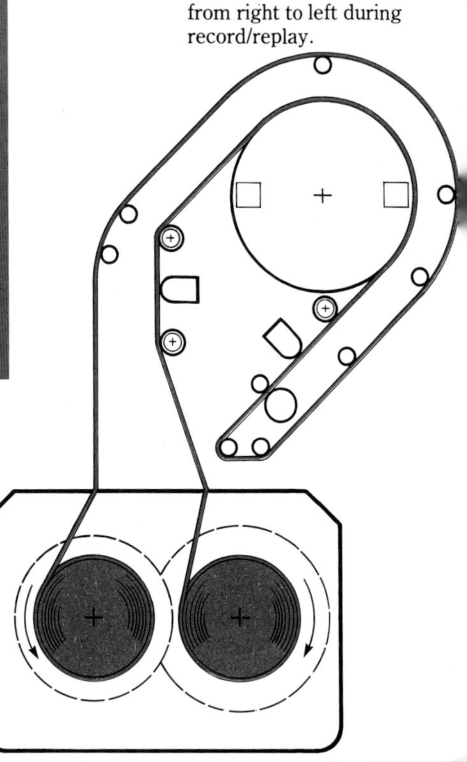

Tape path The tape path on the U-Matic cassette is known as a U-load; the tape runs from right to left during record/replay.

playing tapes that have been recorded on other machines of the same format. The audio and video levels may be controlled either manually or automatically (AGC).

The tape path is lengthy, and the threading process is somewhat slow, but the tape is nevertheless disengaged for rapid rewind and fast-forward.

¾-inch high-performance U-Matic VCRs

The latest generation of ¾-inch VCRs has such a high performance that the machines are entirely suitable for broadcast on commercial networks. They may be expected to have a video signal-to-noise (S/N) ratio as high as 46 dB, and a bandwidth sufficiently high that pictures of adequate broadcast quality can be achieved. In Europe, machines designated 'High-Band' are available which use improved modulation frequencies within the machine to produce these excellent results. Such machines are available as portables, and on return to base after all the filming has been completed the tape may be edited on sophisticated edit machines. The very latest machines include such replay facilities as broadcast-quality freeze-frame, picture-search, and slow motion — this has until now only been possible on the very expensive 1-inch machines.

Editing recorder This highly sophisticated ¾-inch cassette recorder, which is designed for home or studio use, contains no tuner, but it is capable of complex insert and assemble edits as well as remote control by the computer in an editing controller. Both independent audio channels and the video channel may be dubbed and edited separately.

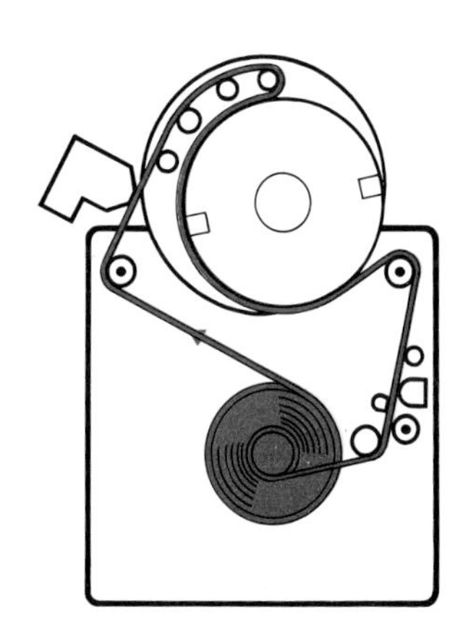

Philips VCR
This was the first of all the home VCRs to really hit the domestic market in Europe. The ½-inch tape is wound co-axially in the fat cassette. The original 1500 series of machines gave one-hour play, but were soon replaced by the 1700 series: this incompatible range of machines gave 2 hours' play at a slower tape speed, referred to as VCR-LP. Even on the VCR-LP, the linear tape speed is more than twice as high as that of VHS: this gives good audio results, but is very expensive in terms of the area of tape consumed per hour. Both this system, and the similar but not quite compatible Grundig SVR systems, have now been replaced by the Video 2000 format.

Reel-to-reel

Cassette recorders are newcomers to the scene of video recording. Until the early 1970s, all such machines were reel-to-reel, from the giant 2-inch Quadruplex machines to the small ½-inch EIAJ recorders. The latter may now be regarded as obsolete, but they will be considered briefly since many are still in use.

2-inch Quadruplex recording

This was the first type of video recording to be made commercially viable (1956) and until recently was the standard workhorse of the television industry. The tape is 2 inches wide, and runs at a linear speed of either 15 ips or 7½ ips. The tape is scanned *vertically* by four spinning heads (each of which accounts for around 17 lines of picture information). There are two audio tracks, one of which may be used for a time-code (pp. 172-3). The tape is sucked into contact with the heads by a vacuum as it passes by, so that the flat tape is curved around the cylindrical drum. The quality is superb; the cost, size, weight of tape, and complexity of maintenance, prohibitive to the amateur.

Helical scan open-reel recording

All other open-reel recorders, whatever their gauge, use helical scanning techniques — developed by Ampex and Toshiba. We need only concern ourselves here with the other principal formats.

One-inch helical scan tape is now rapidly replacing 2-inch in Quad professional work. But the vehicle for amateur and experimental video was for many years the

2-inch Quadruplex A machine such as this would be approximately 6ft (2m) across. The tape moves from left to right past the spinning cylindrical head drum.

½-inch EIAJ open-reel format, and these still have many industrial applications. In between the two fall the ¾-inch ENG and EFP systems (pp. 64-5), but these two are now largely cassette systems, and the trend here is to even smaller tape formats, with one-piece operation.

Several manufacturers have recently announced ½-inch one-piece ENG cameras that are claimed to give results equal or superior to conventional ¾-inch U-Matic tape. Metal or metal-evaporated tape is commonly employed. One such camera was recently carried by Japanese mountaineers to within 90 m (300 ft) of the top of Everest.

½-inch EIAJ standard

All open-reel ½-inch machines conform to this standard, which gives one hour of play at 7½ ips with 730 m (2400 ft) of ½-inch tape. Since the tape is threaded by hand, it is vital that this be done accurately and delicately. The actual tape path varies from one machine to another, so you should carefully consult the threading diagram. Then, with the machine turned off, place the supply reel with a full roll of tape on the deck; holding the very end of the tape, gently draw off enough tape to reach around the drum, through the tape guides, and on to the take-up spool. When the tape is threaded in the correct way around the various components, make quite sure that there is no slack before the machine is operated — slack can cause the tape to pull, stretch, or even tear. This is of course one reason why these machines have now been superseded by cassette recorders.

½-inch EIAJ This format was at the forefront of the video revolution in the late sixties and early seventies. One of the attractions was that the tape could be physically edited, but with the advent of more sophisticated electronic editing and effective cassette design these machines are now largely restricted to industrial and educational use. However, because of their high linear tape speed they continue to give sound quality superior to that of many current machines, though noise reduction circuits promise great improvement.

½-inch portables

A portable recorder is a great deal more than a luxury extra for the person who already has a home VCR and money to burn. The more sophisticated modern recorders offer every imaginable feature that you could expect to find on the large machines, and for home use they can be combined with a tuner/timer, or AC adaptor to make an efficient home VCR. When you are shooting a tape out of doors, the recorder, which has its own rechargeable battery, is detached from the tuner, slung over the shoulder, and the camera plugged in.

The quality of the image recorded on a portable off air should be just as good as that from a normal recorder, while the quality of the camera-generated image is determined initially by that of the camera itself. Properly operated, and in decent lighting conditions, this will be surprisingly high, at a modest cost. A black and white camera will be even cheaper, with, incidentally, rather better quality than an equivalent colour camera.

One option, then, is to buy a portable recorder *instead* of a normal home-based VCR, and also to buy a tuner/timer to go with it so that the machine can record programmes off air. The tuner/timer will function as an AC adaptor for the portable recorder as well, and will also recharge the recorder's batteries. An alternative is to buy the recorder *as an addition* to your existing VCR. In that case you will not need the optional tuner/timer, since there will be one in your other machine, but you will need an AC power adaptor/battery charger. This can be left at home, just like the tuner, as long as you have enough power in the batteries for the duration of the recording.

The addition of a portable recorder to an existing VCR has an important advantage. When you get home, you can connect up the two recorders and, by playing back on one machine and recording on the other, you can edit the tape, removing unwanted, ugly, or unsuccessful sections; rearranging the order of shots or sequences; even dubbing music or commentary. The improvement in pace and content will outweigh the slight loss in quality that you will notice in ½-inch systems when such a second-generation copy is made.

It is vital that the machine that is doing the re-recording (normally the static, home VCR) should incorporate a roll-back edit system or similar control, or else every edit

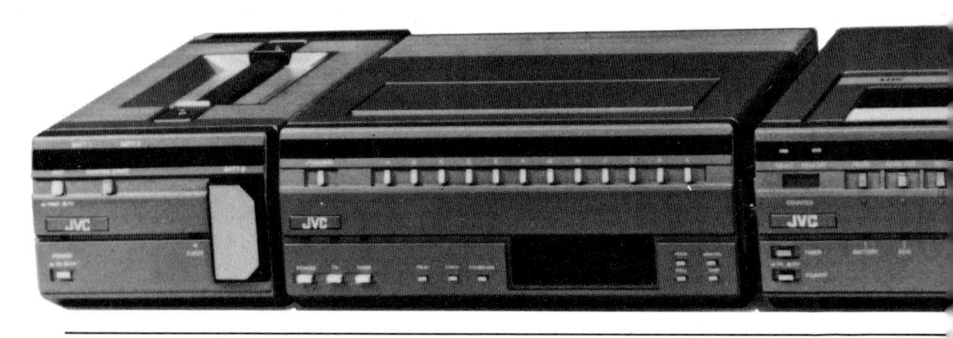

that you make will create frame-roll when the tape is replayed (pp. 170—1). The portable machine will have a Pause control, enabling you to make relatively clean cuts from one shot to the next. It is well worth testing this operation before you buy any given recorder, since it will dramatically effect the final appearance of the tape, and the machines vary widely in their specifications and performance.

Which format?

There is no reason why the portable machine you choose should necessarily be the same format as your domestic machine. A Betamax portable can be played into, and recorded on, a VHS recorder, though of course the cassettes themselves will not fit into the VHS machine. They can still, however, be played directly into the TV from the portable, and you have the added advantage that you will be able to replay either Beta or VHS tapes that you have borrowed or rented. What is more, there is no reason why you need retain the same tape width: the very light Technicolor/Funai portable, for instance (pp. 72—3) uses $\frac{1}{4}$-inch tape, and this too can easily be re-recorded on to $\frac{1}{2}$-inch or indeed $\frac{3}{4}$-inch tape for editing. Your main considerations in choosing an additional portable system are therefore likely to be the features that it offers rather than the format as such.

Connections

The great advantage in using two machines of the same format is that the plugs and connections will be compatible, and you will not need complex adaptors when dubbing or when plugging in the camera. The same consideration applies when you are choosing a camera: there is a great deal to be said for buying a camera of the same make as the portable, as it will plug in without difficulty. There are a large number of connections (pp. 202—7).

On many home machines, even some recent models, the cord that links the camera to the recorder is not integrated into a 10-pin or 14-pin plug: instead, you have separate Video, Audio, Remote Pause, and Power connections to attend to, all of which can quite easily fall out at the crucial moment. Bear this in mind when choosing between rival systems. Go for a camera/recorder combination that combines the features you are seeking with a really convenient cable connection.

The portable set-up This is the most mobile and most fundamental portable set-up. It is entirely a one-man operation, and no help whatsoever is needed from others. Furthermore, he can cover any conceivable event without causing it to be specially staged, since no tripods or recorders need be moved.

Portable recorders work off DC, which means that they require either an AC adapter to work off the mains, or a tuner/timer which also supplies a 12V DC current, or else are run off their own rechargeable batteries (usually Ni-Cad). Typically, one battery might last about 1½ hours, but a tape 3 hours, so that an extra battery would certainly be a useful investment if you are going in for a long taping session. The batteries are charged in either the AC adaptor or the tuner/timer accessory, and they fit into the recorder during the shooting. This in turn delivers power to the camera (only a few watts), from which it receives both a video image and an audio signal if the camera is fitted with a built-in microphone. In any case, the audio signal can be fed to the recorder via a separate audio feed.

The Pause control

To achieve a smooth cut between shots you should be able to use the Pause control: this will arrest the tape without disengaging it from the heads, and will provide a means of recording the next shot without picture break-up or frame-roll. On some portables the Pause (sometimes known as Edit control) can be engaged even when the recorder has been shut down for an hour or so, with consequent savings in battery power. Normally, the camera is so connected that the Pause on the recorder is controlled by the camera's own On/Off button (Remote Pause).

Portability

Weight may well be the most important single factor when choosing a portable recorder. The smallest ½-inch machine currently available is the Sony SL 2000 which weighs only 4 kg (9 lb) with battery. When you add this to the weight of the camera itself — about 3 kg (6½ lb) — the total is still quite substantial. Not surprisingly, many users prefer to put the recorder on the ground as frequently as possible. Though this inevitably reduces the fluidity of the shooting, such a

Flexible shooting For complete flexibility, both camera and recorder can be hand-held (left), but the weight of the combination soon begins to tell. For complete steadiness in a long and predictable taping session, use a tripod with the recorder on the ground (right).

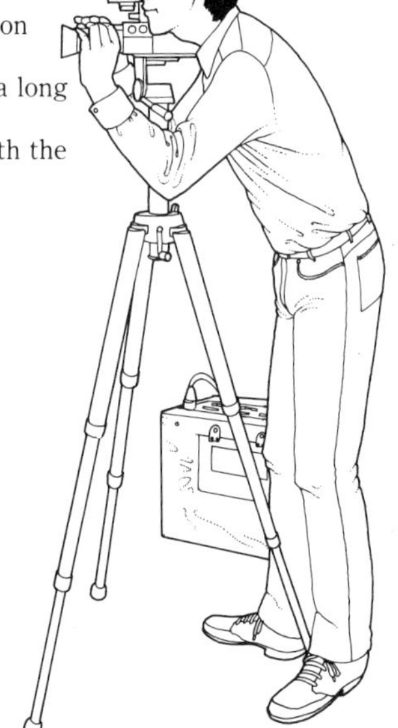

restriction is by no means always a bad idea: the joys of flexible, hand-held (and perhaps wobbly) camerawork should be saved for those occasions when this alone will give the shots you need. There is also the possibility of simply using a longer than standard lead. When it is not required at full stretch, you can just tie a knot in it to keep it out of the way.

Batteries

The rechargeable batteries, which in some cases can be recharged in the recorder itself, are usually connected to a warning circuit of some kind in the recorder or the camera so that you will have a visual indication when the power is running low. Since the battery will be powering the entire system, it is essential to keep an eye on the level of power and preferably to have a spare battery handy. The time required for recharging is an important consideration; for instance, while the JVC HR 2200 recharges in 90 minutes, most others take all night. There is not much point in having a 4-hour tape but only enough power for an hour, so you should investigate the power consumption of any machine, and the provision of power-saving circuitry in the pause mode, before buying.

You should also remember that batteries perform very poorly when cold. In cold weather, keep the batteries warm (perhaps in a pocket) until they are actually needed.

Monitoring

You may wish to replay the shots on location, if only for pleasure. You can do this through the electronic viewfinder of your camera (in black and white), if it has one; or, if you wish to check colour, you may prefer to take along a portable receiver/ monitor such as the JVC 6-inch CX-610. This has its own rechargeable power supply, and accepts a variety of other power inputs, both AC and DC. It also has a VHF/UHF tuner that is switchable from PAL to SECAM. With the addition of a monitor, your portable system becomes truly self-contained, and truly mobile.

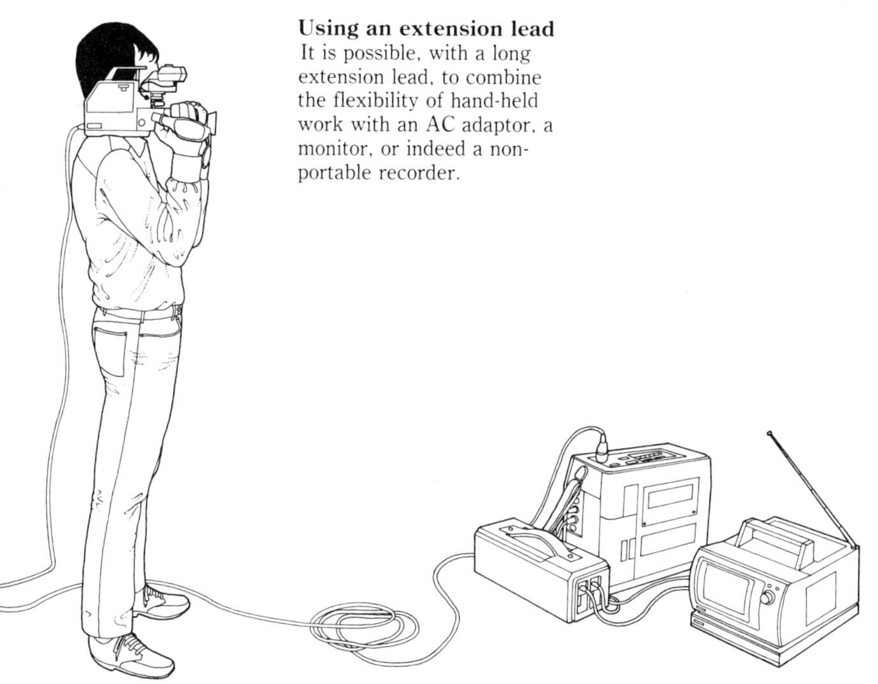

Using an extension lead
It is possible, with a long extension lead, to combine the flexibility of hand-held work with an AC adaptor, a monitor, or indeed a non-portable recorder.

¼-inch portables

The Technicolor/Funai Portable VCR

Technicolor's attempt to solve the problem of portability has led them to part altogether with the ½-inch format: the choice of a ¼-inch tape has made it possible to pack up to one hour of recording time into a cassette that is not much larger than an audio-cassette. The tape speed is 3.21 cm/sec (1.26 ips), with a writing speed, thanks to the helical scan, of 5.1 m per sec. This is perfectly comparable to other, ½-inch, recording systems, and gives excellent results. It weighs only 3.25 kg (7 lb), including the batteries, which is in fact less than the camera provided with the recorder. The batteries last for 40 minutes with the camera, twice that in replay.

There is also an accessory tuner/timer, and an AC adaptor/ charger, which can be used to feed video, audio, or RF outputs from the deck when required. Otherwise, the controls are kept to the minimum needed for lightweight, efficient portable recording. When you return home, the tape can naturally be re-recorded on to your home machine, editing as you go; or else you can just use the Technicolor machine to play through the RF converter on to a home TV. Quality is relatively high, although there is rather greater video noise than on comparable ½-inch units, a disadvantage which many people will consider is made up for by the machine's light weight.

Technicolor/Funai VCR
The cassette format for the Technicolor ¼-inch portable system was developed by Funai in Japan, and it seems likely that it will be adopted by other manufacturers. Some software is now becoming available for this format so that it may be used as the basis for a full domestic system.

The Grundig Portable VP 100

The Grundig VP 100, however, which uses the same Funai cassette as the Technicolor portable, is even lighter: only 2.3 kg (5 lb) including the battery. This makes it the lightest recorder in the world. The normal recording tape speed is 2.25 cm (0.89 in) per sec, as compared to 3.21 cm per sec in the Technicolor machine. More importantly, the writing speed is also rather lower. The Grundig model offers variable speeds for fast and slow motion, time-lapse, audio-dubbing, plus freeze-frame and frame advance. These advanced facilities are not available on the rival Technicolor machine at the present time, but since the Funai format now seems certain to establish itself as yet a fourth contender in the tape-format battle, such sophistications are sure to become commonplace in ¼-inch cassettes.

Grundig portable VP 100

8 mm Video

8 mm Video is the name that the world's major manufacturers have now agreed to give to the newest and most exciting video format. This is a one-piece camera-recorder containing an 8-mm (¼-inch) micro-cassette that can record one hour of sound and video. The whole machine is little larger than a Super 8 sound camera, and when it is considered that the cost per minute of Super 8 film is about the same as that per *hour* of tape, it can be assumed that the days of home movies are numbered. Sony, Matsushita, and Hitachi have all produced prototype systems, and have now agreed with Philips, no less, on the basic parameters of a future 8 mm Video system to be introduced not later than 1985. These are shown below.

The tape widths on all these systems are in the same range as the V2000 format (also a ¼-inch system at heart), i.e. very narrow. In the case of the Matsushita camera-recorder, metal-evaporated tape is used, which is claimed to give a very high recording density — up to ten times that of normal oxide. All such cameras could be fitted with a CCD image receptor in place of a conventional tube (the Sony prototype already is, and the Hitachi is also solid-state) with yet further savings on space and weight. The conventional tube is unquestionably on the way out.

Unless a whole domestic ¼-inch system is to be unveiled based on the technology of this cassette format (which is quite possible), the camera-recorders will be used to record original material, which will then be played back and re-recorded on a conventional VCR, or perhaps just played back directly on to a TV through an RF converter by people who do not have a home VCR. In any case some form of AC adaptor will become necessary. It is immensely encouraging that the major manufacturers seem finally to be moving in a sane manner towards a common new system that could herald yet another video revolution. It is worth noting that Technicolor/Funai have already introduced a combined domestic receiver/recorder for their ¼-inch portable system, with accompanying software to follow.

8 mm Video system

Recording time	1 hour
Cassette size	9 x 6 x 1.4 cm (estimated) (3.5 x 2.4 x 0.05 in)
Tape width	7–8 mm
Tape	metal or metal-evaporated
Recording system	2 rotary-head azimuth
Drum diameter	approx. 40 mm (1.57 in)
Video recording method	FM
Audio	fixed head or rotary head
Writing speed	approx. 4 m/sec
Total weight	approx. 2 kg (4.5 lb)

Matsushita micro The most recent of the three Japanese prototype 8 mm camera-recorders comes from Matsushita. It weighs only 2.1 kg (5.33 lb), and uses metal-evaporated tape. The cassette is diminutive, and the entire unit only consumes 5 Watts DC.

Hitachi This Hitachi camera, which does not contain a recorder, incorporates a CCD chip instead of a conventional tube, with enormous saving in weight. It is highly likely that CCD chips will gradually replace tubes before long, if only for reasons of weight.

ENG system This one-piece ½-inch camera-recorder is the professional equivalent of the domestic 8 mm recorders above. But it gives broadcast quality results, reputedly superior to equivalent ¾-inch U-Matic recorders (which require a second operator). It is designed by Matsushita and RCA primarily for Electronic News Gathering, and the tape, which uses a modified VHS format, runs for 20 mins. It weighs only 10 kg (22 lb) including lens and batteries.

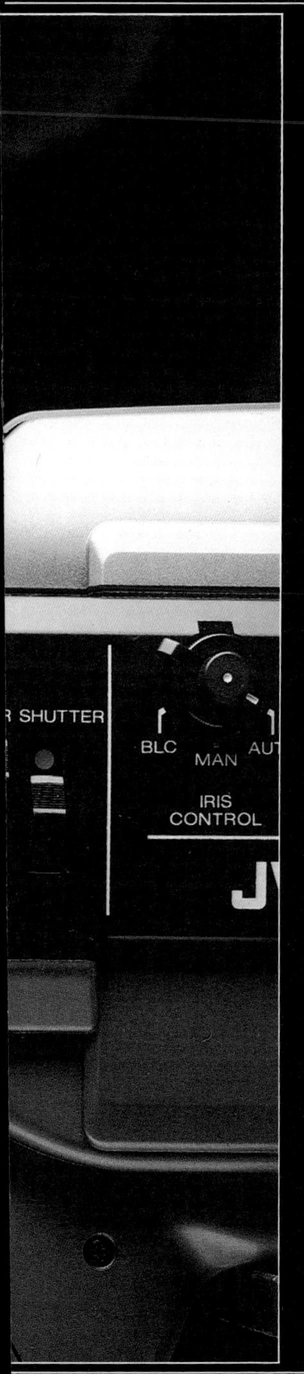

The Camera

The decision to add a camera to your home recorder is more than merely the acquisition of an accessory: it marks a profound change in the attitude that you have towards the medium of video recording. From this point on, you will be actively, not passively, engaged in the enterprise, no longer at the mercy of the networks or the pre-recorded tapes when deciding what to show or view. What is more, you can record the life of your family, your friends, your town, with a freedom and a cheapness on tape that has never before been possible. But it is essential that you have a correct sense of priorities when buying the camera itself.

Camera types

There are many considerations to be borne in mind when choosing a camera, and all too often some form of compromise will result. However, if the priorities are considered in the right order, you are more likely to make the right decision.

Interface It is undoubtedly a great help if the camera is of the same system as the recorder, simply because the plugs will automatically match. Adaptors are available, of course, but there is a great deal to be said for simplifying an already complex piece of equipment. (For example, Sony cameras will not plug directly into a JVC/VHS recorder.) Remember that the cord leading from camera to recorder has to carry not only audio and video signals, but also Remote Pause control and the DC power supply for the camera. It is clearly an advantage to unite these functions: in one 10-pin plug, for instance.

Colour or black and white Black and white cameras are very much cheaper than colour cameras. They are more sensitive in poor light conditions, and less prone to lag. However, there is no question that colour is the way of the future, and indeed the present. What is more, the price, weight, and quality of colour cameras are becoming more attractive each month.

The viewfinder The basic choice is between an electronic and an optical viewfinder, and it must be said at once that despite the extra expense and power requirements of the electronic type, the money is very well spent. It will permit you to balance lighting and assess the exposure directly (though a monitor is more reliable), and will allow replay on location through the viewfinder itself. Other features are battery warning lights, aperture and under-exposure indicators, a 'recorder running' light, and perhaps a white balance indicator. Some cameras with optical viewfinders will accept an optional electronic viewfinder at a later date.

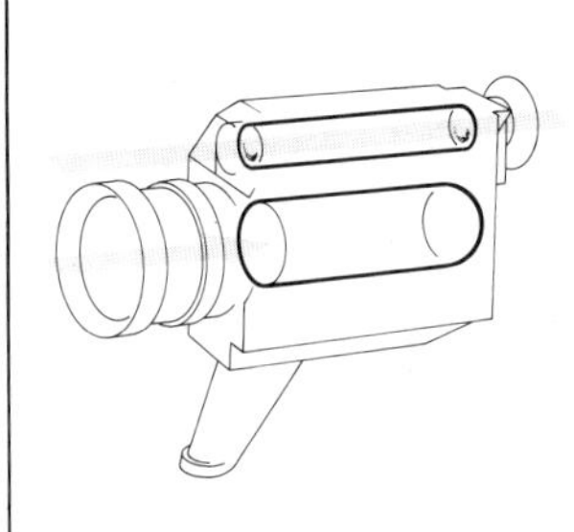

Optical viewfinder An optical viewfinder is the cheapest of the three principal types, but it has the disadvantage that the point of view of the viewfinder is never exactly the same as that of the lens. This is especially difficult in close-up work.

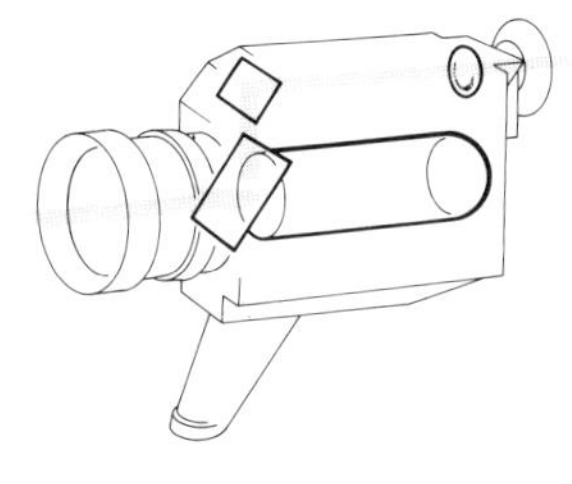

Through-the-lens viewfinder A TTL viewfinder diverts some of the incoming light to the eyepiece, and gives a true idea of the framing and focus that the camera itself is 'seeing'. This does, however, take a certain amount of light from the lens.

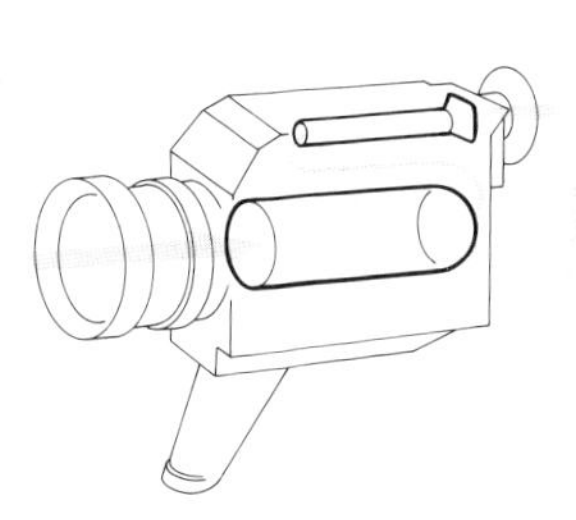

Electronic viewfinder An electronic viewfinder has the enormous advantage of showing the framing, the focus, *and* the apparent exposure and contrast of the image to be recorded, though only in some models.

Sensitivity Cameras vary greatly in this respect and it is a vital consideration for all indoor shooting. The most sensitive domestic-market colour cameras now available will give acceptable results at a minimum of 50 lux, and good results only at 250 lux or more.

Power supply The lower the power consumption, the better.

Weight The same is naturally true, although heavy cameras are sometimes steadier at the long end of the zoom if they are of the type which can be balanced on the shoulder.

Ergonomics Considerations of weight cannot be divorced from the over-all ease of operation, the 'feel' of the camera and the lens. Be sure to handle any camera before buying, and in particular decide between the two basic types: those which rest on the shoulder, and those which do not. The former are often bulkier, but give steadier results in most hands.

Lens Apart from contrast and sharpness, the main factors to consider when choosing a lens are: the widest aperture; and the range of the zoom. It is a great advantage to have a 'fast' lens, perhaps as fast as f1.4, but note that at this aperture the depth of field will be extremely small. Such lenses are invariably more expensive than the more modest aperture of f1.8, which is a good deal more common. The zooming ratio will also have a considerable effect on the price of the camera. Typically, the ratio might be 6 to 1, though 10 to 1 is certainly possible. On no account buy a camera with a lens that has a zooming ratio greater than you need. A macro facility and an auto-zoom may also be offered.

Microphones These vary from make to make. They are usually omni-directional, but it is worth having a camera with provision for an add-on boom microphone which may have directional properties.

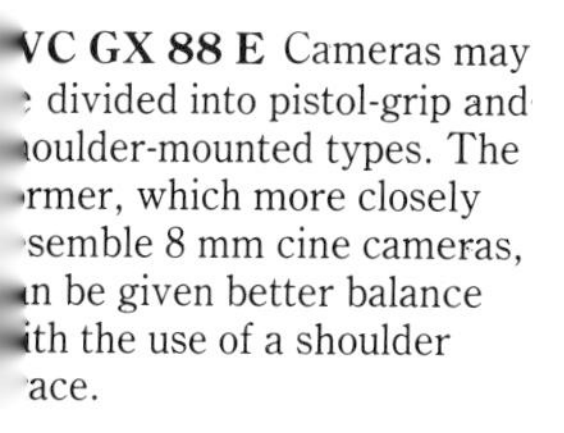

JVC GX 88 E Cameras may be divided into pistol-grip and shoulder-mounted types. The former, which more closely resemble 8 mm cine cameras, can be given better balance with the use of a shoulder brace.

Sony HVC 2000 P
Cameras such as this Sony model tend to have a naturally superior balance, since they rest on the shoulder. The electronic viewfinder can often be rotated for left-eyed operation or for low-level work.

Using the camera

Cameras vary widely in size, specification, and mode of operation, but certain broad principles apply.

Connections If camera and recorder are equipped with multi-pin plugs then the camera need simply be connected to the relevant socket on the recorder. This will supply the 12-volt DC power and will connect the video and audio leads as well as the Remote Pause control. If your recorder does not have the appropriate socket, connect the camera to an AC adaptor, which will provide it with DC power, and run the leads from the AC adaptor to the appropriate Audio In, Video In, and Remote Pause control sockets on the recorder. In either event the power on recorder and/or AC adaptor must be switched on. It is also possible for a TV receiver or monitor to be wired into the recorder for checking the quality during recording.

If you wish to use an external or a boom microphone on top of the camera this should be plugged in to the MIC socket on the camera, and normally this will automatically cut out the built-in microphone. Alternatively, the external microphone can be plugged direct into the recorder in place of the microphone input jack. When all the connections are made, and both recorder and/or AC adaptor are turned on, press the Record, Play, and Pause buttons on the recorder. It will enter the pause mode, and the electronic viewfinder on the camera will be illuminated. Remove the lens cap and proceed to adjust the white balance.

White balance Controls vary considerably but in general there will be a crude setting which enables you to decide on the prevailing light source in daylight or tungsten; then follow the manufacturer's instructions precisely for setting the white balance. This may involve pointing the camera at a white card in the prevailing light, or placing a white translucent cap

Iris and white balance
The two principal controls on a camera are the iris and the white balance. Both controls are a mixture of electronic and mechanical; the iris control is also linked to the automatic video gain, while the white balance is partly a matter of crude physical filtration, and partly a delicate electronic adjustment of the balance between red and blue. It is not usual on domestic cameras for the relative value of green to be manipulable. In addition, there will also normally be a sensitivity setting for the prevailing light conditions.

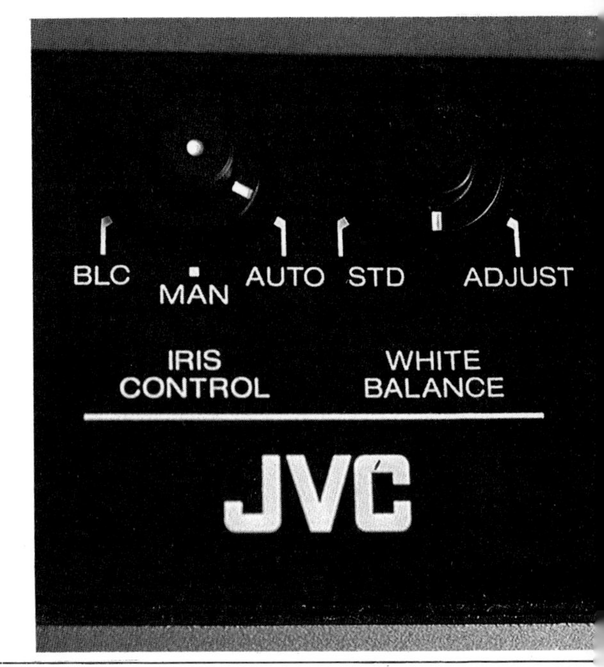

ɔver the lens. There will be an indicator in :he viewfinder which should be adjusted according to the manual setting of a knob on :he side of the camera. In some cameras this ɔperation is automatic.

Sensitivity Sensitivity selections are normally automatic though high and low settings are commonly also available. Avoid exposing the tubes to high levels of light when the camera is on a low setting, as :he tube itself can easily be burnt, leaving streaks on the surface of the image. As a general rule never point a vidicon at a bright ight for any length of time and *never* point it lirectly at the sun.

Iris The iris, which in conjunction with the electronic gain on the vidicon tube controls :he exposure, should normally be set to auto. This may be adjusted manually for special positions such as back lighting, and :he results observed in an electronic viewfinder or on a monitor.

Sound There may be settings for different sound controls which would include sharpness and sensitivity. These two should be selected before shooting, and the earpiece plugged in if you wish to monitor results.

Framing the subject Frame the subject roughly then zoom in, focus up, zoom out, and frame accurately according to your shooting intentions. Check that the brightness and lighting of the picture are satisfactory when viewed through the electronic viewfinder if you have one, and, if all is satisfactory, press the Pause button on the recorder which will now begin recording. It is not a good idea to leave a recorder in pause for more than 2 or 3 minutes at the very most, and if you wish to run the camera off the recorder's power for some time before beginning recording simply press the Record button alone to activate the power without using the pause mode. Unless the Play button is pressed, the tape will not be running and no recording will take place.

Camera hints

- Check that the connections are correct before beginning the recording.
- Allow a short warm-up time for the camera.
- Check that the input selector of the recorder has been set to the camera input position.
- If there is a loud whistle when shooting with a monitor plugged in to the recorder, this can be attributed to acoustic 'howl round', in which the loudspeaker of the monitor and the microphone on the camera are involved in acoustic feedback. Turn down the sound on the monitor until recording is completed.
- Never expose the camera to dampness, dust, or excessive vibration.
- Never touch the front element of the lens with an ordinary cloth or finger.
- Watch the battery indicator light when running the camera from battery power. This will normally begin to flash red in the viewfinder if there is insufficient power.
- The camera will often indicate insufficient light while there appears to be an adequate image in the viewfinder. Viewfinders are not a reliable indication and it is worth checking the results on a monitor before proceeding. After use always replace the lens cap immediately.

Steadying the camera

Any shot that you intend to show on the screen at home should be telling, eloquent, and simple. The technique underlying the creation of the shot should not be visible either in the positive sense (look at this!) or in the negative sense (sorry this is so wobbly...). It is often claimed that purely hand-held camerawork gives a more natural feel to the tape you are making. But, in fact, are you actually aware of a room wobbling when you walk across it? When you focus on a distant scene, concentrating your vision on one element such as a ship crossing the horizon, *does* the target waver in the frame of your eye, as it would if you were shooting on the long end of the zoom with a hand-held camera? It does not. To achieve 'natural' results, it is almost always necessary to resort to some form of artifice, whether you are considering diffusion filters, sound-effects, or make-up. When it comes to steadying the camera, the choice is between good hand-held technique and the tripod.

Hand-held camerwork

The first thing to understand about the use of a hand-held camera is that the wobbliness is partly determined by the focal length. The longer the focal length (i.e. the 'tighter' the zoom), the more visible the wobble will be. With a telephoto shot there are very few people who can maintain a still and soothing image, even with the help of a brace or a handy wall to lean against. When you are also walking with the camera, the use of a long lens is more or less ruled out for all but a few experts. The general rule is

Basic stance In the basic stance the legs should be slightly apart and the elbows held closely into the body so that the camera can be kept quite steady. Most cameras are designed exclusively for use with the right eye and while the right hand should support the camera the left hand may be used to adjust focus. Never place the recorder on the ground unless you are quite certain that you are not going to move in the course of the shot.

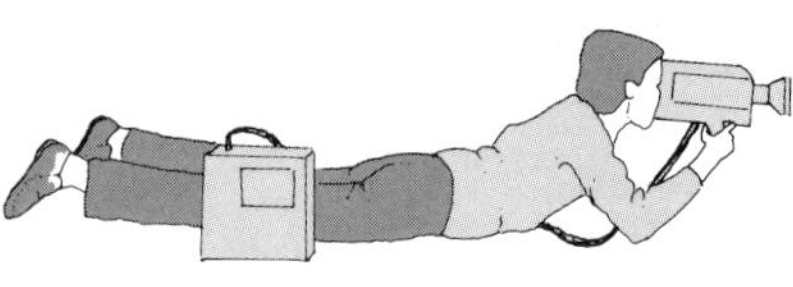

Prone position For low-angle work the prone position gives extremely steady results but remember that the position is also very inflexible.

Kneeling position Kneeling with one elbow on a knee can give steady support for close-up work though a tripod is preferable for true macro shooting.

that if you are hand-holding a camera, you should restrict yourself to the wide-angle (or short) end of the zoom, and get close into the subject. This will not only guarantee steady shots, but will also have the effect of compressing and intensifying the action. Then, when you are immersed in the flow of the action, the mobility and portability of the video recorder will come into its own.

There are many occasions, such as wedding receptions or birthday parties, where the general geography of events may be predicted, but the precise locations cannot. At such times, you would be foolish to harness yourself to a tripod simply because you anticipate one or two telephoto close-ups from that position: there will probably be someone in the way, and in any case the steadiness of one or two shots does not, in such a fluid situation, justify the rigidity of the over-all sequence. Always ask yourself what the real priorities are — in the end, it will always come down to seizing the story you are trying to relate, and if that involves abandoning some fancy tripod work, so be it. Very often, you will only have one chance. Children do not pause, Best Men do not wait, and record-breaking sportsmen do not interrupt their stride while you re-position your tripod. Therefore do not plan to use a tripod, however seductive the beauty of the anticipated results, if you are likely to lose the really crucial shots. But, to compensate, you must have a very good hand-held technique. Fortunately, on video this can be rehearsed and reviewed very cheaply indeed, so that you will soon learn from your mistakes.

Leaning against a wall Always be on the look-out for something steady against which you can lean. This may be furniture or a wall.

Leaning against a car For exterior work a car can also be used as a means of supporting the camera.

Leaning on a chair The back of a chair gives similar support to the kneeling position but with a much higher point of view.

When to use a tripod

A tripod should only, and always, be used in a situation that you can be certain in advance will be under control: it takes quite a while to unbuckle a camera from a tripod if things change unexpectedly. On the other hand, when shooting any form of predictable set-piece, or when a telephoto will certainly be needed, it is a very good idea to plan out a tripod position. Make sure that the tripod is positioned at the correct spot (and convenient height); that it is level in all directions, even when the pan-head is being used (pp. 96-7); and that the view will be unobstructed.

It is worth remembering that steady tripod shots do not readily intercut with wobbly hand-held shots of the same scene; plan your shooting accordingly.

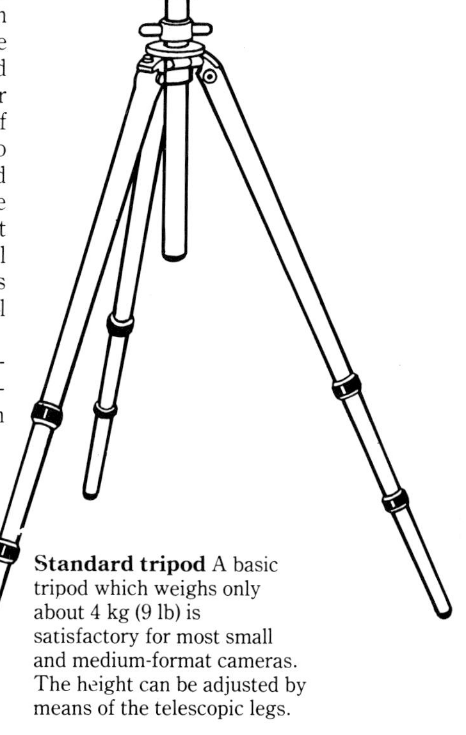

Standard tripod A basic tripod which weighs only about 4 kg (9 lb) is satisfactory for most small and medium-format cameras. The height can be adjusted by means of the telescopic legs.

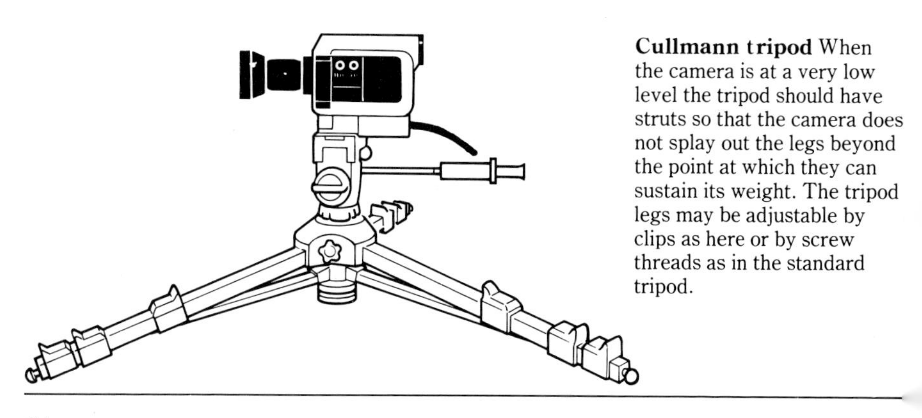

Cullmann tripod When the camera is at a very low level the tripod should have struts so that the camera does not splay out the legs beyond the point at which they can sustain its weight. The tripod legs may be adjustable by clips as here or by screw threads as in the standard tripod.

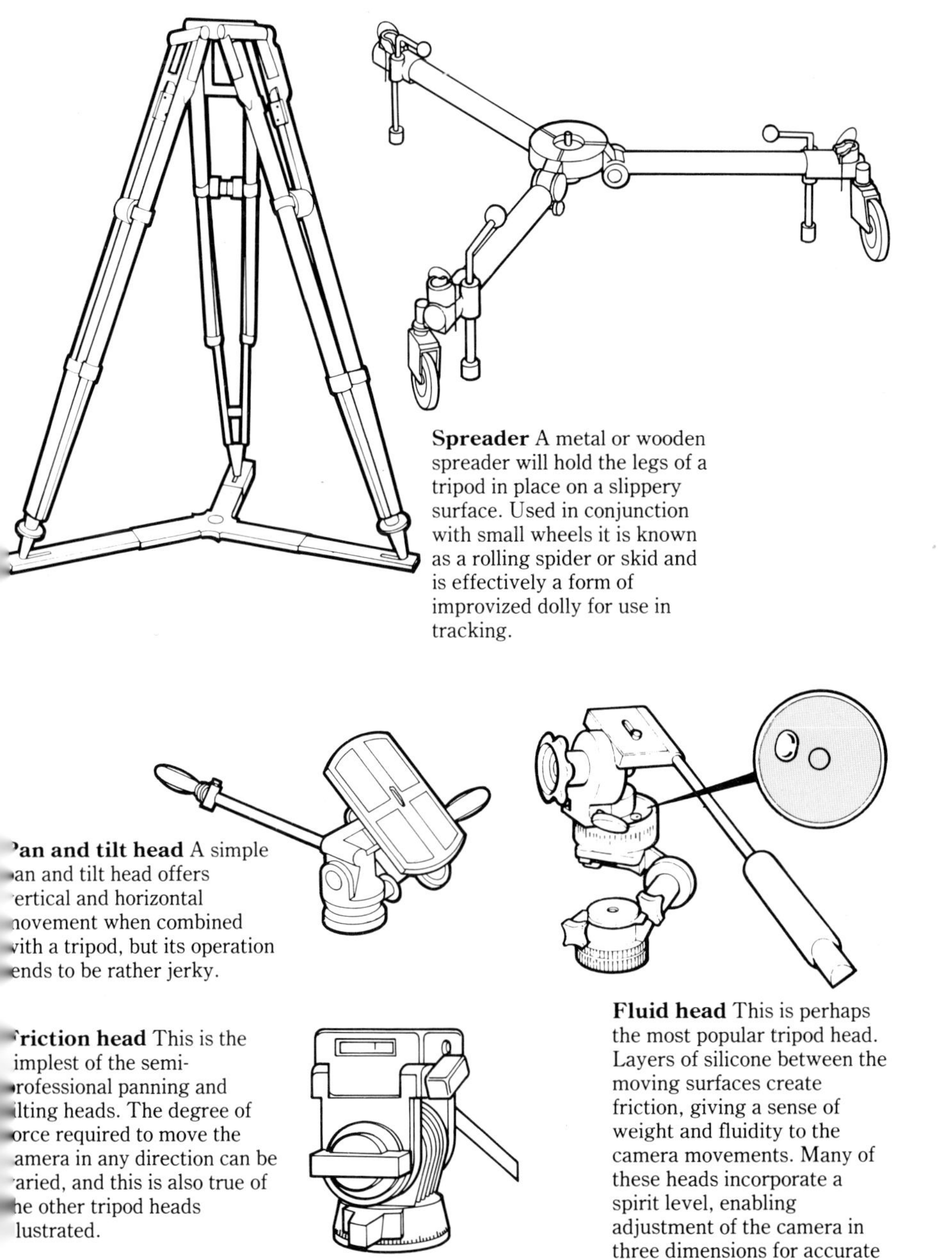

Spreader A metal or wooden spreader will hold the legs of a tripod in place on a slippery surface. Used in conjunction with small wheels it is known as a rolling spider or skid and is effectively a form of improvized dolly for use in tracking.

an and tilt head A simple an and tilt head offers ertical and horizontal novement when combined vith a tripod, but its operation ends to be rather jerky.

riction head This is the implest of the semi-rofessional panning and ilting heads. The degree of orce required to move the amera in any direction can be aried, and this is also true of he other tripod heads lustrated.

Fluid head This is perhaps the most popular tripod head. Layers of silicone between the moving surfaces create friction, giving a sense of weight and fluidity to the camera movements. Many of these heads incorporate a spirit level, enabling adjustment of the camera in three dimensions for accurate panning and tilting.

Basic shots

Very long shot, long shot, mid-shot, medium close-up, close-up, big close-up: the list seems both arbitrary and endless. Yet the jargon used to describe film and TV shots is more than just an exercise for the professionals to sound stylish. It provides an approximate common language which can be used in studios for communication between the director and the cameraman, and more importantly for the amateur, it can lend a discipline to the flow of shots.

In video, as in film, no shot can be thought of in isolation. Every shot, however vivid in its own right, must be thought of in relation to the shot that has gone before and the shot that will follow it. This means that the shots should share a common feel, a common pace, and a common appearance, but *not*, in most cases, a common size of the subject in frame. If you cut between two shots of the same person in which he is the same size in frame, the effect will often be a jump-cut even if the angle has been changed. If, however, you change the size of the shot firmly, but not dramatically, the cut will probably work successfully.

What are they for?

There are three basic shots — close-up, mid-shot, long shot — and though they are loosely defined, they are not so randomly selected as might be thought.

The *close-up* is a shot of *one* individual, of the head and a touch of the shoulders. It gives a personal view, which may perhaps be the point of view of that individual's interlocutor.

The *mid-shot*, which extends to just below the waist, can give just enough room in the horizontal mode to include one other person. A mid-shot can therefore also become a 'two-shot'. Instantly, we are in the realm of society rather than the solitary individual. A mid-shot implies the presence of others, and of surroundings, even if they are not visible in it.

In *long shot*, the figure or figures are related in grand scale to their environment or to the crowd. We see their feet, and so, as they walk on the earth, the frame has expanded to be filled with their surroundings and the crowd, or its absence, or either side.

These three shots stand not only for three practical ways of intercutting a sequence: they might also be thought of as electronic emblems of the individual alone, in society, or against a background.

The basic shots

In a script, shots are referred to by the following abbreviations:

VLS	Very Long Shot
LS	Long Shot
MS	Mid-shot
MCU	Medium Close-up
CU	Close-up
BCU	Big Close-up

The basic shots

VLS

LS

MS

MCU

CU

BCU

Cutting between shots
When cutting from one shot to another the difference in size and/or angle should be decisive but not excessively dramatic. Here when cutting from the master shot to Shot 1 the change of *angle* is insufficient. When cutting to Shot 2, however, the change of angle is just sufficient to give a good cut. When cutting from the master shot to Shot 3 the change of *size* is insufficient, while Shot 4 does provide a good cut. Shot 5 shows a satisfactory change of both size and angle, and this too provides a good strong cut.

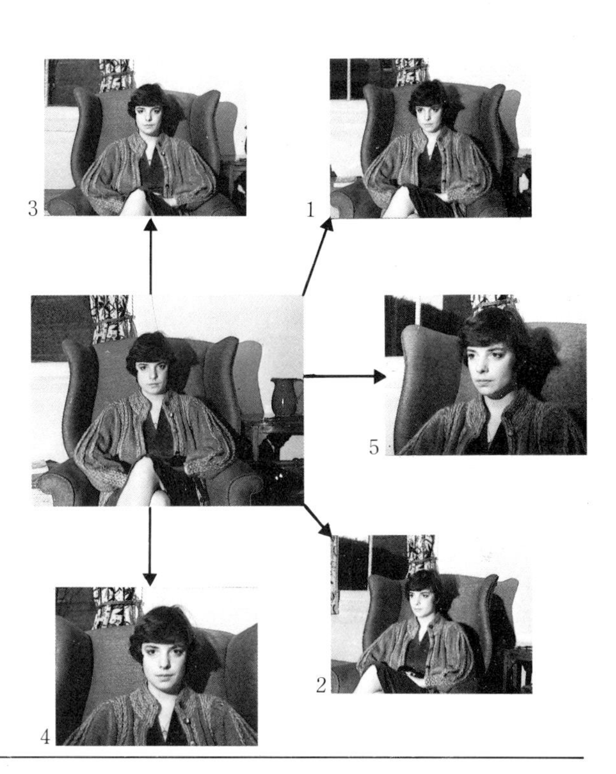

The lens/Macro

In any camera, whether still or movie, video or film, the lens focuses the incoming light on to a plane: this is known as the focal plane, and this is the point at which the target of the video tube will be placed. The image will in fact be inverted, but this will be corrected electronically. The angle of view of different lenses varies according to their 'focal length', which is the distance from the optical centre, or 'nodal point', of the lens to the focal plane. The longer the focal length, the narrower the angle of view — this is known at its extremes as a telephoto lens; while a short focal length gives a wider angle of view — a wide-angle lens. This has a considerable effect not only on the size of the image, but also on the perspective that you will obtain.

It is important to remember that the angle of view provided by the focal length of a lens depends entirely on the target or tube size. The larger the tube size, the narrower the angle of view for any given focal length (see tables, pp. 210—11).

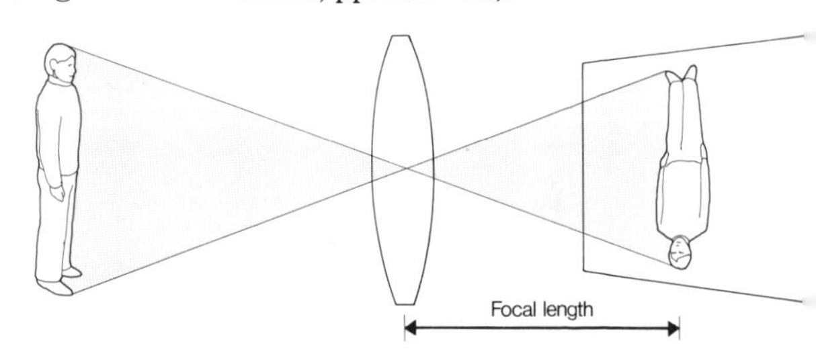

Focal length is the distance from the so-called optical centre of a lens to the focal plane (in video, the target) when the lens is focused on an object at infinity. The focused image is reversed on the target, but this is corrected electronically.

Zooming-in The zooming ratio of any lens is a description of its ability to vary the angle of view: e.g. a 12—120 mm lens is said to have a zooming ratio of 10 to1.

Static camera If the camera is not moved in relation to the subject and the focal length is varied, the size of the subject is changed while the perspective remains entirely unaltered.

Wide-angle

Normal

Telephoto

Wide-angle

Normal

Telephoto

Moving camera If the camera is moved in towards the subject while the lens is zoomed out, or it retreats from the subject while the lens is zoomed in, the subject size remains the same while the perspective changes: in relation to the tree the man is quite a different size.

Macro lens

A macro lens may be either a separate fixed focal-length lens or, more likely, a zoom lens with a Macro setting for very short lens-to-subject distances. Typically, the lens should be adjusted to its widest setting, then the zoom lever may be pulled outwards to engage the Macro position. In this mode, the rear group of lens elements is moved forward, giving very high magnifications at short subject distances. In many cases, focusing is then possible right down to the front element of the zoom. At these high magnifications, a tripod is almost certainly essential, and the depth of field will be extremely shallow, especially at wide apertures. A high level of ambient lighting, such as sunlight, is therefore recommended for macro work.

Focusing

Focal length is calculated for the position of the lens when focusing an object at infinity. For closer subjects, the lens must be moved further away from the tube to permit the rays to converge on the target plate. This is done by twisting either the whole lens or, more likely, only its front elements on a helical thread so that they move forwards.

The zoom

A zoom lens (see pp. 92-3 for further details) is a complex lens with many elements, and it has a variable focal length, giving a choice of angles of view without the necessity of changing lenses. A zoom lens is now standard on amateur cameras, few of which offer interchangeable lenses. Zoom control is often motorized, while focusing is manual on all but professional models.

Aperture

Essentially, the aperture of a given lens is a description of its maximum light-gathering power, and this is expressed in so-called f-numbers. The lower the f-number, the 'faster' the lens, and the greater its light-gathering power when used at maximum aperture. Typically, a fast lens might be f1.4. The aperture is controlled by a *diaphragm,* and the gradations of the aperture are in f-stops. Each full stop represents a doubling or halving in the light being focused by the lens, and the stops are divided logarithmically.

The full stops are:

1.4	4	11
2	5.6	16
2.8	8	22 etc.

See also pp. 130-3 for *exposure.*

The diaphragm is adjusted either manually or automatically, so that the tube is provided with an adequate, though not excessive, input of light.

Selective focus Selective focus has been used to direct attention to the bird sitting on top of the minaret. The background of the harbour is almost completely defocused.

Focus-pull The harbour has its own interest, and this might be preferred. It is possible to change the focus during a shot — a focus-pull. For this effect the depth of field must be minimized. This can be done by increasing either the focal length or the aperture. In video this can only be done by the use of neutral density filters.

Composition

Composition is often described in terms of 'rules', but in truth it can no more be rigidly taught than can any other instinct for beauty. Certain broad generalizations can be made about balance, however, which with practice will improve your shooting. Above all, acquire the habit of critically assessing the structure of each shot before you press the Record button; imagine any possible improvements; frame tightly and go for strong, simple structure.

Rule of thirds This so-called 'rule' dictates that horizontals and verticals should not bisect the frame exactly in the middle. In a shot like this (above) it is often advantageous to place the horizon low in the frame to make the most of the sky. This, combined with a very wide-angle lens, gives the impression of enormous space.

Diagonal emphasis Another convention is that a diagonal is always to be preferred to a vertical or horizontal emphasis. Here (above), the path leads the eye through the grass to the tree on the far right-hand side. In the shot on the right the diagonal cuts through the line of the horizon. The branch below is answered by a small branch coming in from above which brushes, but does not quite touch, the mountain in the distance.

Zooms and zooming

A zoom shot involves the use of a zoom lens, which is a lens with a variable focal length, and therefore a variable angle of view. It can move from wide-angle to telephoto (narrow angle) without the need for a change of lens. The focal length of a lens is nowadays expressed in millimetres, and a typical range for a zoom using a 17 mm (2/3 in) tube might be 11-66 mm. This is a *zooming ratio* of 6:1 and the angle of view on that 17 mm tube can therefore be varied from approximately 8° to 48°.

Zoom lenses are complex optics involving many elements, but they are now standard on all amateur cameras, with varying degrees of sophistication. In addition, the Zoom control will probably be motorized, and many zooms also offer a Macro control for extreme close-up work.

How does it work?

To change the focal length of a zoom lens, only the central portion of the elements is moved backwards or forwards in relation to the film plane; the front elements are used for adjusting focus and the rear group sometimes moved for the Macro setting.

In the non-manual, or auto, mode, there are sometimes several speeds to be selected, and these have a distinct bearing on the impact of the shot. If the auto speed is wrong, use the Manual setting.

Zooming technique

When zooming, always pre-view both the beginning and the end of the shot, both to establish a focus and to define the composition of the final frame, which you will not see until it is too late to alter it.

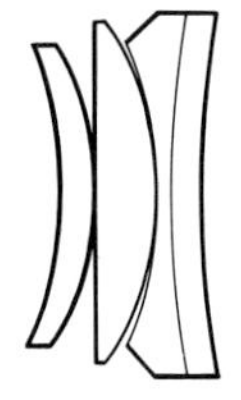

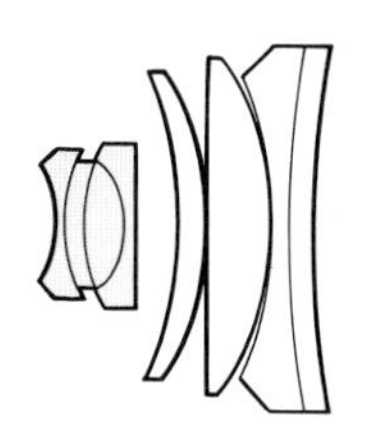

Wide-angle and telephoto
When a zoom lens is moved from the wide-angle to the telephoto position a central group of elements is moved forwards, though both front and rear elements remain in position. This highly complex optical readjustment of the lens does not affect the point of focus. Since the focus is more critical at the telephoto end of the zoom than at the wide-angle you should always pre-focus on a subject if you intend to zoom in on it. It is not so critical when zooming out.

Focusing for a zoom

If you are zooming *out,* there is probably no need to check the final focus point, since depth of field will increase with the angle of view (pp. 94-5). When zooming *in,* especially at low light levels and with wide apertures, *always* pre-focus on the end of the zoom on the final frame. The drill is: zoom in to the close-up you intend to finish with; check for composition and focus; zoom out; check again for composition, and shoot. If the focus on the wide-angle does not hold, you will have to re-focus manually during the shot. This is difficult to perform accurately alone, but is in any case not commonly needed with small-tube video cameras except under the most extreme circumstances or in the hands of very refined operators.

When to zoom

A zoom is a powerful visual effect; it should *not* be used casually, nor should one or more zooms be combined without good reason. This alone of all the common shots is the one which has no parallel in normal visual experience. It is heady medicine which will lose its efficacy if abused. It is therefore perhaps best to consider the zoom as a convenient way of carrying many lenses in one barrel, and to save the effect for when it is really needed.

While a zoom-in concentrates the attention, and would at first sight seem more dramatic, a zoom-out, which reveals more and more as it goes, can in practice be even more theatrical, since everything entering the frame is a new arrival. It is a revelation rather than a concentration.

Pre-focusing In this occasion, if the little girl on the far side of the pool had not been pre-focused she would almost certainly have been 'soft' at the end of the zoom. These shots represent a zooming ratio of 10:1.

Depth of field

Depth of field is the range of distances from the lens to the subject within which the subject appears to be in acceptably sharp focus. For any given distance set on the lens, the depth of field will vary according to the prevailing aperture and the selected focal length.

Aperture and depth of field

The wider the aperture, the shallower the depth of field, and consequently the greater the difficulty in focusing. Since video cameras spend a good deal of the time at relatively large apertures, at least when used in interior work, you should be aware that there is very little margin for error at these large apertures, and focusing is likely to be critical. Indeed, one of the principal reasons for working in good light is that the depth of field is so dramatically increased at smaller apertures. Furthermore, the overall resolution of the lens will improve considerably as it is stopped down, even in those areas which are at the centre of the plane of focus.

Focal length and depth of field

The other factor affecting the depth of field is the focal length. The longer the focal length, the shallower the depth of field. When considering depth of field, remember that it extends more deeply *behind* the point of focus than in front. The other point to remember is that aperture and focus work in concert: e.g. 15 mm at f1.4 gives a shallow but manageable depth of field while 70 mm at the same aperture would yield a depth of field so very shallow that shooting would be exceedingly tricky, and you might have trouble in focusing the whole of one face, for example.

Creative use of depth of field

It is not true that a deeply focused picture is always desirable: you may wish to isolate a subject from its surroundings by throwing them out of focus. To do this, reduce the depth of field by retreating and using a longer lens setting or by increasing the working aperture: in video, this will mean fitting neutral density filters to the lens.

Creative depth of field
Depth of field can be used creatively in a number of ways. It may be used to focus attention on a background (above) or to accentuate the foreground (above right). When focus is changed from background to foreground in the course of a shot, this is known as a 'focus-pull'. This effect may also be used for purely technical reasons, as when shooting through the bars of a cage in a zoo. In all such cases a wide aperture is necessary, and in very bright conditions it may be necessary to use neutral density filters.

\perture and depth of ield At the very widest perture (in this case f1.4) nly one of the peaches is in ocus. As the aperture is rogressively increased nrough f5.6 to f8/11 to the ery small aperture of f22, it ill be seen that more and nore of the row of peaches omes into focus until at the ery smallest aperture (f22) ot only the peaches are in ocus but also a good deal of e landscape behind as well. n this example it could be aid that the eventual depth of eld reaches from the nearest each at 1 ft (30 cm) to nfinity.

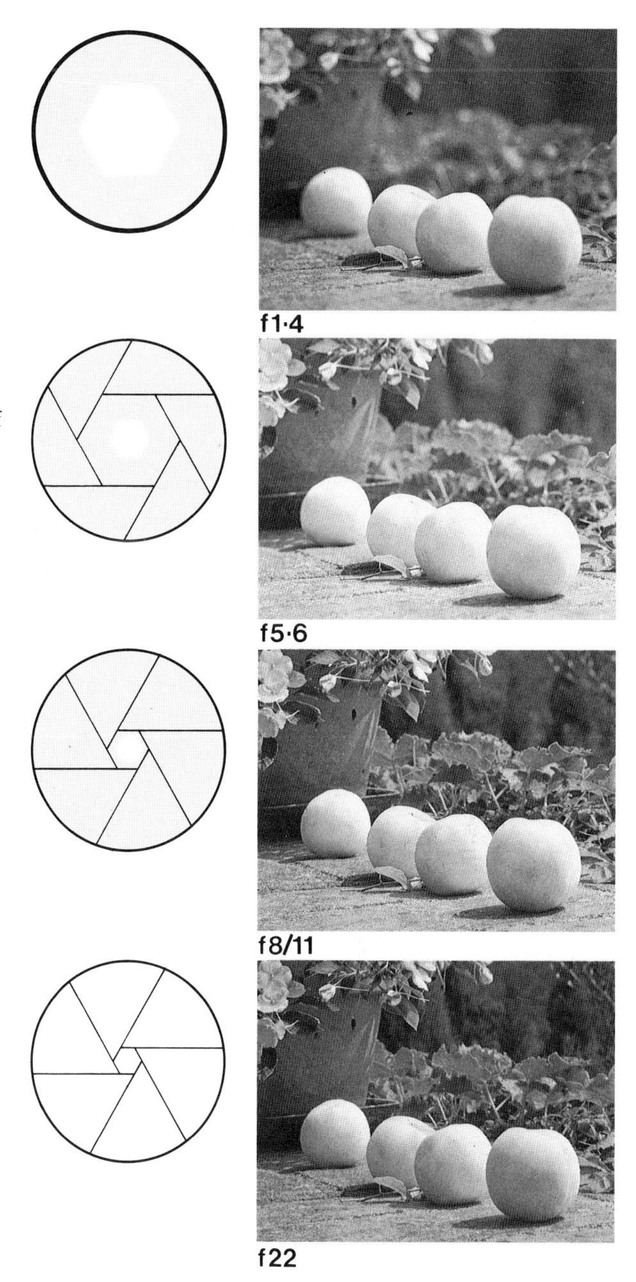

Panning and tilting

A pan is any shot which moves in a horizontal direction, left or right. It may be very fast (a 'whip-pan') or, more usually, sufficiently slow to observe the scene you are panning over. However, if you are following a figure — say a footballer — then the background is unimportant and you can move the camera as fast as you like without losing a coherent image, so long as the central figure is firmly in the frame.

Following a moving subject When panning with a moving subject, always keep the camera slightly ahead, so that the subject appears to be walking into the shot and motivating the movement.

Planning a pan If the pan is not following a moving subject, but is used to cover a larger area than could be encompassed by a single shot, it is important to rehearse the end-frame, as well as the beginning and the middle, before you shoot. There are few more dismal shots than lengthy pans which arrive nowhere.

Tripod technique When panning on a tripod, always arrange the body so that the pan becomes *easier* as you go. In a long pan, this may involve starting in a rath uncomfortable position, but you will or achieve the desired smoothness if yo stance is becoming progressively mc balanced.

Speed and pace Always begin and enc pan with a 'hold' of a few seconds. This w not only give you flexibility if you wish edit; it will also give stability and stature the shot itself.

As for the speed, always err on the sl side: video does not suffer from t 'strobing' problems that affect fil because of the much higher field rate in t camera, but the eye can still only take in much at a time. Consider the speed o given pan in terms of the mood and the pa of the over-all sequence.

Speed and focal length The effective spe of a pan is very much dependent on the fo length. On the long end of the zoom, a p will have to be very slow indeed to followed, and here of course you w certainly need a tripod. On a wide-angle, the other hand, a pan can be fairly rapid y still be comprehensible.

Panning When you are panning with a moving subject, it does not matter that the background is blurred. Aim always to keep the camera slightly ahead of the subject.

Tilting
A tilt is a vertical pan, and all the above strictures apply. Before you start a tilt-up, be sure that you will be well balanced for the end of the shot — this may not be easy if the camera is hand-held, especially if you are carrying the recorder as well. When tilting over buildings, it is often true that a tilt-up tends to accentuate the height, whereas a tilt-down can be very well used as the introductory shot for a sequence. If you are tilting into the sky, be sure to lock off the auto-exposure control so that the sky does not darken automatically.

Tilting With all panning and tilting shots, the opening and closing shots should be equally full of interest and equally well composed. Here, from the couple feeding pigeons in the foreground, the eye is naturally drawn upwards into the church towers.

Tracking

A tracking shot is one in which the camera itself is moving. It may be hand-held, or on some kind of moving platform such as a car, wheelchair, or dolly.

What a track can offer is a true change of perspective and a dynamic sense of movement. Unlike a zoom, a track is a recognizable variant of our normal way of seeing and moving; it can also present a constant flow of new perspectives with an unrivalled sense of realism and drama.

Steadiness

If the camera is hand-held, be sure to use a very wide-angle lens — the wide end of the zoom, at least — and get in close to the subject, whether you are following it or whether you are moving through a static scene. This will minimize the camera shake that is the bane of all tracking shots. Practise balancing the camera, recording the image on a piece of spare tape, and assess the results critically. Get to know just how tight you can go on the zoom before the image becomes unacceptably wobbly. Know your technical limits and work within them. Use a shoulder brace if the camera is not of the shoulder-mounted

Zooming A zoom is the ideal lens when you wish to focus the attention of a viewer on a particular part of a scene yet cannot physically advance towards it. In this example, the river Seine prevents a direct approach to the statue at the centre of the subject, and the zoom lens provides a satisfactory solution. However, even in this very large zoom, the perspective does not vary, and this is particularly unfortunate with a highly three-dimensional subject such as architecture. Although the angle of view changes, the variation in the image lacks dynamism and it fails to convey a true impression of approaching the building.

Tracking Starting from the same position, if the camera is moved towards the central subject (the bronze statue at the top of the monument), the effect is far more dramatic. Compare the final frame of the track with that of the zoom: both have concentrated the attention on one aspect of the scene, but the tracking shot has in the process revealed many three-dimensional aspects of the building, the bridge, and indeed the atmosphere of Paris, which would otherwise have been lost.

type. If all these strategems do not satisfy you, use a dolly or some alternative.

Mobile camera platforms

There is no point in planning a dolly-shot if the scene to be taped is unpredictable. Dolly-shots need rehearsal, and even shots from the back seat of a car tend to go wrong on the first take. In other words, if you are following a mobile and unpredictable subject through a crowd, steadiness is unimportant compared to flexibility; but if you are planning a long architectural tracking shot, it becomes vital. In such a case, there is no substitute for a dolly. If the floor is smooth, a wheelchair is a perfectly good alternative. A second person will be needed to push the chair, and he should mark out the planned beginning and end of the track with a strip of camera tape or chalk.

As with a pan, aim for a very smooth movement, preceded and ended by a static hold. Rehearse the movement thoroughly and, since tape is cheap, do several takes until you are sure of a good result. Tracking shots are spectacular, and well worth the effort.

Wheelchair dolly This is one of the most satisfactory and economical ways of achieving a smooth track though you will obviously need the help of another person.

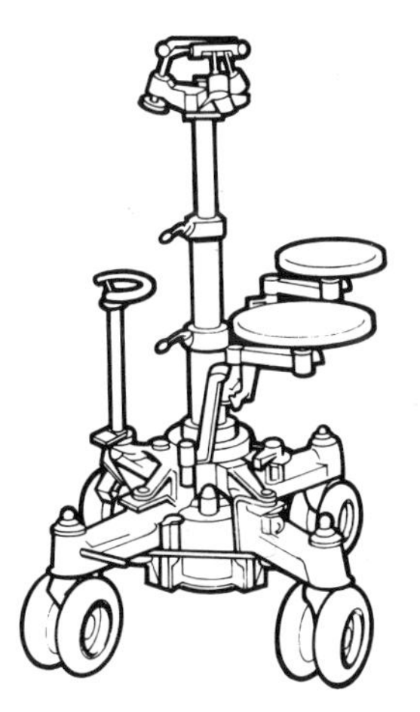

Elemac spyder dolly This is both the most versatile and one of the most expensive professional dollies. The central column can be adjusted hydraulically, and the wheels replaced with metal wheels that attach to rails for more complicated tracking.

Shooting from a car
Use a wide angle to minimize wobble and vibration. The camera can be rested on a bean bag or braced on a small clamp that can be attached to the window frame.

Editing in the camera

If you own two machines, or have access to a second machine in addition to the recording machine, it will be perfectly possible to edit the original tape. Errors and repetitions can be removed, the order rearranged, and the whole tape given a polish that cannot be obtained by any other means. However, there will be a fairly noticeable loss of quality on ½-inch or ¼-inch second-generation tape; the process is somewhat time-consuming; and with present machinery the edits are not always perfectly smooth. The alternative is to edit in the camera. This means shooting as much as possible so that the shots do not clash together on the cuts. There are several techniques.

The Pause control

Most modern portables have a Pause control that can be engaged during recording so that the next shot will not cause a frame-roll on replay. This can usually only be engaged for a brief space of time. Some advanced units, however, such as the JVC HR 2200, have a power-saving switch which will keep the tape locked into position for much longer periods. Domestic machines have a wide variety of Pause controls, and very few of them at the present time have effective Edit controls. If the Pause button cannot be used satisfactorily, you have only the alternative of very long takes. In any case, you should be aware that at the present state of the art no domestic ½-inch or ¼-inch machine gives a completely clean, flash-free edit between consecutive shots.

The long take

It is a good idea to aim for long takes when shooting material that you do not intend to edit. Use the camera hand-held, with the recorder over the shoulder if the weight is

Creative shooting If one single shot is used sufficiently creatively, it can contain within it all the different shots that could be obtained by complex cutting. In this single hand-held track the camera manages to combine long shots of the girl and of the room as well as close-ups of the girl as she walks past. The shot begins as the girl walks down the garden towards the rear door. As she enters the door the camera tracks back to reveal the living-room. As she walks towards the now stationary camera a close-up is achieved, and she then walks away into the kitchen from which the camera has itself just emerged.

ıot too great, so that you have the flexibility :hat is essential if the shot is to be of interest hroughout its length. Make sure that there s room to move around without falling ›ver, and get close into the subject to fill the rame with sustained variety. If the lialogue is important try to listen as :arefully as you are looking: nothing is vorse than an interesting exchange of :onversation which is cut in the middle ›ecause the cameraman, satisfied with his mage, has cut the shot. Keep your balance ;o that the flow of a hand-held shot is not listurbed by an unplanned wobble, and nake the zoom movements or focus-pulls ıs gentle as possible during the shooting. In his context, it is good practice to keep the eft eye open while shooting: not only can ·ou then see where you are going, but you :an also watch the area outside the iewfinder for possible developments in the hot. This needs practice.

Intercutting

If, on the other hand, extensive use is being made of the Pause control, then the principles of true editing come into play. If shots are to be intercut, they must be considered as a constant flow of images; this means that you will have to consider them as notes in the continuous line of visual music. In particular, you will have to consider the *relative size* of the subject in frame; the *continuity* of action, direction, speed, and appearance; and the speed and duration of the individual shots themselves. Many of these subjects are dealt with at great length in the sections on editing (pp. 170—5) and continuity (pp. 102—3), but it should be noted here that when taping one single subject, the variation in size between consecutive shots should be just enough to be a decisive cut, yet not affront the eye. The same applies to change of angle (pp. 106-7).

Continuity

The degree of smoothness that you intend to build into a tape will vary according to the subject: in a drama, it is vital, whereas with children at play the flow will probably be achieved by varying the shot size or the judicious use of cutaways (pp. 104-5). But the principles of continuity should be understood and used.

Continuity may be divided into two types: *action,* which includes literal actions, speed, direction, and position in frame; *appearance*, which includes light, weather, clothes, furniture, and the time of year.

Continuity of action

At its simplest, this means that the same person should not be doing two different things in consecutive shots, unless you are aiming to produce a jolt. This becomes tricky when shooting something like a meal which has a continuous flow to it. In all drama shooting, careful notes are taken of each shot so that continuity can be preserved. At the very least, keep a close eye on the action just as you put the camera into pause, so that the next shot can be matched for intercutting.

Speed is more subtle: if a person is walking slowly in one shot, and fast in the next, no amount of angle change or change of shot size will disguise the discrepancy. The speed of the subject through frame

Continuity of action An activity such as a ball game presents observable problems. Here, when cutting from the wide-angle two-shot to a single shot of the pair at the far end, it is vital that her actions should match in long shot and in close-up. If she is playing a forehand in the long shot (top left), you cannot cut to a subsequent close-up of a backhand (above). If you cut to the close-up when she is playing a forehand (left), the cut will probably work successfully on the screen. It may be possible to disguise glaring errors of continuity by very large changes in shot size and angle.

should also be taken into account.

The direction of movement is if anything even more crucial. It is direction which gives a clear geography to a sequence, and the over-all left/right orientation should be varied only with care (pp. 106–7). If a person leaves frame on the right, you would expect to see him enter on the left in the next shot. There are fortunately many ways around this 'rule', but it remains fundamental.

More subtle is the position in frame of a figure in consecutive shots. If the figure jumps to the left or the right, the effect, as with a very abrupt and violent change of shot size, is one of discontinuity.

Continuity of appearance

This really only applies to shooting over which you have complete control – drama, for instance. It means that a character should be dressed in the same clothes, with the same make-up, the same lighting, at the same time of day, and with the same length of hair, in consecutive shots, even if they are taken a week or so later. The beauty of video tape, as opposed to film, is that the first shot can be played back on the set on a portable monitor to check detail. In this context, the monitor is preferable, since discrepancies of colour are usually the most glaring, and the camera's viewfinder is only black and white.

Direction of movement A common error of continuity is a reversal of direction. Here the man is facing in opposite ways in consecutive shots. The resulting impression of this cut is that there are two similar people facing each other and possibly having a conversation, whereas only one man is present.

Continuity of appearance This is a common error, especially in drama. In this shot, the fact that the woman has removed the jacket between two shots means that one is given a first impression that two different people are playing the game.

Artificial continuity

To sustain the flow of a narrative, to give visual interest, or to compress into a coherent few minutes an event, such as a meal, that may have taken hours, requires the use of a variety of tricks. Among them are cutaways, cut-ins, and buffer-shots.

Cutaways

A cutaway is often confused with a cut-in, and its function can indeed be identical at times: a cutaway is a shot inserted between two shots of the overall master action, which relates to the main shot but which has not been visible in it; e.g. (1) the couple are studying a menu; (2) cutaway of a cigarette on the table; (3) the whole group are shown. Time is compressed, and a jump-cut is averted.

Cut-ins

A cut-in is the insertion of a detail that *is* visible in the main action (this can often be faked for later insertion at the editing stage); e.g. (1) wide-angle with waitress; (2) cut-in to close-up of coffee; (3) very long shot of group at end of meal.

Buffer-shots

A buffer-shot combines a cutaway with the master action; e.g. (1) the master shot of the whole group could be followed by (2) the buffer-shot which begins on the by now empty plate, and then tilts up to reveal the girl raising her glass in a toast. Again, time has been elegantly compressed and the visual pattern varied without a jump-cut. Shots of this kind can be invaluable.

Cutaways

Cut-ins

Buffer-shots

Crossing the line

Whenever a tape is being shot that is supposed to convey a coherent narrative or story, the shots must be linked so that the geography of the action is clear. The most common error is to have the same person moving in opposite directions in adjoining shots – a reverse cut. In such a case the camera is said to have 'crossed the line'.

The line

The 'line' is a convenient fiction to help the movie- or video-maker to organize the flow of images in a comprehensible way. It may be the line of a person's motion; or, in the case of a dialogue, it may run between the two speakers; or it may be the eye-line of one person; or, in a complex group such as a dinner-party, there may be several interlocking lines. In all cases *the line should not be crossed in successive shots without great care*, if the geography is to remain clear. A reverse cut will have the effect of reversing the direction of movement, disrupting a dialogue, or confusing the action.

How to cross the line

It would clearly be intolerable if the line were to dominate all shooting – the camera

The line in this case is established by the direction in which the children are walking. Camera positions 1 and 4, which are on the line itself, can be used for a transition between positions 2 and 3 for purposes of intercutting.

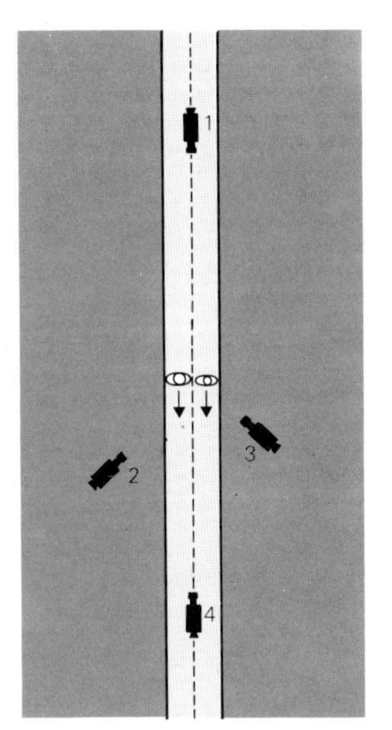

2

2

In this scene, the children's line of movement provides the line of action. If (as above) you cut from one shot to another on the same side of the line (from Camera 2), the cut will work, since in both shots they are travelling left to right.

On the other hand, if the line is crossed during the cut (below), a reversal of direction appears to have occurred. In the second shot (from position 3), they are walking right to left.

2

would be static, the end-result frozen and lifeless. In practice, the line is often crossed, but only in such a way that the ugly cut is either concealed or visually explained. The most obvious way round the problem is to sidestep it entirely by using long takes during which the line is crossed in vision, either by the movement of the camera or the motion of the participants. Then, a cutaway can be inserted between the two shots. Alternatively, if an intermediate shot is inserted in which the camera is on, or very close to, the line itself, it may be crossed in the third shot without offending the eye. Another device to disguise unsightly cuts is to use a very violent action at the moment of the edit to mask a change of direction. This is difficult when editing in the camera.

Once you have got used to thinking of the line as a normal habit when filming, you will soon come to use and manipulate it in the way that is appropriate for the task at hand. It should not become a fetish, but you will never understand the mechanics of the way that visual images are interpreted by the eye unless you come to grips with this most fundamental of all the laws of continuity.

4

3

The line can, however, be crossed by interposing an intermediate shot. This may be a cutaway, a very long shot, or, as here, a shot in which the camera is placed exactly on the line itself.

Above, the camera is dead ahead; below, it is precisely behind the two children. In both cases, the change of direction in the third shot is entirely acceptable.

2

1

3

53. LS
54 C.U.
57 MCU
58 LS

Making a Video movie

The addition of a camera to any home VCR is more than just the acquisition of a new piece of equipment — it marks the transition from the passive to the creative side of video. From then on you will be making, not recording, and the range of subjects will be limited only by your own imagination. However humble your choice of subject, your treatment of it should be guided by a strong sense of form. After all, it is probably intended to be viewed by others at some stage, and a rambling, shapeless tape without a taut narrative line is not likely to endear you to an audience. Unless you intend to edit, therefore, shoot with restraint. If you *do* intend to edit, edit fiercely, and shoot with abandon.

It is perfectly possible to record on to a static VCR using a long extension cable, but most of the examples on the following pages have presupposed the use of at least one portable machine. Where the simpler forms of family video tape are concerned, it may be possible to shoot without editing, but with more complex video movies it is assumed that some form of editing will be employed. This may be a straightforward two-machine assembly edit or a more complex affair involving editing controllers and several generations of tape (pp. 170 — 5).

The family record

Assuming that you already own a cassette recorder and a suitable TV receiver, what do you need to make satisfactory home movies on video? At the very least, you will need a video camera, whether bought or rented, black and white or colour, and probably a portable recorder if you wish to film outdoors. In addition, you can acquire a number of accessories such as Ni-Cad batteries, remote controls, microphones, and AC adaptor kits. But essentially, at this very simple level, you will require a camera, a recorder, a built-in microphone, and the modest intention of placing on tape the particular moment in space or time that you wish to preserve.

What subject?

Choosing a subject for video may appear to be easier than choosing a subject for film simply because the recording medium is so much cheaper, but the results can be equally disappointing if you get it wrong. Unless you intend to view your tape in

If you select a simple subject such as shampooing the family dog, you will find that you have certain very clear problems and possibilities. You must cover the event in sequence while retaining continuity; include shots of the main participants; alternate close-ups, mid-shots, and long shots so that little editing is needed; and try to create a harmonious whole.

The nine shots shown are only examples. They can be intercut without jump-cuts or line-crossing problems, and are vigorous and full of the fun of the occasion.

Go for strong close-ups of dog and children, with narrative long shots. Cover the key moments — the before-and-after shots of the dog, and the pay-off shot of the little girl whisking the shampoo down the drain. Above all, think of each shot in terms of the sequence, and whenever you operate the Pause button remember that your next shot will have to be intercut. Think of the movement, the continuity, the size of frame, and the sound, before deciding to cut or recommence the recording.

1 Establishing shot of unwashed dog

2 Close-up of mother

6 Close-up of dog

solitude, make sure that the subject you select is strong, well structured, lively, and preferably pretty brief. Even when the tape is virtually free, remember the future viewer, and remember the extra work you are giving yourself if you go to the opposite extreme and miss an irreplaceable moment through indecision.

Video tape is not particularly well suited to the kind of intensive editing that is demanded by a montage sequence. On the other hand, it is ideal for recording a specific event such as a party, a wedding, a holiday, a picnic, or any family occasion which is neither so short that a snapshot would be adequate, nor so long as to call for the finely tuned editing that comes only with film or with the very sophisticated video editing suite. Your aim should be to capture the atmosphere of the event while preserving as much continuity as possible and at the same time building into the occasion a structure that will hold the interest of your future audience.

Cut back to the dog – now in the bath

4 Compressing the action, a mid-shot is now possible

5 Get good close-ups of the others

Long shot

8 Close-up

9 Mid-shot: the pay-off

The simple scripted drama

The moment you begin to make a dramatized tape, a fundamental change occurs: instead of searching for the shots, you are inventing them; and you will be involving other people in the process in a quite new and exciting way. One example of this is a drama for children. A simple children's story is not only one of the best ways of shooting tape of your own family, it is also an excellent way of familiarizing yourself with the basic principles of drama.

The script

Whatever subject you choose, bear in mind the obvious limitations of cast, location, and props. It is no good expecting to stage *Star Wars* in a back garden. Keep the story simple, and — just as important — brief, so as not to strain the patience of the junior cast. A script is not merely an optional extra in drama, it is essential, as it organizes the flow of narrative, co-ordinates the shots, and ensures that nothing has been omitted. If there are editing facilities available, the shooting will not necessarily be in the same order as the script: in that case, you will also need a shooting order, which is effectively a rearrangement of the script.

In the example shown, it is assumed that no editing is envisaged: each shot will be separately staged, using the Pause control and thus assembled in the camera. The script is best preceded by a *treatment:* this is a prose outline of the story, giving the basic plot and action. From this, the *script* is developed. In the script, each shot is described, and the dialogue and action is specified. In addition, it is often extremely helpful to draw a *storyboard,* so that the flow of shots is seen as a whole.

In this story, a sailing dinghy is used as a pirate ship; the children are the pirates; a suitcase serves as the treasure chest; the island on the lake is a desert island; and this portion of the action comes at the end of the story. As the pirates celebrate the capture of the treasure on shore, our two heroes (boy and girl) creep out from hiding, seize the treasure and escape in the boat. In the script, the end of the action might become

Shot No.	Description	Action	Dialogue
53	LS	Pirates feasting on beach.	General noise of festivity
54	CU	Bottle raised to lips.	
55	MCU	Two heroes peering through leaves at pirates.	'Now's your chance... Come on...'
56	LS	Over pirates' heads, the heroes are seen tiptoeing towards the treasure.	
57	MCU	Chest. Four hands enter frame and lift chest. Tilt-up to reveal boat, to which the chest is carried.	
58	LS	Over pirates' heads. They see the theft, point, jump, and start running.	'Stop them! Quick, the ship!'
59	MS	Heroes running towards camera, panning with them. They jump in boat and push off.	
60	LS	Camera in the boat, over the heroes' heads. They wave to the outraged pirates stranded on the shore.	

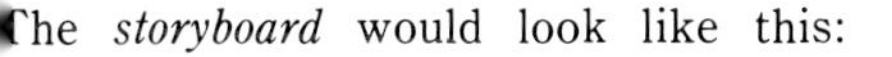

The *storyboard* would look like this:

If the drama is being shot without the intention of editing, it is particularly vital that you keep a close eye on continuity. The shots here have been selected deliberately to represent very large changes of shot size and angle. This makes for far easier continuity (pp. 102-3). Since in this type of story you will only have one chance to get each shot right, it is essential to rehearse beforehand.

It is also worth noting that the Pause button can only be engaged for a limited length of time, which means that shooting under these circumstances would have to be uncomfortably rapid. Furthermore, some machines tend to emit, and record, a loud click at the beginning of each shot. This is an atrocious effect on replay, and is yet another reason for preferring some form of editing when shooting all but the simplest drama.

Complex drama

To shoot complex drama on video tape you must be prepared to invest a great deal of time and effort, both at the shooting stage and in the editing. Every shot will have to be considered, lit, and shot with care, and you should not expect to get more than a few *minutes* of cut tape recorded in a working day, unless very long shots or multiple cameras are being used. What is more, when working with serious actors — and perhaps designers, make-up artists, and costume designers — a great deal of the creative attention of the video movie-maker will be on a human, rather than technical, level. This kind of operation is above all a collaborative enterprise.

The director's job

In the end, however, it is the job of one person to co-ordinate the various talents that are working together, and the director may or may not also be the operator of the camera.

The director will cast the actors, rehearse them, engage their confidence, and incorporate their creative suggestions. He or she must be sure that the actors are matching the scale of their performances to the size of the shot — one of the most common mistakes of actors who are more used to the stage is to overplay a scene, not realizing that on a small screen the flicker of an eyelid can be a grand gesture. The director should lead the actors without bullying them into a performance that they are unable or unsuited to give. It is the director's job to marry the actor's performance to the location and the shots that have been selected, and to give the actor the right action and 'business' to allow his characterization to come through.

Shooting a scene

Any given scene can be shot in a hundred different ways, and the creative possibilities can only be investigated through experience and, above all, by studying work that you respect on both television and the commercial cinema. However, there are two fundamental ways of shooting a scene. In the first, the scene is covered by one master shot, with cut-ins and cutaways shot separately to be intercut later; in the other, the whole scene is broken down into separate shots, which are subsequently assemble-edited to make up the finished tape. The first system calls for insert editing, though it is probably faster to shoot and certainly presents fewer problems of continuity; while the second system, though more laborious, can at a pinch be assemble-edited, and offers greater finesse and variety. In practice, a combination of the two is usually employed for any given scene. It is, however, *vital* that the way you shoot should be determined in the light of the editing facilities that you have at your command (pp. 168–73).

'he professional studio
n this kind of professional -camera drama studio, large umbers of people are ıvolved, quite apart from the ctors and cameramen. There vill also be a microphone oom operator, scene shifters, esigners, make-up artists, a oor manager, and so on. ach camera will be assigned coherent series of shots, yet ıust not itself be visible to nother camera. Accurate cripting and rehearsal are vital.

ontrol room In a rofessional studio, the ontrol room — known in the ade as a gallery — will ontain a director, the rector's assistant, a vision ixer, a sound mixer, and at ast two technical operations ıgineers to control lights, ımeras, connections, and ectronics. In addition, there ill be remote access to video pe and telecine controls. All ese (and the cameras) are ontrolled through the rector's microphone.

You may well find it easier to adapt an existing story into a script than to write your own from scratch. A novel will probably be too long for your purposes, but there are hundreds of short stories that have never been adapted, and which would make excellent viewing. Before you choose a subject, you should look into the question of copyright. If the tape is purely for your own amusement, copyright may safely be ignored, but if you ever hope to sell it, the copyright must be cleared. This varies from country to country (e.g. fifty years in UK).

When choosing a story, remember that powerful interior feelings, which may be very accurately described in print, must somehow be made visible when you come to shoot. Memories, impulses, and desires, which form the basic motivation for most human actions, are by their very nature invisible, and until you have become very skilled you would do best to concentrate on plots in which the action itself is important, with a fairly small cast and with dialogue that can be used as it stands.

The process of adaptation requires that the interior is made into an externally visible act: anxiety about the time might mean a glance at a watch; rage might entail white knuckles; or, more obliquely, happiness can be expressed by lyrical shooting of the natural world. A more complex problem is the manipulation of time and space.

Flashback and parallel action There are a number of ways in which the simple course of a narrative can be expanded and made more complex. You can manipulate time by the use of flashbacks (or indeed premonitions), and by using parallel action — two simultaneous but separate events — you can expand space too.

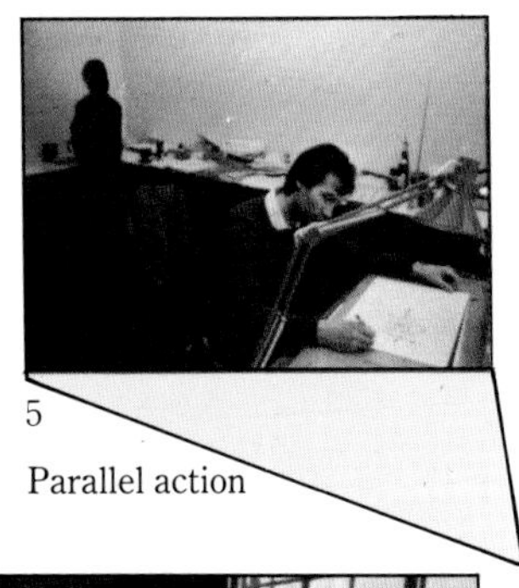

5

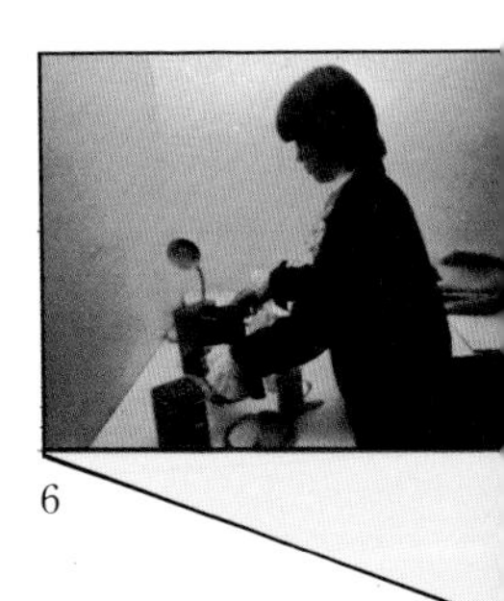

6

Parallel action

1

2

Master shots

Flashback 9

Manipulating time and space

The simple phrase 'two weeks passed' presents a challenge when you come to translate it into visual terms. A straight cut to the events of two weeks later might well be confusing, and so over the years film-makers have developed a series of conventions to deal with transitions through time and space: they apply to video tape in just the same way, and though they can often be dispensed with they can be a useful extra item in your visual vocabulary. The *fade-out* and the *fade-in* traditionally indicate the passage of time. Some cameras now incorporate an automatic fade device, and this will be linked to the sound so that it, too, fades down or up as desired. Alternatively, a fade can be generated at the editing stage. A *dissolve* cannot be generated in a video camera, and as it can only be generated by means of a complex three-machine edit it is therefore only of more academic interest for the average video-enthusiast.

Parallel action

A far more practical way of manipulating space is the use of parallel action. This is the intercutting of two simultaneous actions that are taking place in separate places. It can be used to heighten tension, or to juxtapose contrasting scenes for ironic effect. An intercut sequence may also be used to indicate a memory, or a flashback.

7

8

3

4

10

Here, the master action is very simple (1, 2, 3, 4). A man is sitting at a desk, drawing a picture of the Taj Mahal. Then he drinks a cup of coffee. But parallel to his drawing, a girl is making the coffee. These shots (5, 6, 7, 8) could stand as a sequence in their own right, but on the other hand they could equally well be intercut, as follows: 1, 5, 2, 6, 7, 3, 8, 4. In this way the two parallel activities are placed in the same time reference.

Alternatively, the master shot could be expanded by a glimpse of what was in the draughtsman's mind. If a close-up of his face was followed by a shot of the Taj Mahal itself, these two could be inserted between the shots of the drawing process: the sequence would then go 1, 2, 9, 10, 3, 4. This would have the effect of a flashback to a memory of the building, which given the correct equipment could be reinforced by a brief fade up and down before and after the Taj Mahal shot.

A video album

Children are at once the best and the worst subjects for a video-tape record: they tend to veer between unselfconsciousness and petrified shyness, with brief periods of strained play-acting in between. Another problem arises not with the subject, but with the loving parent taking the pictures: the inability to judge what is likely to be of interest to a less devoted viewer when screened at some future date. The solution is simple — even if you intend to view the tape alone, you will still enjoy it far more if you bring to bear all the disciplined planning and creativeness you can. Try to give each scene a shape, a coherence, and a form of story-line. Don't just blaze away at everything that moves, but when you have found a good scene, enjoy the cheapness of tape to the full by letting the action develop naturally and at leisure.

As for putting children at their ease, the best advice is to attempt nothing of the sort: they will just become even more self-conscious. Instead, *always* find them something to do. Tape them at play, at a party, sailing, playing football, or painting, and never make them do anything specially for the camera. For this reason, a tripod is not advisable. Most shooting with children will be hand-held, with the recorder slung over a shoulder.

The only reason for using a tripod would be if you are planning to use the long end of the zoom to make the camera even more inconspicuous. Otherwise, a tripod will be found to be hopelessly clumsy and restrictive. It does have one advantage, however: the camera can be set up and left to run remotely, thus guaranteeing an unselfconscious 'performance'.

First child

A new sister

Easter eggs

Holiday snapshot

Airline ticket

Making an album A cassette can be set aside to be used as a video album. It may be the growth of one child, or the whole family; it could include snaps, tickets, Christmas cards, drawings, bathtimes, holidays. With the advent of one-piece 8 mm Video and the increasing use of ½-portables, an album will include moving video material as well. Each shot can also be frozen in frame, and it could accept stills from a video stills camera such as Sony's Mavica.

What subject?

The act of getting out your video equipment and organizing a recording requires a fair amount of effort, and is a good reason for thinking carefully about your choice of subjects. But you should also give thought to the arrangement of the recordings within your collection. For instance, it is a good idea to set aside one entire tape for each child. On a four-hour tape you could easily include all the most significant moments of the first five years of its life, literally from birth onwards if you like. It might include the christening, birthdays, holidays, Christmas celebrations, learning to walk, first day at school, learning to read, and so on. This would be a wonderful thing for the child to have in the future, even leaving aside your own present enjoyment.

Alternatively, the sequences involving the child could be included in the tapes you make of your family. If the tapes are not very well organized, it may be a good idea to dub small patches of commentary (pp. 168-73), if only to identify date and place when you come to look at them in ten years' time. (Remember that tape, unlike film, does not deteriorate in colour balance and, with the kind of use that such a tape would expect, would not experience physical damage either. It is an ideal medium for a family record.) Finally, if you wish, the tape-album can be supplemented with still photographs or other visual signposts such as birthday cards, invitations, calendars, road or street signs, tickets, luggage labels, and so on. These will all help to 'pace' and to assist the flow of what could be a potentially messy collection of valuable material.

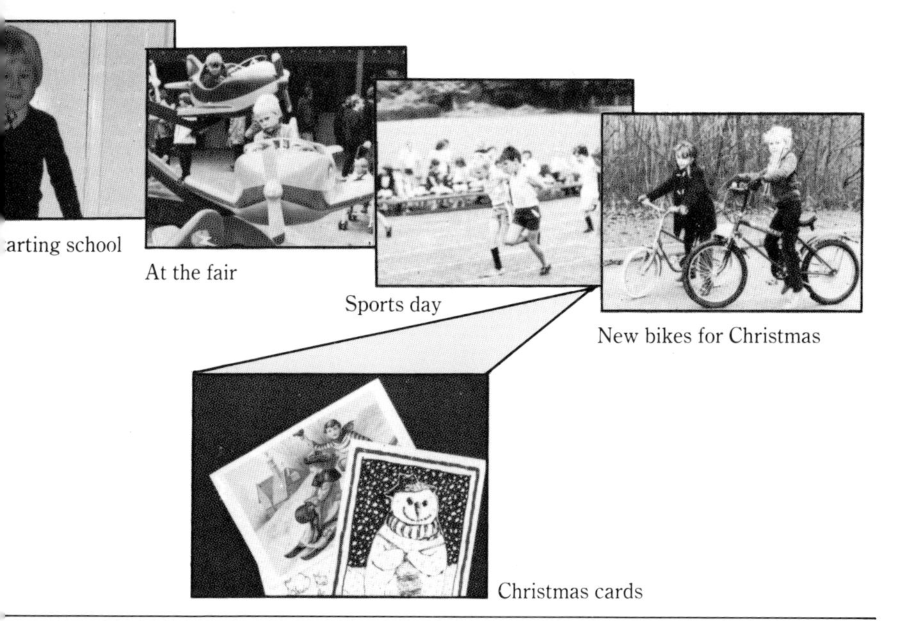

arting school

At the fair

Sports day

New bikes for Christmas

Christmas cards

Documentary

A documentary may be anything from an affectionate study of your home town to a musical master class or a study of the sex-life of mice. In all these cases, you will be intended to show the finished tape to others with pride, and you must therefore bring to the planning, the shooting, and the editing all the skill and care you can muster. Certainly, you will need to reckon on extensive editing — a documentary must exploit the greatest virtue of tape (its cheapness) by shooting with freedom and editing ruthlessly to a compelling final tape.

This kind of form can scarcely be scripted, unless the material you are working with is unusually predictable, but it is a very good idea to work around some form of written treatment. At the very least, you should have some notion of a beginning, a middle, and an end before you start to shoot. Then look critically at the treatment to see what elements are missing; where the tension flags; what technical requirements present problems; and whether the story-line of the documentary is strong. Then you can begin to shoot with confidence.

The place of objectivity

Television documentaries are sometimes praised for their 'objectivity'; for the appearance of impartiality with which the programme-maker has approached the subject. Yet in truth this feeling of neutrality is more likely to be a conscious effort of style than a reality, and this is especially true where very emotive issues are involved (nuclear disarmament, for instance). The person who sets out to make a documentary is bound to have some views on his chosen subject, though not necessarily well-balanced ones, but he has decided that one-sidedness is self-defeating. Instead, the role of the maker is played down so that the subject is apparently seen through glass.

There are several ways of doing this, and they can all be used to a greater or lesser degree according to your personal style. For example, you can shoot interviews in such a way that all questions are to be cut out — leave pauses after the subject has finished talking and before asking the next question; do not interrupt; shoot over the interviewer's shoulder; to encourage the subject, nod but do not grunt during the replies; in other words, let people talk for themselves. This neutral style would tend to go with an unemotional, minimal commentary, or no commentary at all, letting the choice and content of the material tell the story unassisted. At its best this kind of treatment can have an inexorable effect.

At the opposite extreme is the committed polemic directed straight at the camera, with the video-maker well to the front of the scene, interviewing, popping up with comments and judgements at every turn, guiding the viewer's response. This may be superficially more effective, but people resent others making their judgements for them, and you may feel that the quieter approach is in the end a subtler way of getting your view across.

Many documentaries, of course, are just that: documents that seek to record on tape an event, a community, or an activity without political or artistic coloration of any kind. Here, though, even the simplest activities have to be carefully planned: suppose, for example, that you wanted to make a tape of a friend who was a sculptor. You would have to follow the growth of one sculpture from the earliest models through to the final work, shooting in such a way that time is compressed yet retaining the flow of the work's development. Processes of this kind appear easy at first sight, but in practice require just as much forethought as drama. The difference with documentary is that so much less is under your control: you are there to record, not alter the nature of your subject, and yet at the same time the finished work should bear the unmistakable stamp of your own taste

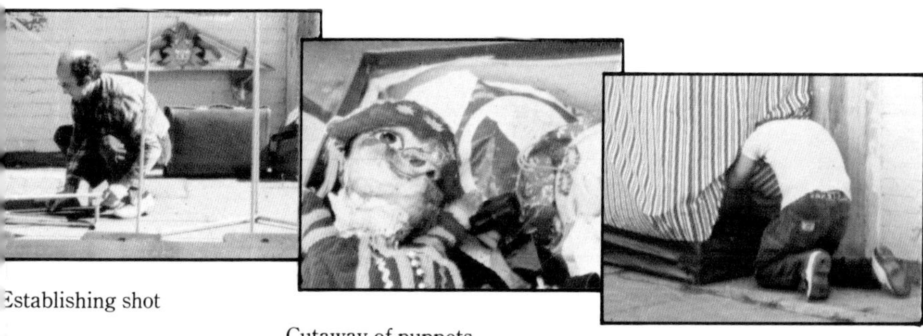

Establishing shot

Cutaway of puppets

Time has elapsed — entering the tent

The show begins

Reverse cut

Wide-angle

ig close-up

Long shot — applause

Packing up — end of show

ı this sequence, the shots are ɑried, and the action is ɔvered in such a way that the me can be compressed ithout strain. In such a ɔcumentary, you could also include shots of the audience reaction, a voice-over commentary (on tape) from the puppeteer, and a wildtrack of music.

Special events

More and more people are using video recorders for taping weddings, very often renting them on a daily basis. If the equipment is rented, it is vital that you spend some of the previous day experimenting with it and viewing the results critically. A wedding consists of a few crucial moments that you miss at your peril, and an offer to shoot a wedding should not be made lightly. For one thing, you can forget all notion of enjoyment: the entire day will be very hard work, and this can only be made bearable by careful preparation.

What equipment?

If the equipment is being rented, and if you have the possibility of subsequent editing, it is advisable to make the original recording on a U-Matic ¾-inch portable VCR. This is more expensive to rent, and the recorder is almost too heavy to carry, but the results, when dubbed on to an edited second-generation or third-generation ¾-inch or ½-inch tape, are good. There is little to choose between the rival ½-inch and ¼-inch systems as far as quality is concerned, and the new 8 mm Video systems have yet to show their true paces.

If you are in a position to choose between cameras, go for one with a good aperture — say, f1.4 — and be sure that you have ample charged batteries available to cover the full duration of the tape you have selected. It is so easy to run out of power half-way through the groom's speech.

It is at the reception that you are likely to have the most practical problems, since you will almost certainly require additional lights. Quartz lights may be hired which give ample illumination but do very little for the atmosphere. You may well do better to

1 The arrival is one moment that you must be certain not to miss.
2 If you can get into the church, and there is enough light, tape the exit.
3 Go for strong close-ups.
4 At the reception, choose a good tripod position, and make sure the batteries are freshly charged — even good speeches tend to be quite long.
5 and 6 Cutting the cake is another moment that you must capture.
7 Look for plenty of good cutaways and don't forget the relatives.

bounce them off the ceiling. This gives a soft light, though of course more lights are required for a given level of illumination.

You should also visit the place where the service is to take place. Can you get permission to shoot at all? Is there enough light? If not, try the vestry for the signing of the register. Plan a good camera position from where you can see both the service and the congregation, and keep your spare batteries handy at all times.

Shooting on the day

It can be pleasing to aim for a slow build-up to the climax of the ceremony, opening perhaps with a shot of the wedding invitation (you will need a tripod), then seeing the bride and bridesmaids getting prepared. The hectic bustle is often more fun than the wedding, and serves to build up a tension that can be reinforced with shots of the groom waiting, the packed church, and so on. From the arrival of the bride onwards, the cameraman will have a desperate scramble just to be in the right place at the right time, fighting through crowds of well-meaning guests to catch one very rapid moment – the kiss, the confetti, the car, and gone. In these moments, although long takes would seem to be appropriate, you may well find it impossible to sustain them: the action is just too fast, and a tripod is really out of the question. This is where good hand-held technique pays off. However, a tripod is practical during the set-pieces of cutting the cake and speeches, and here a directional microphone will be found valuable because of the considerable ambient noise (p. 158). By this time, in any case, you will probably be having trouble lifting the camera, let alone holding it steady!

5

6

7

Sport and action

Video has one enormous advantage over film when recording sport: you can simply ignore the amount of footage that is being shot, and concentrate on the subject. The duration of the shot is limited only by the battery endurance, rather than by the cost of the film or the length of a film magazine. What is more, video gives you the option of not only multiple cameras fed into one recording, but also of slow motion at any point in the subsequent replay if you wish. This, however, raises the single greatest difference between amateur and professional coverage of sport: professional sports coverage *always* uses more than one camera, even when taping a game of chess.

Multi-camera operation

Multiple cameras give you a flexibility that is virtually indispensable when dealing with any sporting activity. In football, for example, if you have only one camera you can only be at one end of the field at any one time, and the over-all view from dead-centre, though comprehensive, lacks drama. The professional director will cut between several cameras, in close-up and long shot, covering the action on the field, and he will also include reaction shots of the crowd, plus replays, shots of the scoreboard, and so on. However, he is still constrained by the laws of the line of action, and these apply to sport almost more than to any other form of action except warfare, and for the same reasons – if we become confused about the direction in which a person is travelling, we will soon become confused about which side he is playing for.

In the case of football, or any other right-to-left game, the cameras should always be placed to one side of the line or at the most exactly *on* the line itself. This applies equally to tennis, with the interesting variation that here the prevalent view is normally exactly on the line *from one particular end.* This is the master camera position, and it is worth considering how it is arrived at. If the camera were in the

Football The camera can be positioned in the centre so that each side is covered equally, or to favour your own team goal, or (for more dramatic shots), next to the goal. Here four cameras are used giving:
2. A high master shot
1. A low-level camera close to the pitch for action shots (and possible close-ups for both goals)
Cameras 3 and 4 cover both goals from the goalkeeper's point of view.

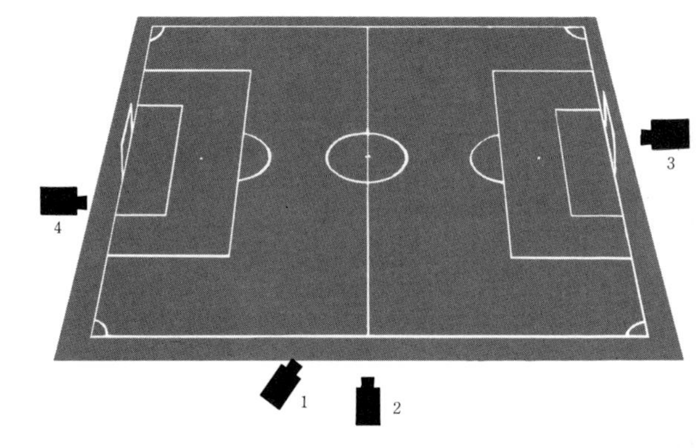

Camera 1 | Camera 2 | Camera 3 | Camera 4

niddle of the court, it would be panning vildly from one side to the other, with haotic results. If one camera were at either nd, all sense of direction would be lost. If he camera were too low, the fall of the ball nto the service court would not be visible; if oo close, the zoom would not be wide nough to cover the action; if too far, not ight enough for a good close-up of the layer at the far end of the court.

These are complex considerations which ny professional would take into account vhen planning the master position for a amera in a tennis game, and they are the ind of thing you have to think about when hooting any sport with only one camera.

Jsing one camera

'here are relatively few sports that can be omprehensively treated with just one amera — golf, some forms of athletics, kiing, boxing, or any of the essentially solo ports such as weight-lifting or hang-liding. In all of these, the video camera does not have to choose (as it does in football, for instance) between a boring over-all coverage and an exciting but incomplete series of impressions: it can cover the whole event, since only one thing is happening at a time. What is more, in these events in particular, the video tape is an invaluable aid to coaching.

Video and coaching

The slow-motion facilities of video are not the only aspect of the medium to have been appreciated by coaches and teams across the range of sport. The instant replay means that moves can be analysed over and over again — the New York Mets have had a video replay system since 1971, and the Boston Red Sox now use a three-camera set-up for their analyses. For the amateur, the pre-recorded video-tape market now offers every imaginable kind of coaching tape, from fishing to badminton. The only tape on the art of bull-fighting is presumably more for information.

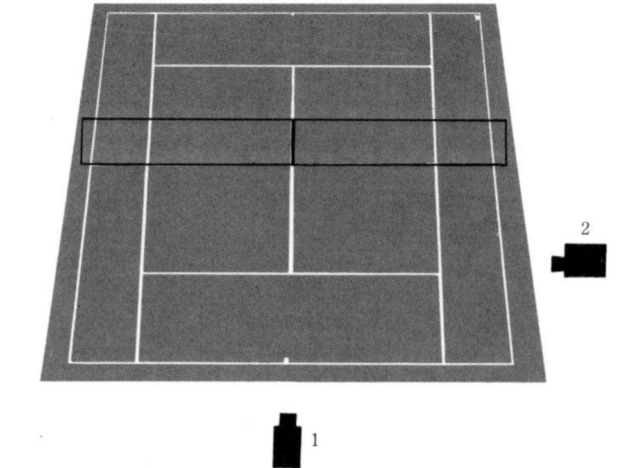

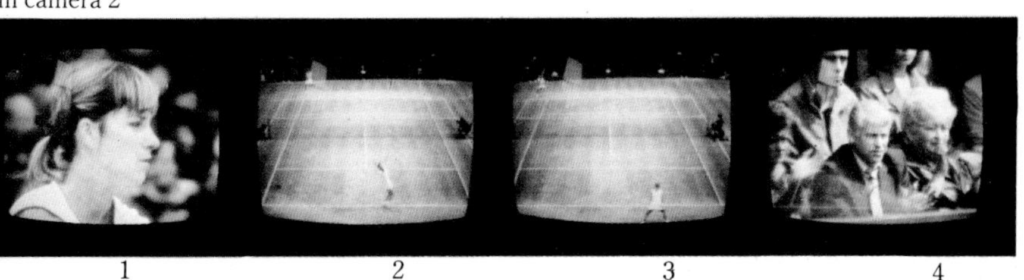

'ennis The position of the ıaster camera is strictly etermined (see text). Camera can also cover close-ups of ıe player at the far end; ımera 2 gives a more :amatic viewpoint from close the court.
Close-up of the server from ımera 2
The master shot from ımera 1
This can also cover the ceiver of service
A cutaway of the crowd om camera 2

Wildlife

A portable video recorder is clearly indispensable, and the camera lens should have as good a telephoto range as possible. It is even better if the camera can be fitted with a variety of lenses so that you can use really long optics that may have been primarily designed for 35 mm stills cameras. For instance, an 800 mm lens, which is powerful enough when used on a 35 mm camera, gives truly colossal magnification on a ⅔-inch vidicon tube—so much so that a very heavy tripod is needed to minimize vibration.

If you are filming insects, a Macro setting is equally essential: the macro world actually provides one of the liveliest and wildest locations to be found within reach of the ordinary home, and can be very challenging (pp. 88—9).

For a great deal of wildlife work, you will probably need an extension microphone, which can be placed a good deal closer to the subject than the camera, and this will normally be of the directional type. It may even be necessary to use a parabolic reflector in order to capture elusive bird song.

Studying life-style

To capture the life of an animal on tape, you will have to immerse yourself in every aspect of its life-style — when it feeds, mates, migrates; where it sleeps; how it reacts to the presence of man. Only with the greatest patience will you ever record those crucial moments that appear so natural when we see them on television. Here, the video-maker has one tremendous advantage over the film-maker. The tape is extremely cheap, and you can get on with recording (in silence, what's more) in the hope that the animal will do just what you are hoping for. Once the animal's habits are known, you will be in a position to set up

ıide, or you may use food, water, or decoys :o persuade it to change its behavioural ›atterns.

You can even lure an animal quite ;uccessfully with tape-recorded calls from ınimals of the same species, though you nust be sure that they are not distress calls, ›r, in the case of large animals, mating calls.

Building a hide

The simplest form of hide consists of four ·ertical posts, with horizontal cross-pieces t the top. This is then covered with brown ›r green tarpaulin — depending on the pre-'ailing vegetation — leaving ports for the amera to peep through. The hide should be ›uilt as quickly as possible, at least a day or o before you plan to use it, so that the nimal is not disturbed too much. You hould count on a lengthy stay so you will robably need a folding chair, notebooks, ›od and drink, and binoculars.

Filming from a car

It is well known that many animals, especially in Game Reserves and National Parks, accept cars where unmotorized human beings would cause flight or be in danger of attack. If you intend to shoot from the car, the camera can be braced on a small clamp that can be attached to the window frame, or it can be rested on a bean bag. These are available from good photographic shops, and are essential if you are to use the full range of the zoom lens without shake. It is also worth remembering that many animals could make very short work of a car if they wished; for instance, you should always reverse towards a herd of elephants, keeping the engine running, in case your presence becomes unwelcome. The other golden rule, especially when dealing with rare species or nesting birds, is never to disturb (and perhaps destroy) the life of the animal itself.

ideo and wildlife ırprisingly interesting video ›es can be made of animals zoos. Video tape has an ıormous advantage in all ıldlife shooting in that it is ent (unlike film) and, also ılike film, is extremely eap in operation. This is of estimable value, since ldlife shooting requires ›re patience than any other :m of video work.

Shooting with a long lens A long lens is almost indispensable in wildlife shooting, and this entails the use either of a tripod or of a very heavy brace. When shooting from an impromptu position such as a car window, it may be found that a bean bag rested on the window-sill of the vehicle provides a satisfactory makeshift alternative.

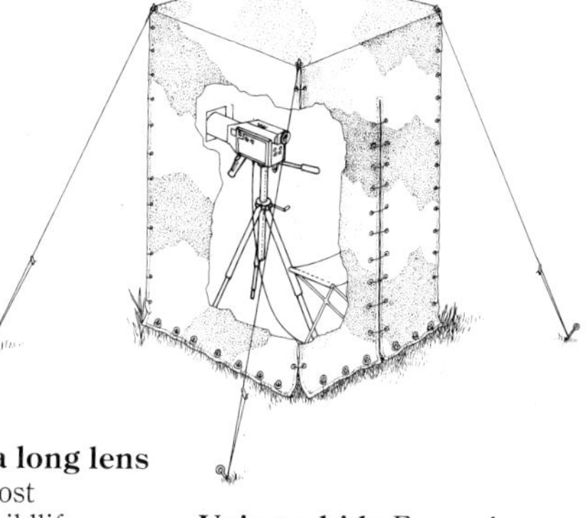

Using a hide Even when a satisfactory hide has been constructed it is possible that the animal will be aware that you are inside. One ruse is for two people to open the hide and for one, an hour or so later, to leave it. The animal can sometimes be deluded into thinking that it is then empty.

Light and lighting

'Lighting' covers a whole range of operations, from simply augmenting existing light — for example with reflectors, or by uprating the light bulbs — to a fully comprehensive lighting set-up. In any case, the video camera is critically limited by the prevailing level of light, and at the present state of the art normal domestic lighting will give indifferent or even unacceptable results. Lighting is therefore not just for the expert — in some degree it should be understood and considered by anyone who owns or rents a video camera.

Lighting and exposure

The quality of a video image is affected by the level of illumination in much the same way as film, but there are important differences in both the way the light is measured and in the way the camera uses that measurement. In video, the light intensity is measured in either foot-candles (ft-c), or lux (lumen per square metre), there being 10.76 lux per foot-candle. A foot-candle is derived from the imagined level of illumination that would fall on a subject one foot away from a 'candle' emitting one lumen of light; lux is the metric equivalent. Because of the inverse square law a doubling of the distance from the light source will produce a quartering of the available illumination on a given subject. In practical terms, this reveals that your shooting is critically limited by the level of light, since normal domestic cameras will not produce acceptable results below about 50 lux, which is the light level of a brightly lit living-room, and they will not give good results below about 250 lux.

Lag and noise

Under-exposure is apparent in video in a progressive rise in the level of visual 'noise' as opposed to the proper signal from the vidicon tube. Then, as the sensitivity of the tube is automatically raised to cope with dark images, so the tube becomes sensitive to 'lag'. Lag is the delay caused when bright objects are in motion relative to the tube at low light levels, and is the most serious defect of the vidicon tube. Newer tubes such as the Plumbicon and Saticon are vast improvements from this point of view, and can thus be used effectively at lower light levels than their crude specifications would imply. At the present time, however, they are rather expensive.

Gain and aperture

The output from the camera is governed by three main factors: the level of illumination; the degree of gain of the camera (the electronic amplification of the video signal) and the aperture of the lens. On a video camera the Automatic Gain Control (AGC) will increase the gain until a satisfactory output has been achieved, and only then will the aperture be stopped-down to reduce the light reaching the tube — in bright sunny conditions, for example. This is because of the noise and lag problems encountered in high-gain conditions. Most cameras have two or more AGC settings from high to low sensitivity, and these are selected according to the prevailing light. There may or may not be a manual override of the automatic operation, but this is an invaluable facility and you should not purchase a camera without it. The combined effects of the AGC and the Iris control can be seen immediately in a camera with an electronic viewfinder, but if it only has an optical viewfinder you must rely on the AGC to an even greater extent, along with the exposure indicators provided. These vary from model to model.

The maximum aperture is determined by the lens fitted to the camera, or, in the case of interchangeable lenses, by that selected by the user. The smaller the f-number, the wider the aperture.

Inverse square law
Because of the so-called 'inverse square law', the doubling of distance between a light and the subject results in a *quarter* of the level of illumination (rather than a half, as you might expect). This effect is minimized when spot-reflectors are in use, but must always be borne in mind.

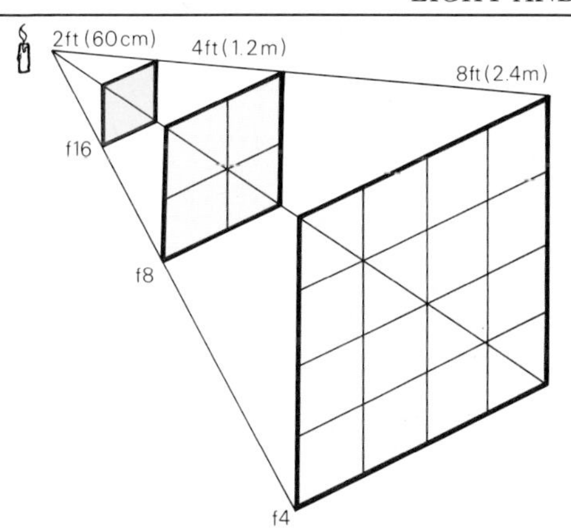

Lag All camera tubes suffer from 'lag', to a greater or lesser extent, when shooting moving highlights in low light levels. This takes the form of a 'comet-tail' stretching behind the bright highlight. Modern tubes such as the Saticon, Plumbicon, and Cosvicon are less susceptible to this defect than the old vidicon tube.

Noise Video 'noise', which occurs at low light levels owing to the consequent high level of video gain required, takes the form of mottled coloration, especially in shadow areas of even density.

Controlling exposure

In video, the camera is itself used as the exposure meter, since it will register (with either an electronic viewfinder or by means of a monitor) the exact quality of the light being recorded. If the camera has only an optical viewfinder, it will be equipped with some form of exposure indicator in the viewfinder which will at the very least indicate a state of under-exposure. Because the tube in a video camera is itself subject to electronic variations in the degree of 'gain' (effectively varying its 'speed' if it were film), in addition to the variations in aperture that are often effected automatically, conventional light meters are not commonly seen in video work: the camera is the meter.

An *incident meter* can be used to check the over-all evenness of lighting, pointing the diffusion bulb back towards the camera from the subject, and with a little practice such a meter can also be used during a reconnaissance, if the camera is not with you, to assess the light levels of a given location. If you are using it for this purpose, and if the meter is not calibrated in lux or foot-candles, set it at some arbitrary ASA such as 100, and some typical speed such as 1/25, and find out what is the lowest level at which your camera can operate successfully — it may, for example, be f2.8 at such a setting on the light meter. Once you have established that, you will have a readily portable way of checking the minimum level of illumination in an area that you plan to shoot in, without the weight of the camera.

Back light and manual override

The AGC in the camera will only monitor the average light level of a subject; but in the case of, say, a girl standing in the snow with the sun behind her, this would give a pure black silhouette on the face. The camera would treat the snow as a mid-grey and the face would therefore be black. In this and in all other back-lit or predominantly white subjects, you should override the AGC and open up the aperture by 1½ stops. On many cameras there is a Backlight button which does the same job. Conversely, with a subject on a very black background, the lens should be stopped *down* a stop so that the blacks retain their richness. On an electronic viewfinder these effects may be judged roughly, though in order to obtain really accurate results a monitor will be required.

Back light There are several occasions on which the camera's exposure controls will be fooled by the prevailing lighting conditions. In this shot of the boy not only has the snow defeated the electronic circuitry, but the fact that he is standing against a bright sky has also meant that his face is exceptionally dark. If this is corrected by use of the backlight control the exposure is increased so that the face tone becomes normal. The backlight control is equivalent, in film terms, to about 1½ stops extra exposure. If no backlight control is fitted to the camera the manual override may be used to open the iris, and the results judged through an electronic viewfinder.

Lighting equipment

The equipment you buy will determine the size of scene that can be taped, and have a crucial effect on the quality and subtlety of the lighting. Lights vary in output, the way they are focused, and the degree to which that focus can be manipulated. They differ in the accessories they can accept, which enlarges the possible range of diffusion-effects and shadow-masking (pp. 140-1).

For amateur use the most common form of light is a photoflood or quartz. Quartz lights give very high output for their size and weight, and several models also offer variable beams, from flood to spot. An alternative design is the softlight which contains two 750-watt quartz bulbs which face inwards, bouncing their light back into the reflector. The Tota-Light is a convenient way of carrying around a fairly powerful set of lights in one compact kit.

Power supply

It is vital to know whether the power supply is adequate for the lights that will b plugged into it. Even the small quartz Tota Lights range from 300 to 1000 watts, an when several are plugged in at once th circuit can be overloaded. Add up the tota power required; split the load on t different circuits if possible; and never us ordinary circuits for high-powered lightin — at the very least it will blow a fuse. Whe estimating the power requirements remember that you may need an extensio cable to run in power from another rin main, and be sure to have one handy. Als have spare bulbs, fuses, wire-stripper electrical tape, screwdriver, and gaffe tape. See Lighting Accessories, pp. 136-7

Safety

Cables should be taped to the floor and lai so they cannot be tripped over. Avoid we areas. Sandbag high stands so they cannc be overturned. Never overload circuits Remember that quartz lights get *very* hot.

Fresnel spotlights The bulb has a reflector behind it and the front element of the lamp is a Fresnel lens. This combination means that the beam may be flooded or spotted by moving both lamp and reflector backwards or forwards. A Fresnel is invariably fitted with barn doors and will also accept filters, wires, or scrims.

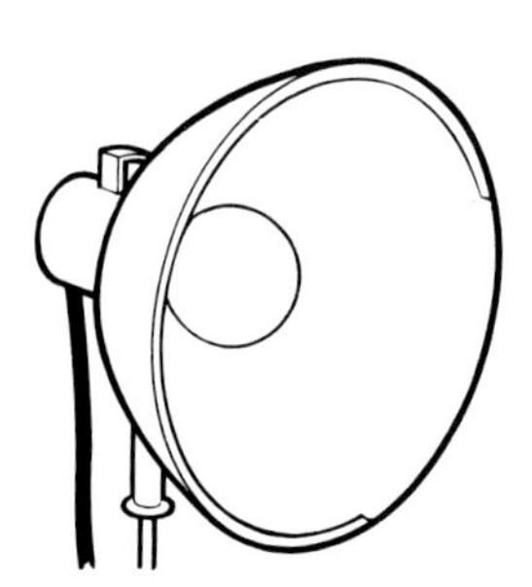

A Floodlight contains a single tungsten bulb set in a dish-shaped reflector and is designed to cast an even ligh over a fairly wide area. Thes lamps are not expensive and are not too difficult to transport.

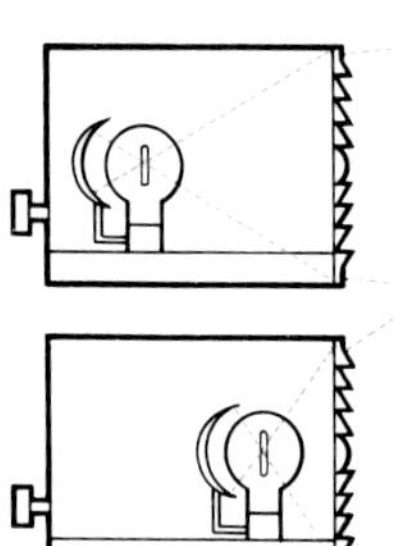

Variable positions When the bulb and reflector are moved backwards the effect is to produce a spotted-up light. When the bulb and reflector are in the forward position the effect is a flooded beam. When Fresnel luminaires are in an overhead position the main control may be adjusted by a pole.

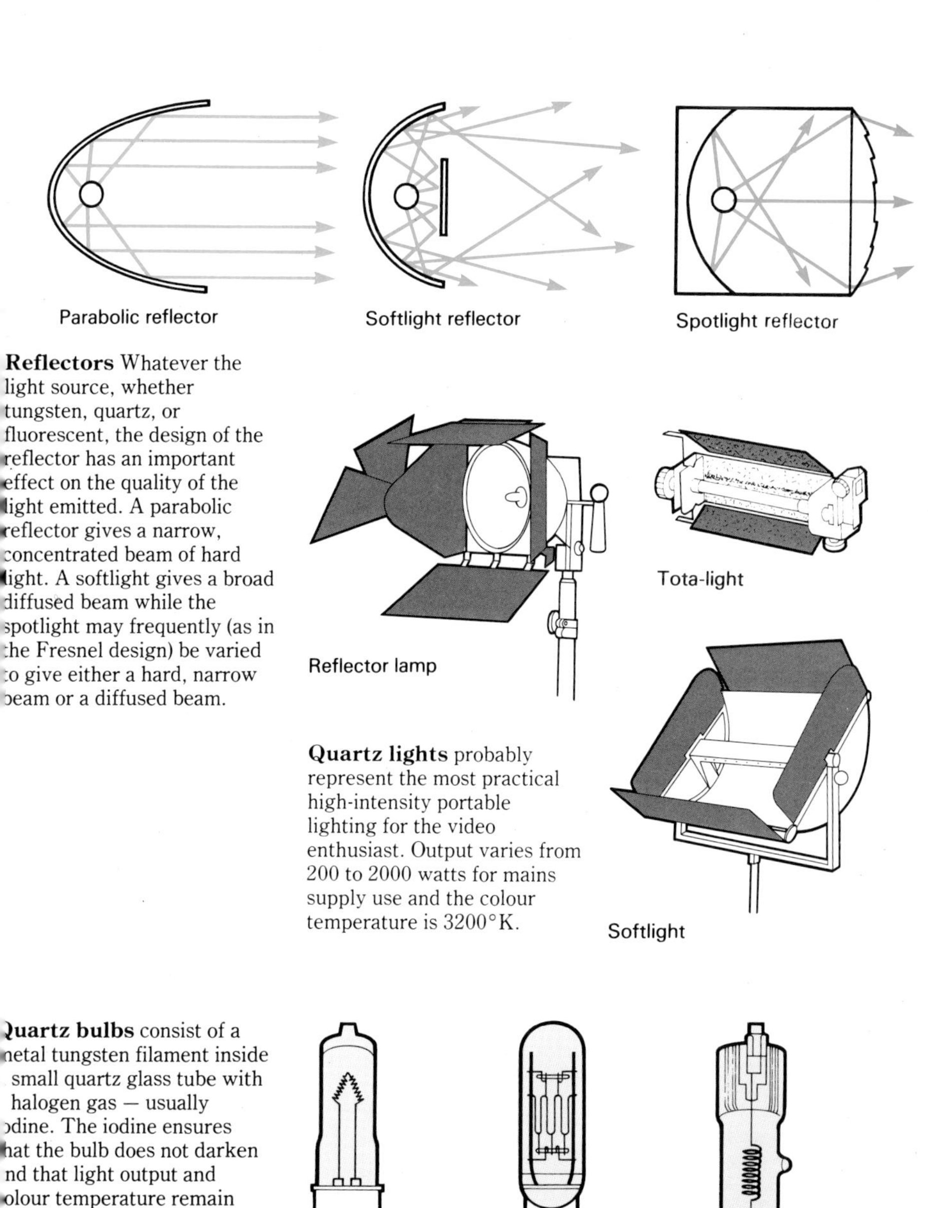

Parabolic reflector

Softlight reflector

Spotlight reflector

Reflectors Whatever the light source, whether tungsten, quartz, or fluorescent, the design of the reflector has an important effect on the quality of the light emitted. A parabolic reflector gives a narrow, concentrated beam of hard light. A softlight gives a broad diffused beam while the spotlight may frequently (as in the Fresnel design) be varied to give either a hard, narrow beam or a diffused beam.

Reflector lamp

Tota-light

Quartz lights probably represent the most practical high-intensity portable lighting for the video enthusiast. Output varies from 200 to 2000 watts for mains supply use and the colour temperature is 3200°K.

Softlight

Quartz bulbs consist of a metal tungsten filament inside a small quartz glass tube with a halogen gas — usually iodine. The iodine ensures that the bulb does not darken and that light output and colour temperature remain constant. Do not handle the bulb directly as contact with the skin can cause premature failure. Never touch it until it has cooled down as it becomes very hot during use.

Lighting accessories

Barn-doors are hinged metal flaps which clip on to the front of the lamps, and enable you to restrict the fall of light in any direction. When they are closed horizontally, the position is known as 'Chinese'; vertically, 'English'.

Snoot A cylindrical funnel which slips on to the front of a lamp to give a very tightly focused beam.

Scrims and half-scrims, sometimes referred to as 'wires', are inserted behind the barn-doors to reduce the output of a lamp. They may be doubled up.

Spun glass is the most common form of broad diffuser. A square sheet is torn off and clipped to the barn-doors in front of the lamp. Two sheets may be used if less light is required.

French flags are simply opaque black panels on long hinged arms that can be attached to a lamp to block off a portion of the spilled light.

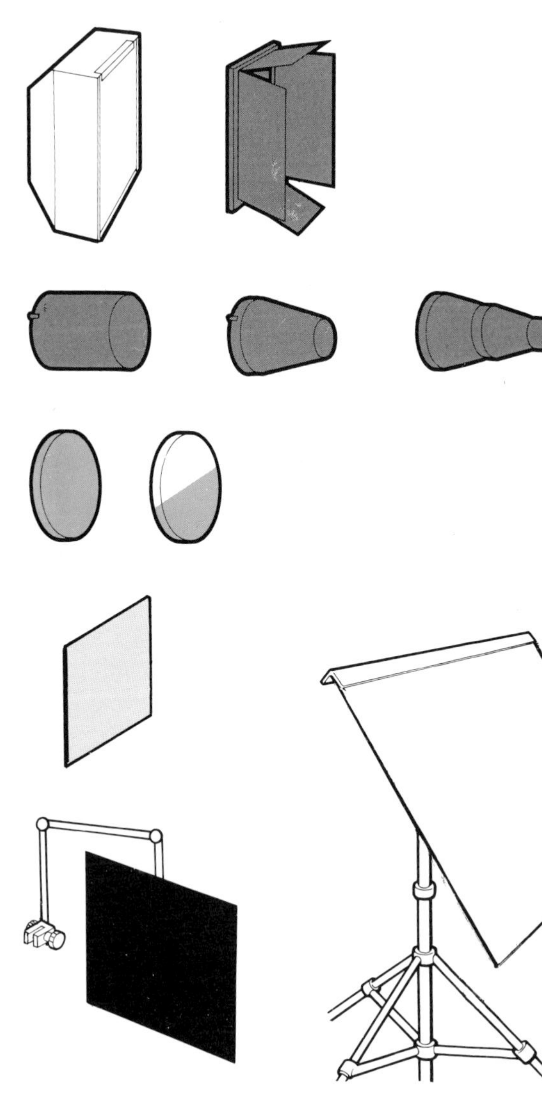

Cucaloris A shading device of opaque material which, placed in front of a lamp, gives a mottled distribution of light.

Reflector May be purpose-built, or could be a sheet of foam polystyrene coated on one side with aluminium foil; this gives one hard and one soft reflector and is very lightweight.

Filters The most common filter is the blue dichroic glass filter used on quartz lamps to raise their colour temperature. Gelatin filters are also common, and they may either be 'full-blue' or 'half-blue', depending on the degree of colour correction intended. Other filters may be for effect (red, orange) or may be designed for colour correction of other sources such as arc lamps.

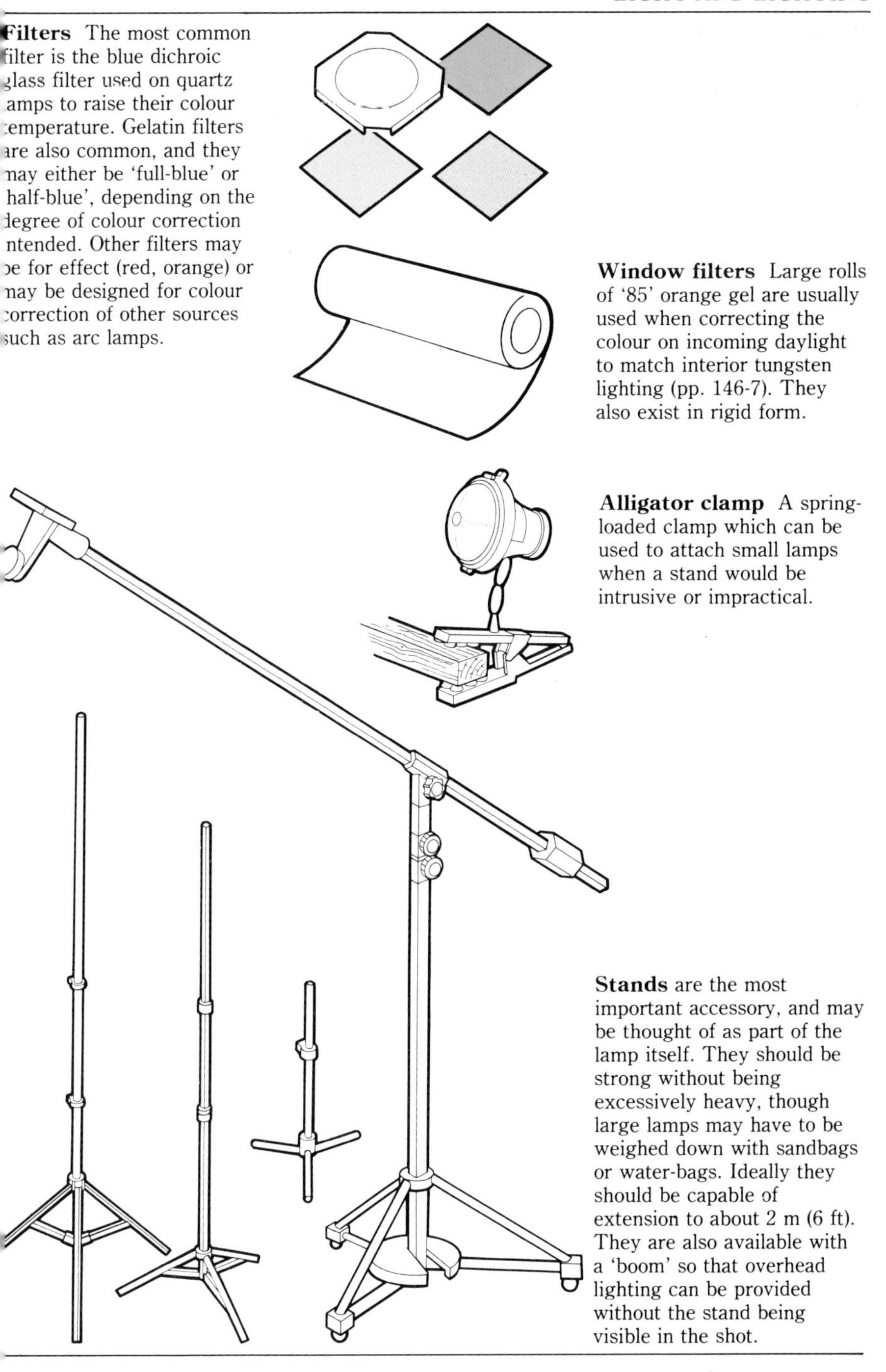

Window filters Large rolls of '85' orange gel are usually used when correcting the colour on incoming daylight to match interior tungsten lighting (pp. 146-7). They also exist in rigid form.

Alligator clamp A spring-loaded clamp which can be used to attach small lamps when a stand would be intrusive or impractical.

Stands are the most important accessory, and may be thought of as part of the lamp itself. They should be strong without being excessively heavy, though large lamps may have to be weighed down with sandbags or water-bags. Ideally they should be capable of extension to about 2 m (6 ft). They are also available with a 'boom' so that overhead lighting can be provided without the stand being visible in the shot.

Using available light

Outdoor lighting

Available light outdoors is, of course, daylight, but daylight comes in many forms and colours. The whole question of colour temperature, so vital in all colour video, is dealt with on pp. 142—3. Here, we are concerned with exposure and contrast. Video cameras and receivers can only cope satisfactorily with a limited range of contrast. If a subject has very bright highlights and very deep shadows, it is said to have 'high contrast', or a high 'contrast ratio'. As the camera can be adjusted for either the highlights or the shadows, but not both, the result will be either burnt-out highlights or blocked-up shadows. With a low-contrast subject, the camera can easily encompass the range of contrast, but the image is flat and undramatic.

To compensate for excessive contrast, use either a reflector to fill in the shadows; or a portable quartz Sun-Gun with blue filter; or a large gauze screen between the sun and the subject.

The only way of correcting low contrast is to supplement the available light with large quantities of tightly focused spotlights (with blue filters). In professional work, these would often be arc lamps, which can even simulate sunshine. The volume of light, and therefore power, required for such an effect is so large that it may be more

Sun-Gun and gauze screen In very high-contrast exterior conditions, particularly with powerful back light, satisfactory exposure on a face will often only be obtained by adding light from the direction of the camera or by diffusing the prevailing light. To fill in the shadows on the face, use a battery lamp or Sun-Gun with blue filter and a sheet of spun glass to diffuse the light. With a very harsh noon-day sun the prevailing light can be diffused by a large gauze screen suspended on a boom over the subject.

advisable to wait for another day. In all thee attempts to manipulate light the intention is not merely to 'improve' the appearance of a scene, but also to create, and sustain, a mood over several days of shooting.

Indoor lighting

Indoor lighting is just as variable in its range of contrast as daylight, if not more so: the pools of light that are created by table lamps or spotlights may give just enough illumination in their immediate area, but the spaces in between will be black on your tape. The over-all level of light in a domestic setting can be raised easily and cheaply by replacing the bulbs with higher-wattage units or with photofloods. In addition, to reduce the contrast, and to raise the over-all level of illumination still further, it is good practice to place one or two photofloods *without* shades behind the camera. These will bounce light off the walls and ceiling and will help the exposure in the shadow areas. These simple procedures require no investment in lighting equipment except for the bulbs, and the original effect of the room lighting will, generally speaking, be preserved. If you are seekng a natural effect, and do not wish to intrude on the scene with glaring spotlights, this solution is certainly preferable to the use of a battery light on or behind the camera.

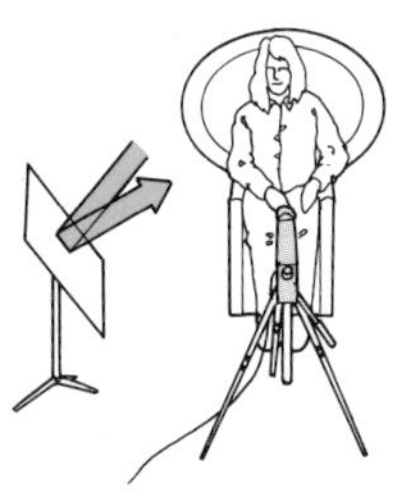

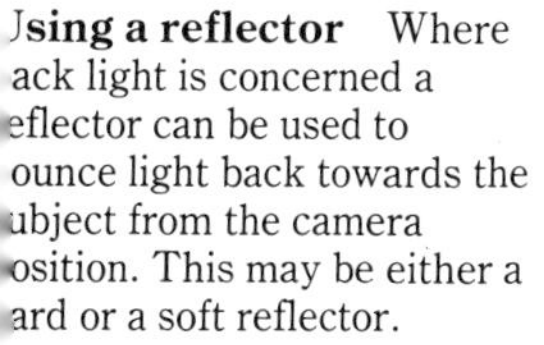

Using a reflector Where back light is concerned a reflector can be used to bounce light back towards the subject from the camera position. This may be either a hard or a soft reflector.

Available light indoors Very often available light in a living-room is exceptionally flat with pools of high contrast. In this case the subject is in one of the flat areas, and the light gives no modelling whatsoever.

Bounce lighting Bounce lighting provides a compromise between the excessive brilliance of direct high-key lighting and the flatness of available light. It lifts the ambient light level in a pleasing and natural way.

Basic lighting

Every lighting set-up presents a challenge, and must be considered on its own merits. You have it in your power to vary the intensity, direction, height, balance, and degree of diffusion of the lights, with a consequent range of effects. There are, however, certain basic principles which are common to all situations. These can be identified by taking as an example the lighting of a face, which offers a surprisingly large range of possibilities.

Balancing the lights

Always begin with the key light, and then add the filler and back lights, in that order. The ratio between the key and filler light is crucial, and may be accurately judged with an incident meter, measuring each in turn. The ratio may then be repeated in matching subsequent shots if necessary. Alternatively, the balance can be assessed directly through a monitor or through an electronic viewfinder.

Key light Both the height and the angle of the key light have a crucial effect on the kind of lighting that you are aiming for. This is the first light that should be set — if the light is too high the nose will give a shadow running down towards the mouth; if it is too low the effect can be ghoulish. Similarly, if the light is too far to one side of the subject unattractive shadows can be thrown by the nose. The angle with respect to the camera should be determined partly by the direction in which the subject is facing.

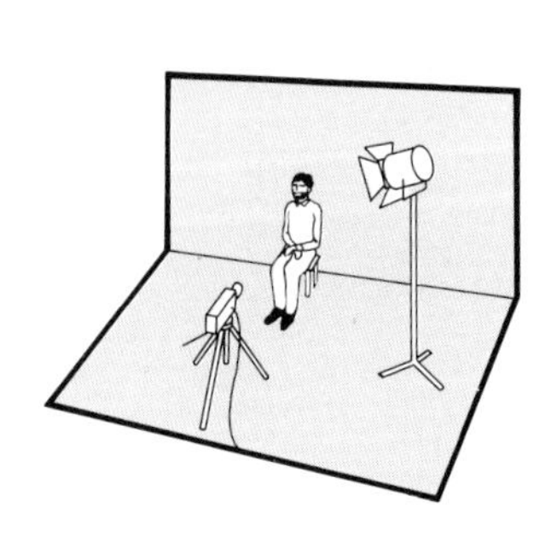

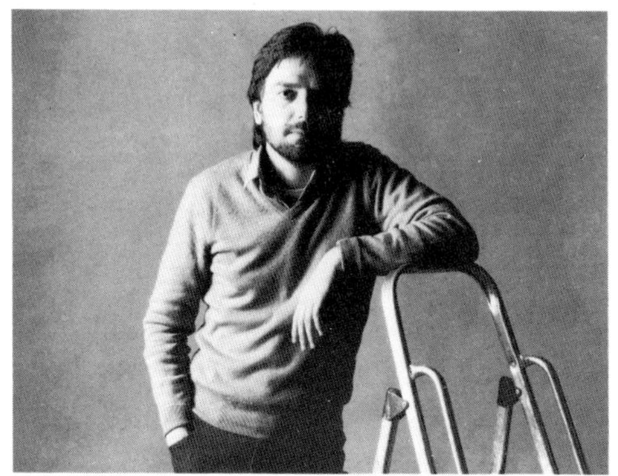

One light The crudest form of lighting is provided by one light mounted on top of the camera or behind it. This is also the very worst position, giving no modelling or depth to the subject. If you are restricted to just one light, it should be diffused with 'spun', and positioned high up to one side of the camera. This will at least give some modelling without blinding the subject.

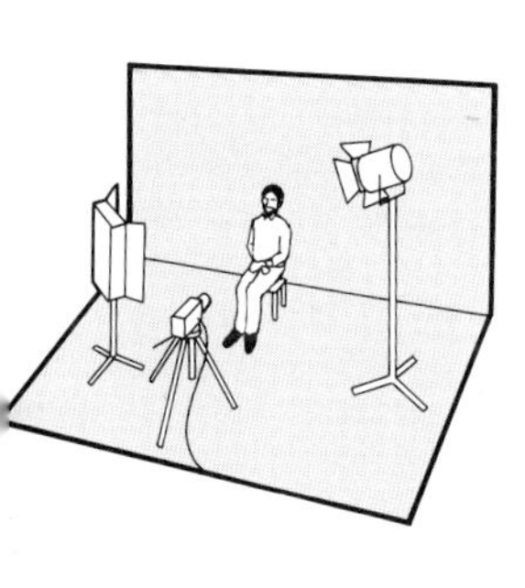

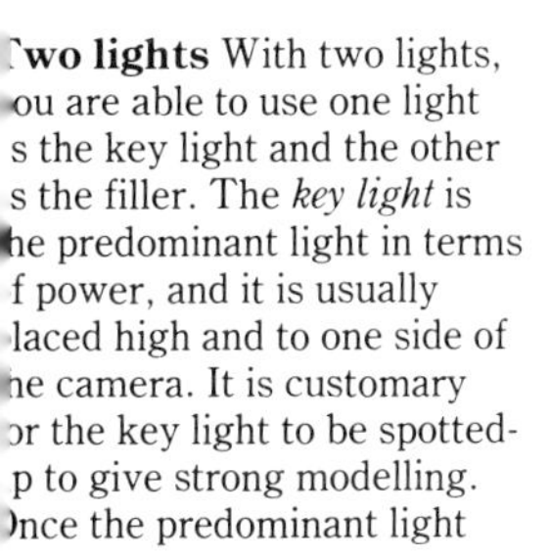

'wo lights With two lights, ou are able to use one light s the key light and the other s the filler. The *key light* is he predominant light in terms f power, and it is usually laced high and to one side of he camera. It is customary or the key light to be spotted-p to give strong modelling. Once the predominant light has been set, a *filler light* is positioned on the other side of the subject to soften the shadows in the face. Ideally, this light should be a diffused source which does not modify the over-all exposure.

These two lights may be balanced in any number of ways, and their relative intensity will have a potent effect on the dramatic impact of a scene. When positioning the key light, take particular care that the nose does not cast an ugly shadow, and that the light is not so high that the eyes are hooded. These faults can be masked by the filler light, but ideally they should not be there in the first place.

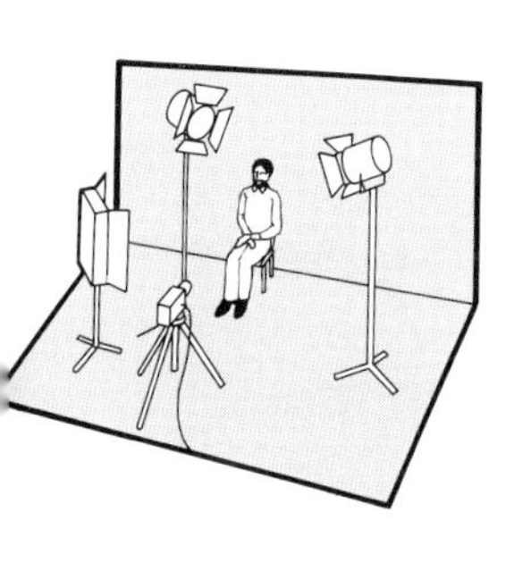

'hree lights If a third light available, it can be used as back light. In this position it 'ill form a rim light around e head, separating it from e background and giving dded relief and visual terest, but at the price, in me circumstances, of a ther more theatrical effect. the back light is very strong, or even predominant, the effect is very artificial indeed, although this may well be what you require. When placing the back light, take care to avoid lens flare. The light may be shielded from the lens by barn-doors or a flag; remember that flare can still be caused even if the light is not actually visible in the viewfinder. A back light is usually a spotlight.

A fourth light may be added in some circumstances to give mottled light across the background (shining through a cucaloris, for instance), or as an additional eye-light, but in normal shooting this is an unnecessary complication.

Colour temperature

All light sources have a colour cast of some sort, and in general these sources vary from red to blue. For instance, lamp-light is reddish, whereas the light from a north sky at noon is blue. A system has been devised whereby the range of colour is expressed as *colour temperature* in degrees Kelvin. Ordinary lamp-light is as red as the light at sunset, and noon daylight gives a colour temperature ('white light') of 6500° K. It is at this level that TV monitors are adjusted, so that peak white on a TV should have the neutral white of noon daylight.

Both film and video cameras are more sensitive to the deviations of colour in a light source than is the human eye, and unless some compensation is made at the time of recording, any tapes made in a ligh that diverges greatly from the norm wil produce highly coloured results. Colou cameras therefore have filters an circuitry, usually in combination, to balanc the colour of the recording. Typically, thi might consist of four settings (tungsten fluorescent, sunny, and cloudy-bright) with a fine-tuning knob for mino corrections. The latter would be tied t some form of viewfinder indicator. Som cameras now have automatic white balanc controls: the camera is pointed at a whit subject (a piece of paper; even a white shirt in the prevailing light; the auto whit balance button is pressed, and the camera' electronics perform the rest. Large

Kelvin scale The Kelvin colour temperature scale is based on the colour of a theoretical 'black' body at any given temperature in degrees Kelvin (K). It ranges from the deep red of sunset or candlelight to the blue-white of a northern sky at noon. The human eye adapts speedily to these variations but both film and video have much less tolerance of variations from the norm in colour temperature and some compensation, either through filters or electronically, is invariably required to return the over-all balance to the norm of 'white light'. This is established around 6000° K, and this is referred to as daylight colour temperature.

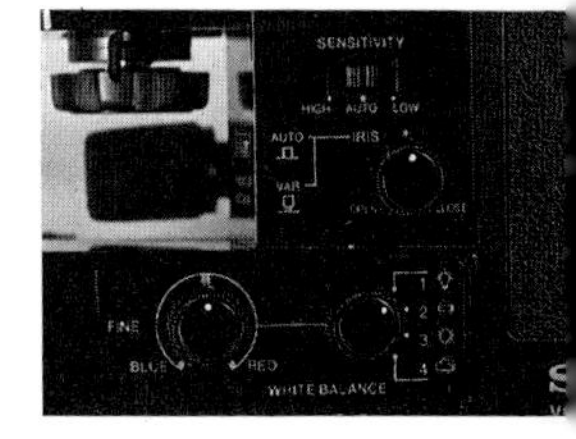

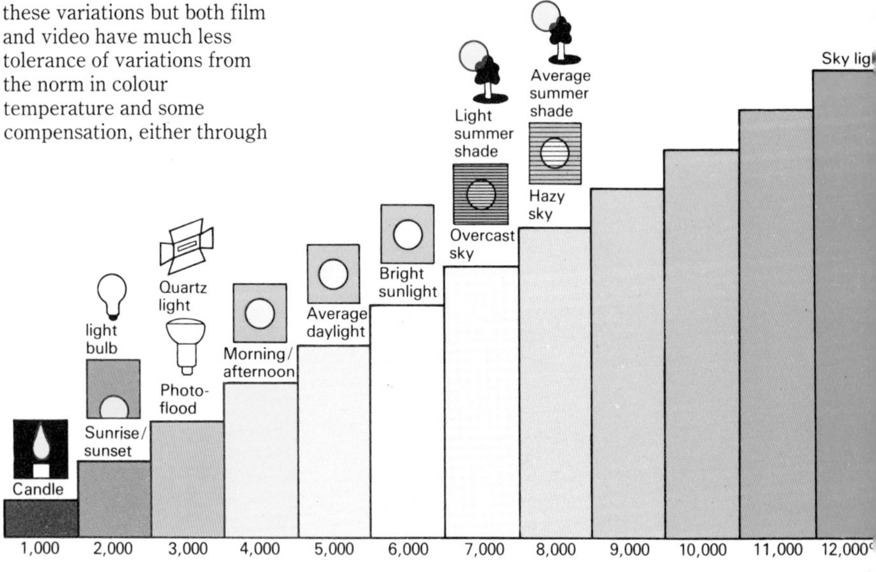

cameras usually require a separate Camera Control Unit which contains the colour balancing circuitry.

Setting up with a monitor
The eye is particularly sensitive to the colour of skin tones, and a bluish or flushed face can be quite alarming on display. It is therefore just as well to double-check visually before an important taping session that the colour balance is correct. If you have a colour monitor/receiver near to the camera, hook it up so that the camera video output is fed directly to the monitor, and, pointing the camera on to some skin-tones or other critical subject, fine-tune the camera to your satisfaction. If this operation is to be of use, it is naturally vital that the monitor should have been set up correctly in the first place. In particular, NTSC users should beware of maladjusted receiver/monitors.

Fluorescent lighting
Fluorescent lights tend to create several problems with video cameras. They can cause r f interference, visible as a black interference bar on the screen, and in any case they tend to be greenish. Since the fine adjustment on most cameras runs from red to blue only, this greenishness is not subject to correction. The only solution is some form of mechanical filtration, whether over the lights or over the lens.

Colour control The colour balancing circuit on most cameras only enables the user to vary it between red and blue — corresponding to the difference between tungsten and daylight. If the balance of the camera is found to be too magenta or too green, it is usually only possible to adjust this by internal means. More complex cameras have colour control units (CCUs) which enable colour correction to be made in any given direction. In the camera illustrated a crude filtration is applied according to the colour temperature of the prevailing light source, and this is then refined by means of a fine colour control. An optimum position for the white balance can be judged through an indicator in the viewfinder, though for really accurate results the use of the colour monitor is strongly recommended.

Colour correction The general range of colour correction in domestic colour cameras is between red and blue. In practice, this means correction between daylight and tungsten illumination. Daylight tends to be bluish, while tungsten is reddish. The results may be assessed critically on a colour monitor. Many cameras have automatic white balance to achieve natural effects. The lighting in these shots is tungsten.

Too blue

Correct

Too red

Lighting for effect

Very low key

Very low key lighting is one of the trickiest effects to achieve convincingly: you have to create an impression of utter darkness while giving the camera enough light for an exposure, and at the same time introducing enough strong visual elements to give structure and interest to the scene. One answer is to use rim lighting on very selected areas of the scene — the edges of furniture, the glint of metal — and to avoid frontal light as much as possible. Use side or back lights, and perhaps include the light source in the picture — a candle, or moonlight streaming through the window. For a very dark effect, take care to place the lights low, so that the minimum illumination spills on to the floor.

Dramatic lighting

Here the light should be very contrasty, with the filler practically non-existent. The sharp shadows are thrown by hard spotlights in a low position that also give a melodramatic under-lighting to the face. In turn, these can be used to throw dramatic shadows on to the walls.

Romantic lighting

For the kind of romantic scene that was perfected in Hollywood lighting of the 1920s and 1930s, the light is high contrast, and diffused by gauzes on the camera lens itself. Also, the back light is exceptionally powerful in relation to the frontal lighting, giving a halo of radiance around the hair. In addition, the eyes glimmer through the gauze, being picked out with a tightl focused 'eye light'.

Day for night

This is the technique of shooting during th day in such a way as to create the illusion o night. First, you must have a sunny day then, shoot *into* the light, having stoppe the camera down manually until the imag in the electronic viewfinder appear plausible. (A manual override is of cours essential here. For optical viewfinders reckon about two stops under-exposure. It may also be effective to alter the colou balance slightly towards the blue or to use blue filter such as a Wratten 80A. It is we worth checking the effect on a colou monitor before shooting.

'Natural' lighting

Video tends to exaggerate the contrast of scene as compared to the way it would b perceived by the eye, so that simply addin a wash of diffused filler light to an existin scene can often have the effect of restorin a 'natural' contrast. Alternatively, if yo are seeking the effect of the grey light fror a north window (this is a gloomy but rea istic light), the lights can be bounced o walls and ceiling, or else shone through large suspended sheet. The result is almos shadowless, with no trace of artificiality and is strongly recommended fo documentary, or for any setting wher more 'theatrical' lighting would be a intrusion. It also allows great freedom movement.

'ery low key

Dramatic

omantic

Natural

ay for night (before)

Day for night (after)

Colour balancing

While the camera can be accurately adjusted to cope with any given over-all colour balance, you should be aware of the problems that are created by mixed lighting. This is true of any scene in which the light sources have different colour temperatures: at the most extreme, this might be a room lit by both daylight and tungsten interior lighting, which are respectively blue and red. In these circumstances, if the camera is adjusted for the interior light, the window and the area lit by it will be deep blue; or, if adjusted for exterior light, then the interior lamplight will be deep orange. In such a case, the decision must be made to unify the colou temperature of the lighting, either b raising that of the interior or by lowerin the exterior. This involves placing blu filters on the lamps (and balancing fo daylight), or else covering the window with large sheets of orange gelatin ('85 gel), and balancing the tungsten light. Bot methods involve some loss in the total leve of light falling on the scene, but the latter i usually to be preferred: daylight is normall more plentiful than artificial light, and th reduction of contrast is therefore welcome

Frequently, however, it may be prefe able to meet the problem only half-way. I

Interior lamplight If lan light is shot with the camera set to daylight the effect is overpoweringly yellow.

Adusting for daylight This scene was adjusted on the camera for daylight, though the exterior is still somewhat blue because of the time of day. The interior is quite yellow, but this is acceptable since the lighting clearly represents a mix of interior and exterior.

'half-blues' are used on the lights, for example, some warmth will be retained on the interior lighting that can be used creatively to give a glow to the lamp-lit portion of the image. This is something that can best be judged on a portable colour monitor at the time. It is certainly pointless to rely on the apparent evidence of your eyes, since the colour response of a video camera is so much more extreme. The same could equally well apply to unmixed lighting such as a sunset. It is perfectly possible to adjust the camera or CCU so that a sunset looks like midday — and this is what would happen if the auto white balance were used too literally — but a sky-blue sunset is hardly desirable. This is only one of many cases where technical and artistic requirements conflict, or at least have to be delicately reconciled. In this connection, it should be noted that all these difficulties would be enormously eased if cameras were equipped with accurate colour (rather than monochrome) viewfinders. That development, which is presumably only a matter of time and technology, is nevertheless overdue. The problem is apparently that colour viewfinders would emit excessive X-ray radiation so close to the eye.

Interior light In this shot blue filters have been placed on the quartz lights in the interior and the over-all lighting balance has been raised so that the exterior is visible. The colour temperature of both interior and exterior matches in a natural way.

Evening light It is possible to correct the warm light of evening so that it looks like noon. This may or may not be desirable, but it is certainly an effect that is at the video-maker's disposal.

Lighting for movement

The kind of lighting described on pp. 140—1 works perfectly well in the case of one single shot of a stationary subject; but that is hardly the stuff of exciting viewing, and in practice the subject is very frequently in motion. What is more, the camera may well be moving too, whether on a dolly or hand-held. Finally, if you are using a multi-camera set-up, the over-all scene will have to be lit so that it can be shot satisfactorily from several angles at once. These problems can only be solved by compromise, which is why the feature cinema has adopted the laborious method of lighting each shot separately. This is feasible in video too, but you may feel that in the interests of speed you would wish to move the lights as little as possible.

The moving subject

In this example, the subject is walking forward in a straight line towards the camera. The decision has been made to concentrate the most effective portrait lighting on the points at the beginning and end of the shot. The filler lights not only serve their normal purpose for the two major positions, they also ensure an even over-all level of illumination for the duration of the subject's walk forward. The evenness of the lighting may be checked by walking through the scene with an incident meter pointing towards the camera: the reading should not vary appreciably from beginning to end. Alternatively, both key lights could be on the same side, if the subject was always looking straight ahead. In all such set-ups be on the look-out for dark 'holes' in the lighting through which the subject will have to pass. An alternative is to flood the entire scene with a diffused wash of light.

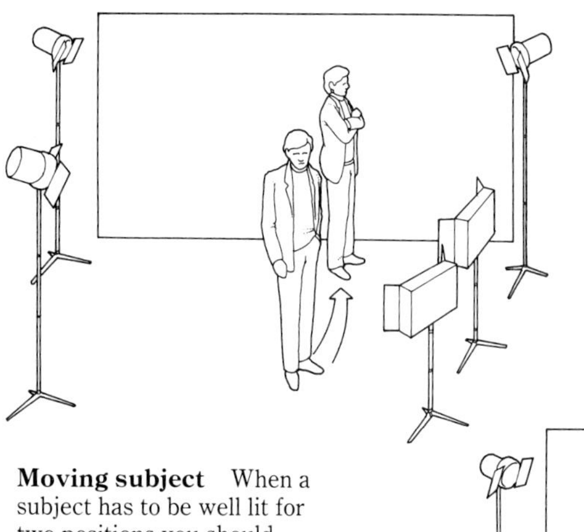

Moving subject When a subject has to be well lit for two positions you should consider the position of the key light both before and after his movement. Here he is provided with a key light and filler for both front and end positions.

Moving subject and moving camera In some shots both camera and subject may be on the move, and while the subject should have a good key light in both positions it is important that the lights are not visible in the shot as the camera moves.

ither bounced or from soft fillers, but this s fairly crude illumination.

The moving camera

Vhen the camera is also moving, great are has to be taken, to retain even xposure and to avoid shooting the lights nemselves. Since it is very ugly to have all ne lighting from behind the camera, it nay be best to clamp the back light high p on a wall behind the subject. Another ossibility is to add a small supplementary amp to the top of the camera to cover any ark spots during the movement. This hould be diffused with 'spun'.

Multi-camera lighting

ighting for more than one camera is omplicated not only by the necessity for reating attractive lighting for several ngles at once, but also by the increased difficulty of hiding the lights themselves. This is of course why TV studio lighting is almost always suspended from overhead gantries. If overhead lighting is not available, both cameras (and therefore the lights) will have to be grouped in a fairly narrow arc — perhaps 120° — around the subject, which could be lit adequately by a combination of keys and fillers, with high back lights clamped to the top of part of the set. The trick in this kind of lighting is to maintain over-all covering power without losing all gradation of tone and modelling. For this kind of set-up you will need not only experience but also a good deal of fine-tuning as the lights are being rigged. The lighting should be viewed through the camera viewfinder, or preferably on a good monitor, as it is being built up, so that the effect of the electronics can be incorporated into the set-up.

Multi-camera lighting In multi-camera set-up one of he most difficult tasks is to nsure that no lights are isible by any of the cameras, nd that the cameras hemselves do not wander into hot. In practice this means hat they are usually arranged an arc around the subject, nd that the lights are placed igh and out of view.

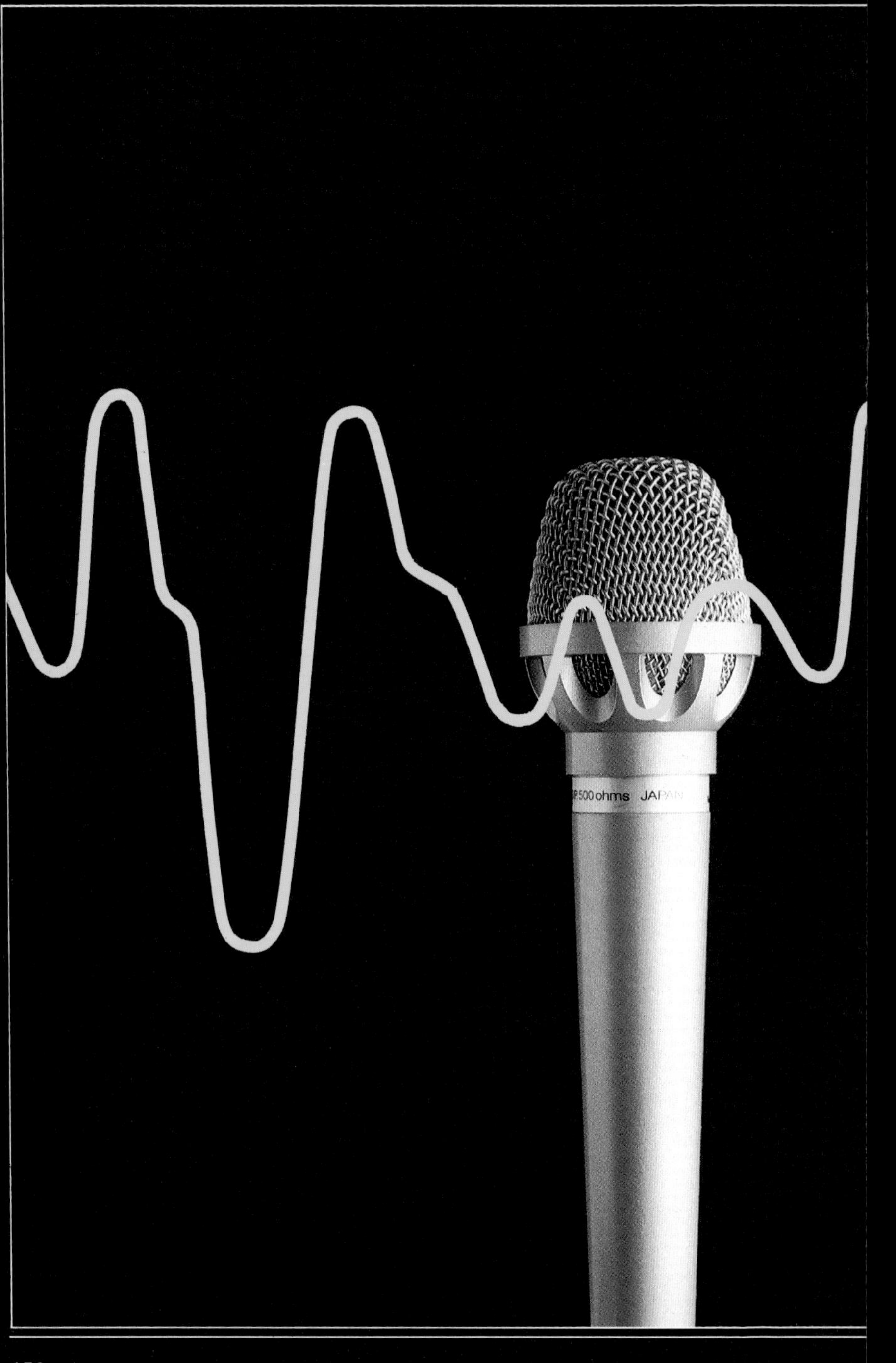
500 ohms

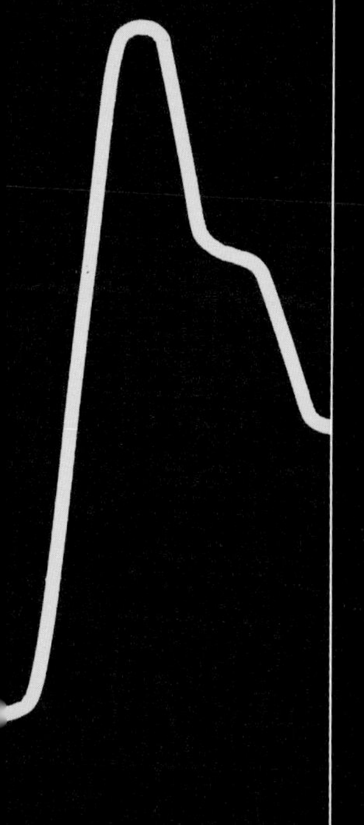

Sound

Video cameras are visually so exciting when they are used for the first time, that it is easy to forget the element of sound. Yet more often than not, it is the *sounds* of an event, whether a party, a wedding, or a drama, which will determine the lasting value of a tape. You should therefore give it as much attention as the video. Even if the microphone is built into the camera, the sound can usually be monitored and controlled as you shoot. In audio, as in video, a little extra care will yield disproportionate rewards.

The basics of sound

Although sound and vision are transmitted as one composite signal, and although we experience both as one coherent whole when watching a TV programme, they must be considered separately when discussing video recording. Indeed, except for the rf modulated signal stage of the TV process, audio and video channels are physically separated by the cabling.

In all VCRs, whether helical or Quad, the sound track or tracks run in a linear way, while the video tracks run at an angle. This is because the bandwidth required for the video signal is so much greater than that required for the audio signal, and the sound head can therefore be stationary while still giving acceptable frequency response at present tape speeds. However, since the full range of hearing runs from about 25 Hz to more than 16 kHz, and since the best ½-inch VCRs will only reproduce frequencies below 10 kHz, the sound quality of replay is at present distinctly inferior, even with noise reduction systems such as Dolby.

When considering the relative merits of

Harmonics Any musical instrument produces both fundamental tones and 'harmonics', which often extend up into very high frequencies. These harmonics are vital to the fidelity of recorded sound, which is why a good frequency response is essential to all sound recording, even when low notes are being recorded.

Dark blue = approx. fundamental range (and lower harmonics)

Light blue = approx. range of relatively important harmonics (subjective by necessity)

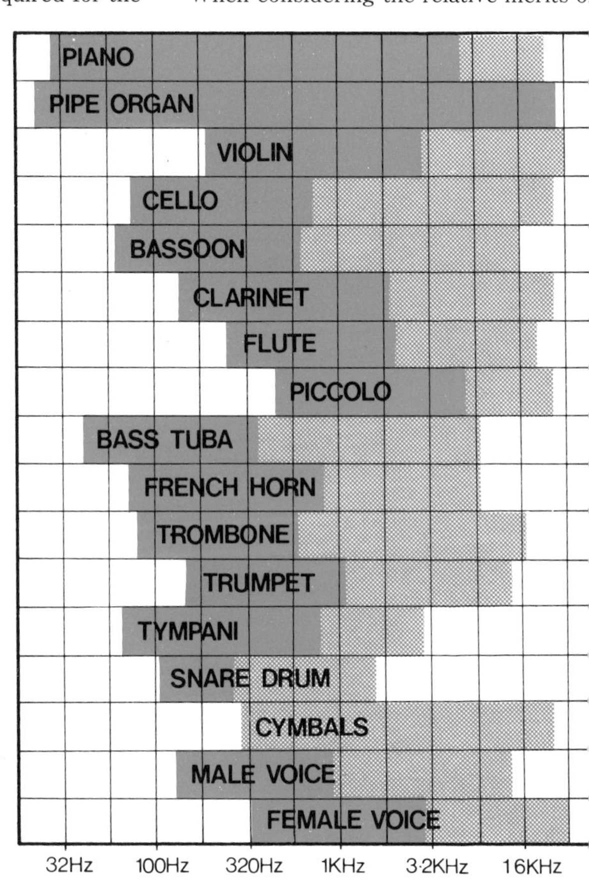

any recording system, you should look at the signal-to-noise ratio (43 dB would be good on ½-inch, or perhaps 50 dB with Dolby); the frequency response (10 kHz is the very best you can hope for on ½-inch); and *both* are partly a function of the actual tape speed. The linear tape speeds of the three main ½-inch systems are: Betamax 1.873 cm/sec (0.74 ips); VHS 2.34 cm/sec (0.92 ips); V2000 2.44 cm/sec (0.96 ips) — see table of International Standards, pp.208-9. A conventional audio cassette runs at 4.76 cm/sec (1.87 ips).

Finally, both the size of the head gap and the composition of the tape will greatly affect the quality of the eventual sound, and it is to be expected that the newest tape formulations will improve the rather dim performance of current ½-inch equipment.

In the ¾-inch gauge, with a speed of 3¾ ips, very good sound recording is possible, and signal-to-noise ratios could be expected to rise above 48 dB, with frequency response up to 15 kHz. But the quality of the recording will be determined primarily by the quality of the input.

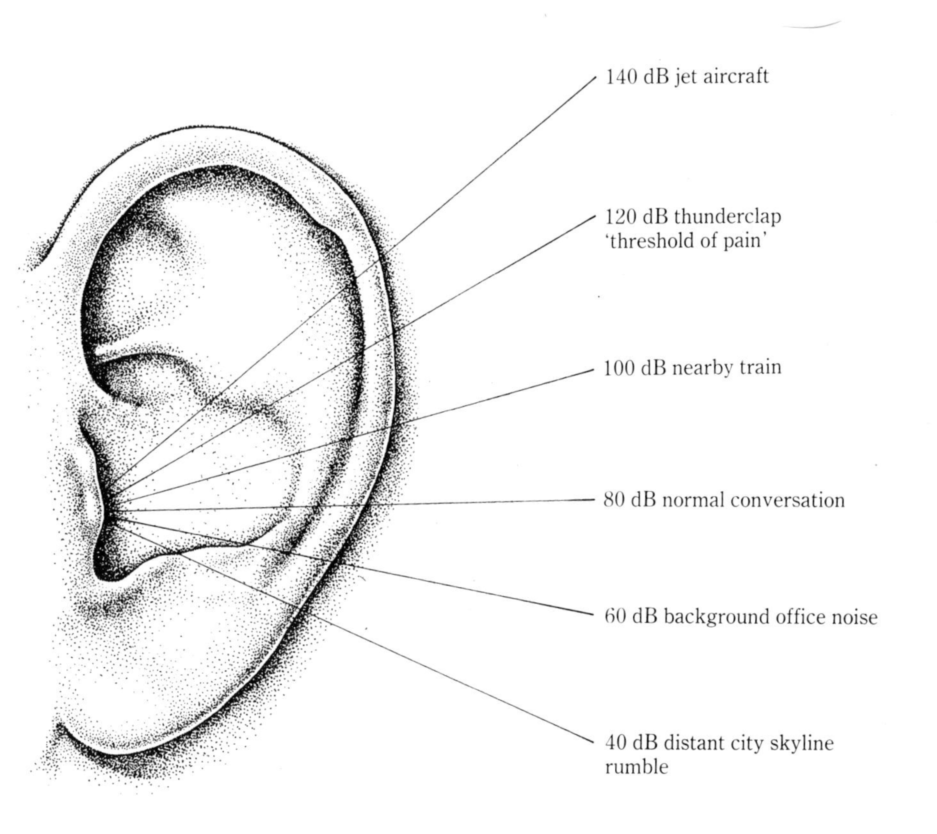

Off-air recording

The quality of the sound transmitted on conventional TV channels varies widely, but at its best it is much better than commonly supposed. The main reason for the inferior sound from home receivers is the quality of the receiver's amplifier and speaker. Therefore, if your VCR is equipped with an Audio Out socket (as virtually all are), run a lead to a spare Aux In socket on an audio amplifier, and play back the TV sound through the larger speakers. Not only will the sound be astonishingly enhanced, but you will also be able to use the tone controls on the amplifier to vary the frequency response curve.

The principal defect of off-air sound, whether it originates on film or video tape, is *noise*. This is heard as a high-frequency hiss, and if it is objectionable the worst of it can be removed by the amplifier filter. It is unlikely to be noticeable on a normal home receiver, since the built-in speaker usually has very poor high-frequency response. However, when the same programme or film is taped off air on a ½-inch recorder, a considerable amount of extra tape-hiss is added, and even with Dolby noise reduction in operation the combined hiss will be noticeable.

On all the smaller-gauge recorders the sound level is controlled automatically by Automatic Gain Control (AGC), and on some machines this may cause quiet passages to be raised unacceptably in recording level, together with an unpleasant rise in the level of hiss. On more sophisticated machines, the level can be controlled manually, via a VU meter.

The VU meter

The object of the VU sound meter is to prevent the tape being overloaded by the recording level, which would cause distortion. The needle should remain predominantly in the white areas of the scale, rising slightly into the red areas for very transient peaks of high-level sound only. This should ensure that both loud and quiet sections of the tape are accurately rendered. Except in the case of very wide

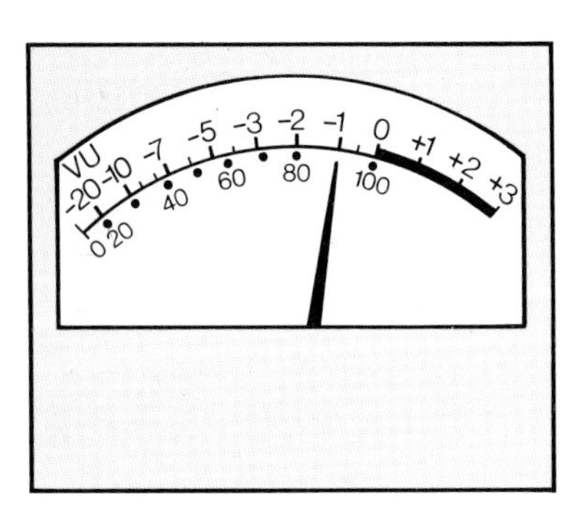

Connecting the VCR to an amplifier On the back of every VCR there is an Audio Out socket which may be used to connect the recorder to the Aux Input of a domestic amplifier; this may be a DIN socket or a phono socket. The speakers should not be positioned too far from the receiver, or you will find that the sound source is inadequately identified with the image.

VU meter All current domestic ½-inch machines have AGC which prevents accidental overloading of the sound signal during recording. More sophisticated industrial and professional models feature VU meters so that the sound can be monitored manually. The VU meter is calibrated in decibels and should be set so that the needle does not peak into the red except for very brief moments of high volume.

variations in the volume of the sound input, the Recording Level control should not be 'ridden': this would tend to even out the dynamic range to an excessive extent, and is in fact the main defect of AGC.

It is vital that the loudest parts of the recording are not heavily over-modulated; when a setting has been established for off-air recording, it should not need revision unless the channel is changed. The same should also normally apply to tape-to-tape transfer. Live recordings are of course another matter, since the level of the ambient sound varies greatly from one scene to the next, and the Manual control will have to be intelligently — and gently — ridden throughout if AGC is not being employed.

Stereo

Some cassette recorders are now coming on to the market which can record in stereo, on two tracks. There are corresponding stereo transmissions in Japan — on quite a large scale — and in one or two European countries on an experimental scale. New receivers are being introduced worldwide which can replay these transmissions, and it may be supposed that stereo sound will soon be as common a facility on TV as on FM radio.

Simulcast

This is the term for simultaneous broadcasts on radio and TV, in which the sound is transmitted in mono on TV and in synchronous stereo on FM radio. When positioning the speakers, do not place them too far apart, since the stereo separation of the FM audio is greater than that of a normal screen: you can have too much of a good thing. These broadcasts can naturally be recorded by a suitable VCR which has a 2-track recording facility. In all these examples of stereo recording, it may be necessary to leave the receiver's own loudspeaker on at a low volume, in addition to the surrounding loudspeakers from the audio amplifier, to help to identify the sound-source with the screen.

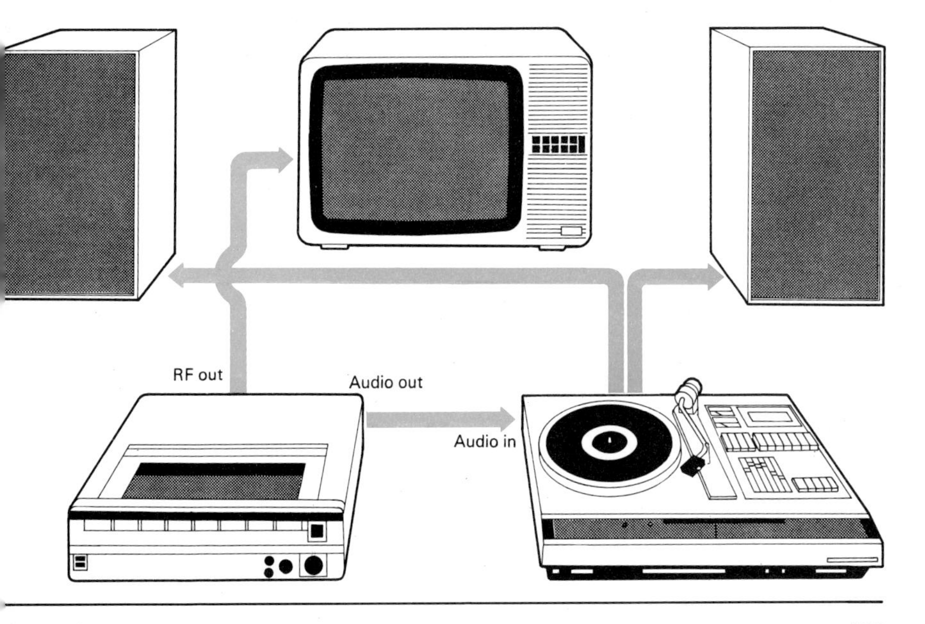

Recording live sound

Most amateur cameras come equipped with a microphone in the body. This is usually an omni-directional type, unfortunately, though there are almost always provisions for mounting a more directional boom mike on top of the camera. This cannot be too highly recommended, since the boom mike will not only be more selective in the sounds it records, but it will also be well away from the taps, grunts, shuffles, and breathing of the camera operator, to say nothing of the whine of the servo-zoom.

An additional hazard with many portable recorders is the very audible 'clonk' sound as the Pause button is released on Remote Pause. The effect is that any visible flash that you may perceive on a cut is made even more objectionable, since it is loudly reinforced on the sound track. Recorders vary quite considerably in this respect, and it is well worth investigating their performance before buying. If the machine in question is particularly noisy, the only solution is not to wear it over the shoulder, but to use a long camera lead instead. This is hardly ideal, and in the case of the very light JVC 2200, for example (which is also very noisy on cuts), it may undermine the whole point of the design.

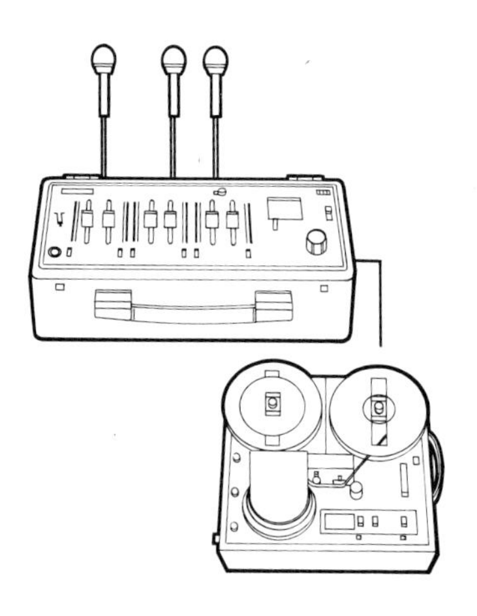

Mixers If more than one microphone is being used, the outputs should be fed through a mixer before being passed on to the video recorder.

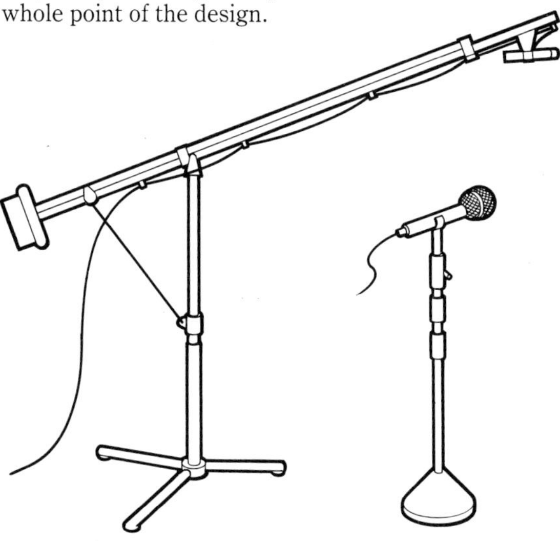

Stands Microphones can be mounted in a variety of ways: on a boom which can be adjusted for both the angle and the length of the arm; on a floor stand which is also adjustable for height and angle; or on a table stand (this should be placed on a firm mat). All these mounts commonly contain some form of shock-absorber.

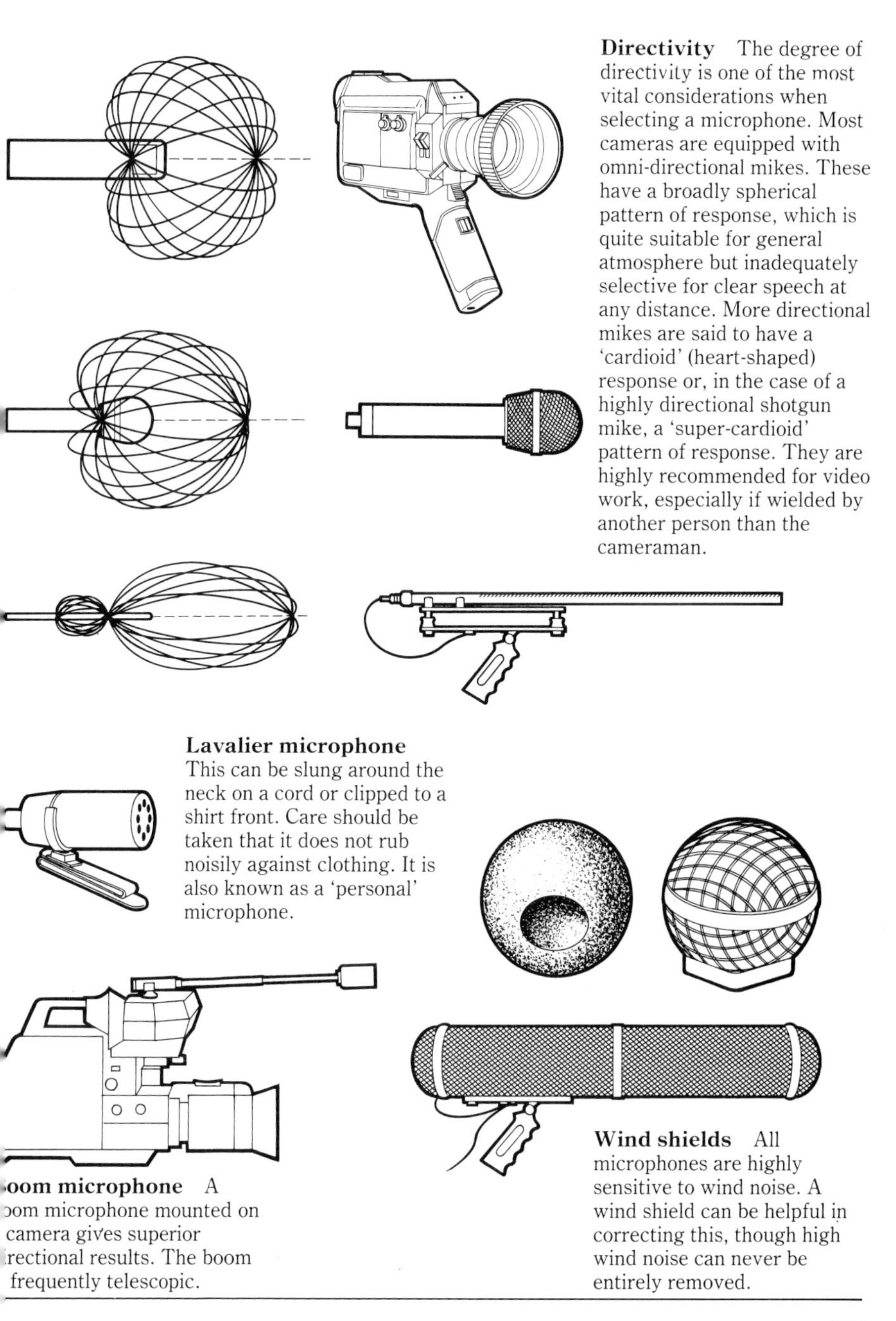

Directivity The degree of directivity is one of the most vital considerations when selecting a microphone. Most cameras are equipped with omni-directional mikes. These have a broadly spherical pattern of response, which is quite suitable for general atmosphere but inadequately selective for clear speech at any distance. More directional mikes are said to have a 'cardioid' (heart-shaped) response or, in the case of a highly directional shotgun mike, a 'super-cardioid' pattern of response. They are highly recommended for video work, especially if wielded by another person than the cameraman.

Lavalier microphone This can be slung around the neck on a cord or clipped to a shirt front. Care should be taken that it does not rub noisily against clothing. It is also known as a 'personal' microphone.

oom microphone A oom microphone mounted on camera gives superior rectional results. The boom frequently telescopic.

Wind shields All microphones are highly sensitive to wind noise. A wind shield can be helpful in correcting this, though high wind noise can never be entirely removed.

Manipulating sound

A *sound filter* selectively removes one portion of the sound spectrum to a greater or lesser extent. The degree of correction is expressed in decibels — for example, a treble filter might introduce a cut-off of −10 dB at 12 kHz, or a bass filter might come into operation below 100 Hz. The function of the former is primarily to reduce hiss, while the latter would mostly be used to remove rumble. The two could also be used in conjunction: for instance, the treble could be raised to clarify speech, while the bass cut could be introduced to eliminate the rumble of traffic. Sound filters can be introduced into video recording at the initial recording stage, if they are inserted into the

Stereo mixer In this Sony 5-channel stereo mixer, each individual input can be adjusted in level, as well as the over-all output and the relative balance of the left versus right channels.

Graphic equalizers A graphic equalizer provides a highly sophisticated way of modifying the character of recorded sound. Each fader is assigned to a specific narrow frequency band, which can be boosted or attenuated according to your needs.

recording chain between the microphone and the recorder, or interposed between two recorders during a tape to tape transfer.

Graphic equalizers provide a far more flexible and subtle means of modifying the frequency-curve of a recording. They can be used to remove one very precise frequency, to re-balance the tonal texture of music, and to clarify speech. Since each sector of the frequency-spectrum is allotted a separate fader, the degree of correction can be rapidly judged by eye and ear.

Other sound manipulation features such as echo-chambers and compressors are rare in video, though there is no actual reason why they should not be used.

Adjusting the faders
These three positions represent, respectively, a boost of the middle range, a reduction of both base and treble, and a lift of the upper treble range.

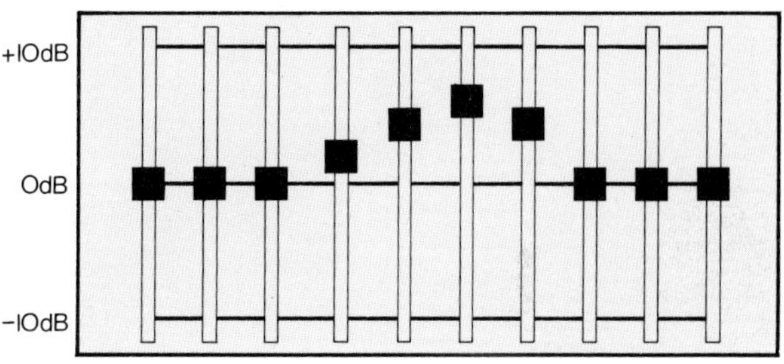

Middle boosted

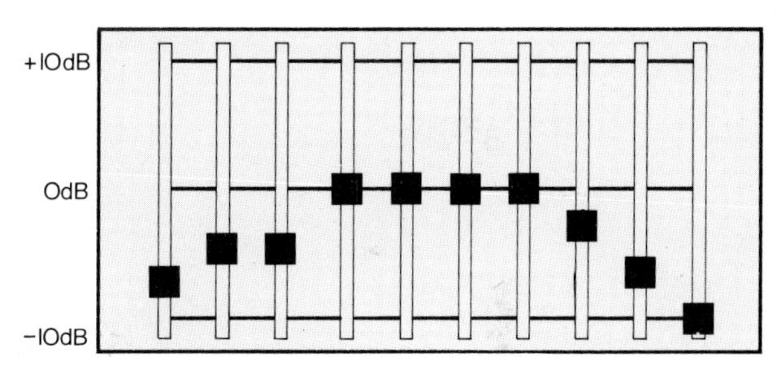

Bass and treble reduced

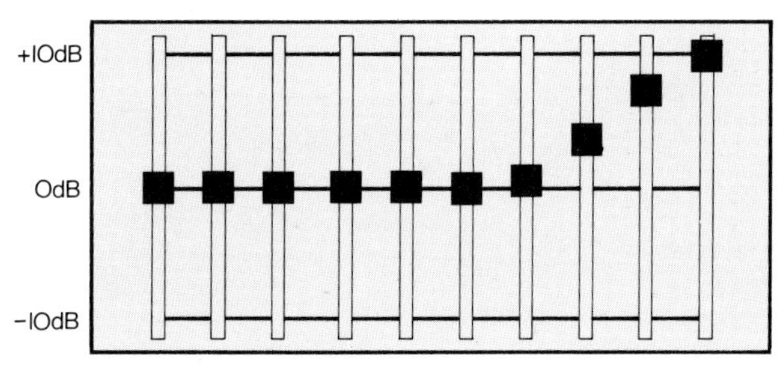

Treble boosted

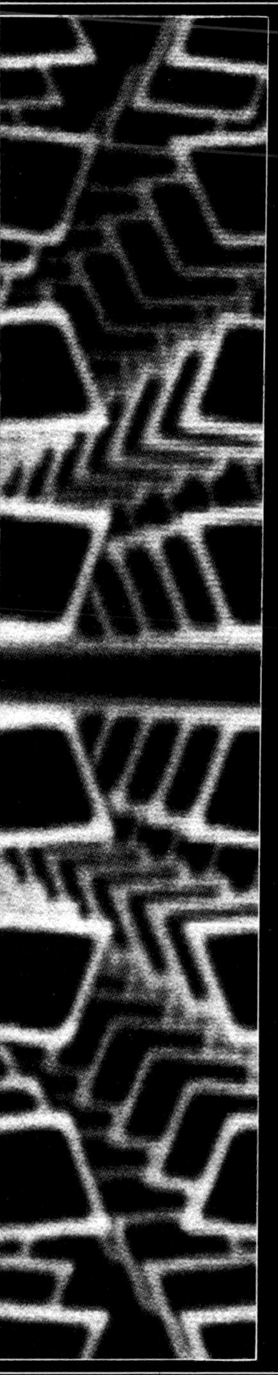

Expanding the Image

Although straightforward video shooting, editing in the camera as you go, has considerable appeal, it only hints at the true possibilities of video as a creative medium. Once you decide to expand and manipulate the original recording, the doors will be opened on to wholly new areas. For instance, you might begin by editing the tape; slides or film material could be added through a telecine converter; other tapes could be copied or dubbed; special effects could be added through a special effects generator; or, most radical of all, the single camera of the original recording could be replaced by a multi-camera set-up. This is effectively a small studio, and will allow you to intercut at the moment of shooting.

Multi-camera techniques

In the earliest days of video — indeed until the late fifties — all video editing was effected in the studio itself by cutting between two or more cameras, and the resulting video signal was transmitted 'live'. The advent of video recording and tape editing, which now spreads to the very smallest tape gauges, has meant that comparable results can in some cases be produced with just one camera. However, there are many occasions that can only be covered with multiple cameras. There are several advantages: an unrepeatable event such as a rock concert, a wedding, or a football game can be covered from several angles; a drama can be shot with perfect continuity; the resulting tape is a firs generation copy; and editing should nc necessarily be needed. The disadvantage are: the capital expense; the complexity c the set-up and lighting; a lack of flexibilit

What you need

When two or more cameras are used the must both be capable of accepting a external sync pulse so that their scanning c the field begins and ends synchronousl The best way of arranging this is to lin both cameras to a Special Effec Generator (SEG). This not only provid the cameras with a common sync pulse; also provides the facility to cut or m

Simple set-up This simple three-camera set-up is suitable for interviews or discussions.

etween them in such a way that there is no lashing or frame-roll between shots. Such n accessory has a number of other features oo (see pp. 168–9). If, in addition to the nultiple cameras, you wish to add extra nputs such as a VCR, they will need to be ed in through a 'genlock' – this ensures hat the sync pulse of the VCR is amplified nd serves as the dominant sync pulse for he cameras too: in this way you can mix rom tape to live action without picture reak-up.

et-up

n a multi-camera set-up the audio and ideo leads are usually entirely separate. Clearly, once you have decided to use more than one camera, you have made the jump from a one-man operation to a collaborative venture. One person will be needed for each camera, one for the sound and one for the 'direction' and the cutting between the cameras. If there is audio talk-back to the camera from the director, some kind of glass-fronted sound-insulated booth is required. In addition, each camera should have a separate preview monitor so that the director can select the shots for cutting to them, as well as a 'programme' monitor which will indicate the actual output from the mixer desk or from the Special Effects Generator.

amera use Each camera . a multi-camera set-up may e assigned to a separate dividual contributor to a scussion.

Studio direction

It is unlikely that many amateurs will attempt these semi-professional set-ups, but they are certainly applicable to schools, universities, or industrial training schemes. The set-up will probably contain the equipment described on pp. 162-3.

With this kind of investment it is strongly recommended that the master recording is made on ¾-inch U-Matic high-band tape so that subsequent editing is possible; ½-inch tape can be used if you do not anticipate that any editing will be required. A good deal of the advance work can be done on paper by imagining the shot that each camera will be able to cover. Effectively you will be editing in advance and the problems that you encounter when cutting between cameras are the same as those when intercutting shots at the editing stage. Therefore the same principles of continuity, shot size, and crossing the lin will apply. In addition, you should also b aware that it is extremely easy for on camera to be in the shot of another camer and again you should try to keep a groupin of three cameras on one side of a line.

When preparing a studio of this kind it i vital to have a script, even if the subject is a interview, since this will enable you t envisage the shot that each camera i expected to cover. Each cameraman shoul be given a separate camera sheet whic refers only to his own particular shots an which corresponds in shot number to th master script.

In rehearsal go through every shot th each camera is to be expected to cover an make sure that it is to your satisfactio Each cameraman should be in contact wit the director through headphones, thoug

Control functions Even in a small-scale studio it is a great help if the various control functions are spread out between several people, leaving the director free to concentrate on content.

Control room The studi control room often, but not always, has a view of the studio floor through soundproof glass. The outpu of each camera is visible on the monitors.

he or she will not be able to reply. It is customary for a cameraman to answer yes or no by either nodding the camera or shaking it from side to side. These signals will of course be visible to the director on the monitor even though he cannot hear anything the cameraman is saying. In the studio communication is absolutely essential. It is the director's job to make his vision felt through every word he says to the cameras. Above all he should be acutely aware that they cannot speak to him. He should imagine that they are in constant need of advice, correction, and approval. When complicated movements are required such as zooms, tracks, or focus-pulls, these should be rehearsed in advance, and it is perfectly possible even during recording for the director to 'talk through' a given camera movement.

Anticipating the next shot

Perhaps the most crucial job that a director has is to look forward to the oncoming shot while monitoring the shot that is in progress. Very often a camera has to zoom in to a subject in a forthcoming shot, and this subject must be pre-focused before such a zoom is possible. In such a case the cameraman must have foreknowledge of what he is expected to do and the director must line up the shot accordingly *before* cutting to that camera.

As all this would indicate, a director's lot is not necessarily a happy one. He must both sympathize and control; anticipate and listen; take both the longer and the shorter view; and perhaps, if it is a one-horse show, operate all the vision mixing equipment at the same time. Whatever else may be said of studio direction, it is never dull.

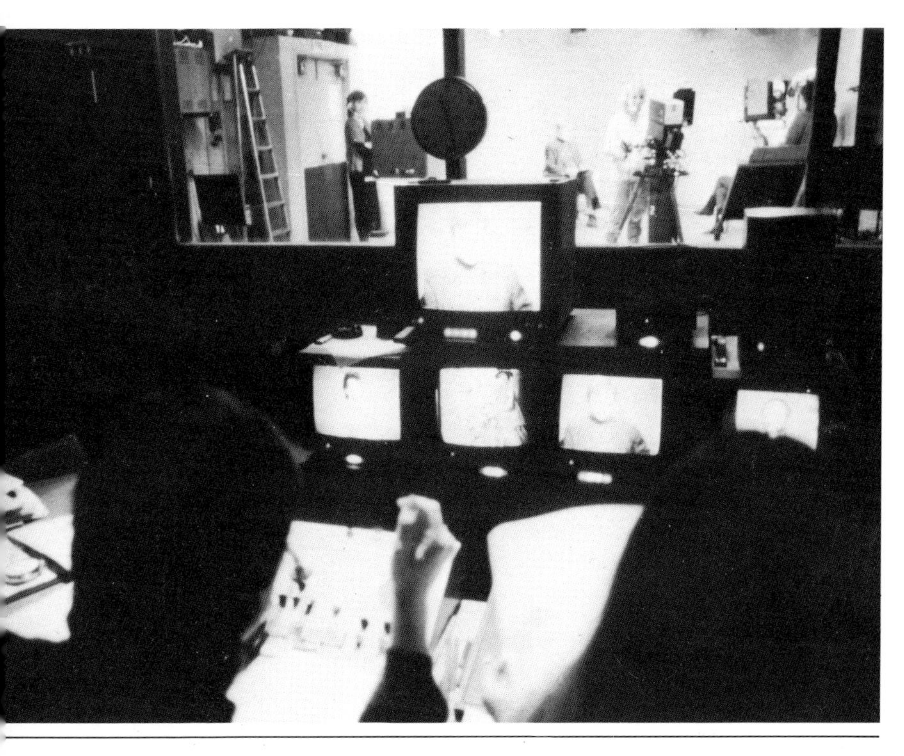

In-camera effects

In-camera special effects are naturally limited in their scope but are available to the humblest user. The most common of all is the *fade*. This may be included in the specifications of the camera, in which case both sound and vision may be automatically faded up or down at the press of a button. This is a useful facility especially if your recorder does not have a very effective Pause control, and it may be used to indicate a transition of either time or place. Alternatively, a *matte-box* may be used to create a crude form of wipe or to contain filters if they are not of the correct size for screw-thread fitting to your camera.

Filters

There are a number of special effects filters that will create really spectacular images at a minimum of expense.

Mattes A matte is any form of physical, optical or electronic device which excludes part of an image. Here a matte-box is used on the front of a camera for specific visual effects – a keyhole, binoculars, a window, a hole, a star.

Matte-box A matte-box, which is fitted on to the front of a lens, has an extendable bellows. The matte may be fitted either to the rear or the front of the bellows, though in the case of filters they are always slotted into the rear.

Filters Any filter that you buy must match the size in millimetres of the screw thread on the front of the lens on your chosen camera. Filters should be handled and treated with as much care as the camera lens itself.

)iffusion filter

Graduated filter

Multi-prism filter

tar filter

Editing

Video-tape editing is the rearrangement of images and sounds from one tape on to another, enabling rubbish to be discarded and new alignments made. It is without doubt the single greatest improvement you can make to a tape.

Two machines are always involved in modern, electronic editing: the 'record' machine and the 'replay' machine. The replay machine (possibly a portable) will contain the original tape that has been recorded on location. The record machine (called an editing recorder) must be capable of producing cuts from one shot to the next without flashes or frame-roll. No ½-inch machine except some of the industrial Betamax versions gives absolutely clear edits. At the worst with domestic machines you will receive a 'crash' edit, in which the picture breaks up entirely between consecutive shots from a separate replay machine.

The control track Any continuous video recording contains a series of regularly spaced pulses on the control track. These ensure that the sync pulses on the receiver correspond to those in the original camera

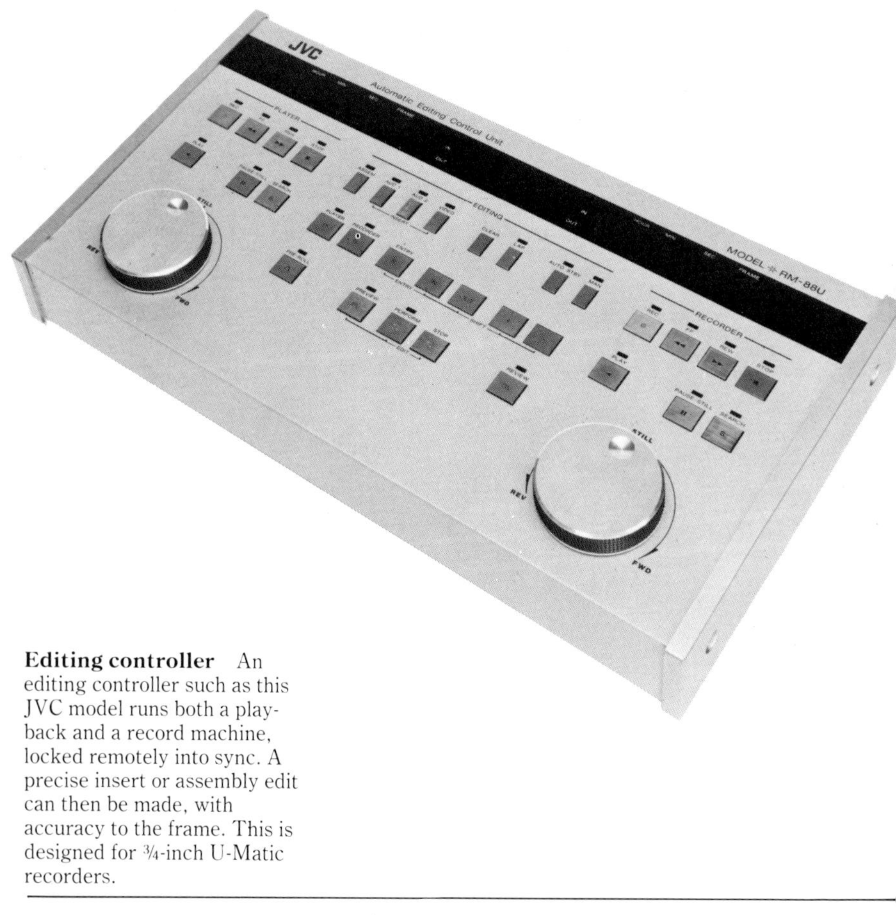

Editing controller An editing controller such as this JVC model runs both a play-back and a record machine, locked remotely into sync. A precise insert or assembly edit can then be made, with accuracy to the frame. This is designed for ¾-inch U-Matic recorders.

and that, as a result, the picture remains stable on replay. In a 'crash' edit, the incoming sync pulses from the replay recorder may not (almost certainly will not) correspond to the existing spacing of pulses. The result is a visual hiccup which may cause severe disintegration of the picture at the moment of the cut. The only satisfactory remedy is to roll back the tape on the recording machine for, say, five seconds and to 'pre-roll' the recording tape and the replay tape in synchronization so that the editing recorder can synchronize its control track with that of the incoming new shot. In this way the regular sync pulse on the second-generation tape will not have been interrupted.

This facility is currently only available on ¾-inch U-Matic editing recorders, though a simplified version is becoming available on the more sophisticated home machines in both Betamax and VHS formats. On domestic ½-inch machines the editing function is always engaged by use of the Pause control. This produces highly variable results from one brand to another, and it is worth investigating its efficiency before purchasing a given machine.

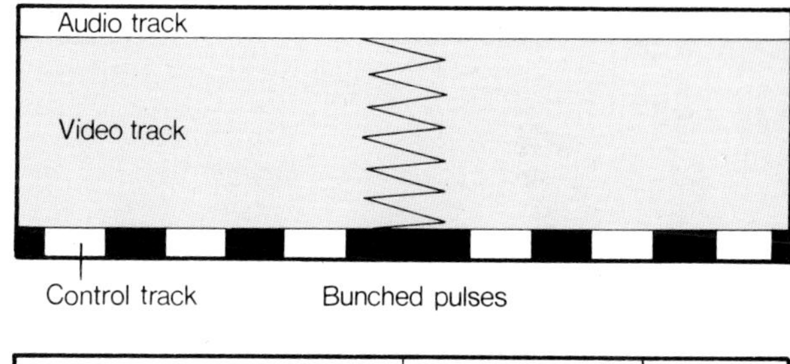

Crash edit In a crash edit, the regular beat of the sync pulses is interrupted, giving possible picture break-up or frame-roll.

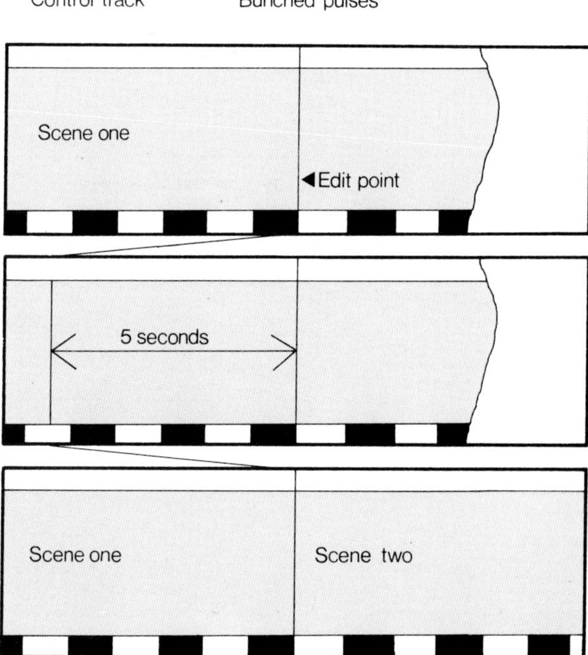

Roll-back editing In roll-back editing, both tapes are rewound a short distance from the edit point, then rolled forward together, so that their sync pulses match by the time the edit point is reached. The record machine is 'slaved' to the pulses of the replay machine via a capstan servo.

The generations The tape that you have recorded on a portable or direct from a camera on to a home recorder is known as the *master tape*. When you come to edit this on to another machine the second tape is known as the *composite master*, and this is referred to as a second-generation recording. If the composite master is used for copying, those copies will become third generation, and the smaller the gauge the greater the loss of quality. It is definitely not recommended that ½-inch tape should proceed beyond second-generation editing if you wish to retain acceptable audio and video quality.

Assembly and insert edits The most basic form of editing is known as an *assembly edit;* here separate segments of the master tape are reassembled in a different order (or in the same order with defective portions removed) on to a virgin piece of tape which then becomes the composite master. The record machine may be left in the pause mode while the next shot is found, rehearsed, and accurately located on the replay machine. The replay machine is then rewound for a few seconds, set into the play mode and when the chosen entry point is reached the record machine is released into record. At the end of the section required for that shot the pause is again pressed on the record machine and the replay machine used to find the next shot on the master.

Insert editing requires much more

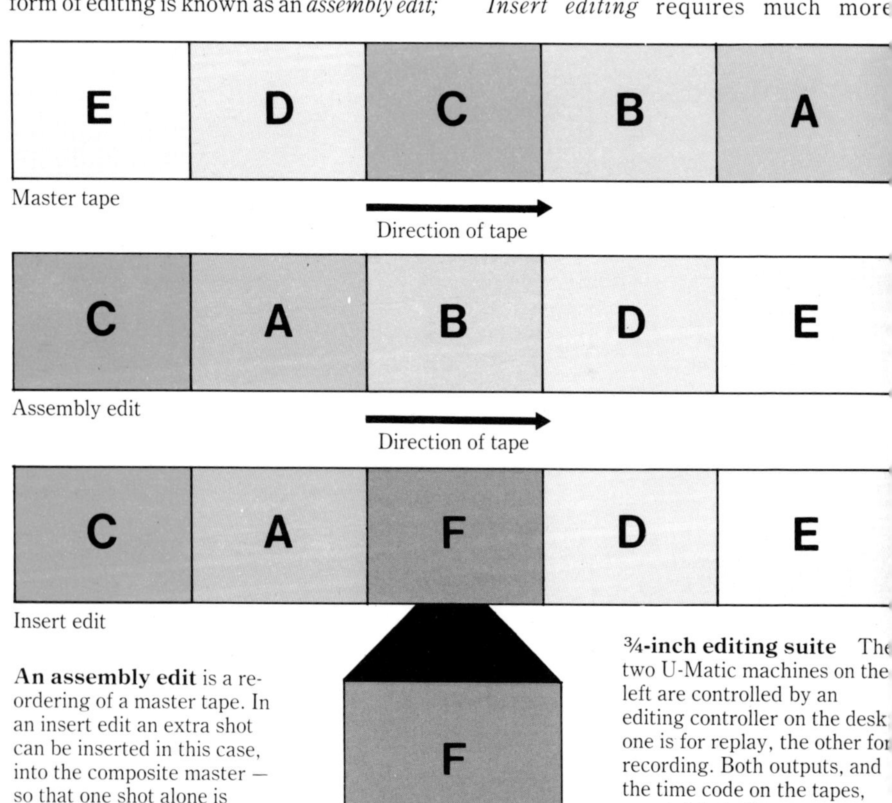

An assembly edit is a re-ordering of a master tape. In an insert edit an extra shot can be inserted in this case, into the composite master – so that one shot alone is replaced without interrupting the flow of sync pulses.

¾-inch editing suite The two U-Matic machines on the left are controlled by an editing controller on the desk one is for replay, the other for recording. Both outputs, and the time code on the tapes, are visible to the operator. Commentary, music, or effects can be added at this stage.

sophisticated equipment and involves the insertion of audio and video (or perhaps video alone) on to a previously recorded tape. This may be one shot or an entire sequence, but can only be done without picture break-up if the record machine is truly suitable. It is inevitable that ½-inch recorders will soon be introduced with flying erase heads, enabling them to perform insert edits, which are at present out of their grasp.

Editing on to a ¾-inch composite master
Unlike ½-inch machines, the ¾-inch U-Matic format offers genuine editing recorders, which can produce flawless assembly and insert edits. This is achieved in a number of ways: the machine may roll back a few seconds from the edit point and, by locking its tape speed (via a servo system) to the incoming signal, ensure a smooth cut; or two or more machines may be locked into a common sync through an *editing controller.* Here the replay and record machines roll back and forth in interlocked sync.

Increasingly, video houses are offering an hourly rental service of an 'editing suite' for domestic users. At quite reasonable rates you can gain access to ¾-inch editing facilities, and the ¾-inch composite master can then be copied any number of times on to a ½-inch cassette. Although this is a third-generation copy, quality should still be acceptable. Until ½-inch VCRs come of age, serious editing *must* be done via ¾-inch.

Editing controllers In a two-machine edit, the editing controller controls the replay machine from one side (usually the left) of the console, and the record machine from the right. The edit is established by rocking each tape back and forth, monitored individually, until an exact frame is decided upon for both an 'in-point' and an 'out-point'. These coordinates, which are read off the control track on each tape or off a time code, are fed into the controller's computer memory. Then, with modern machines, the edit can be rehearsed without the recording being made, and judged for its suitability. Final adjustments, to the frame, are then made, and if all is well the actual edit is carried out. In a three-machine edit, two machines are used for playback, and it is possible to mix between them on to the recorder.

Finding an edit point In an assembly edit, it is vital that the point at which the cut is made be chosen with care, and with attention to *both* incoming *and* outgoing shots. The composition, speed, and direction of movement in one shot will either glide into the next or collide violently against it. Either may be the effect you seek, but in general the aim should be to make the cut as invisible as possible.

An action cut requires the greatest care. For instance, if you are cutting from a long shot of a woman walking across a room to a close-up of her legs, she must be on the same foot as in the long shot, her speed must match, and she should not reverse direction. This means that perhaps only two frames can be found that match perfectly.

When you are satisfied, make the edit and play in the new shot on to the composite master. In an assembly edit, record more of each new shot than you think you really need, so that you have plenty of spare shot for the next cut. In ¾-inch insert editing you will have to decide both the in-point and the out-point before proceeding — this is made a great deal simpler by the memory on the editing controller.

Cutting and continuity
When cutting from a long shot to a close-up, it is important to pay attention to continuity of action. In this case, the girl should be walking on the same leg in the close-up as in the long shot. The speed and direction should also match in the two shots.

Audio dubbing

Almost all ½-inch VCRs permit you to replace a recorded audio track with new sound, leaving the video unaffected. Unfortunately, the original audio is totally erased on all current ½-inch models, though there is no technical reason why a 'partial erase' or 'trick' recording system should not be devised in future. Audio dubbing enables music and commentary to replace sync sound or, if the shooting was silent, to provide some form of audio backcloth to the images.

The technique is fairly straightforward. Music and commentary may be pre-mixed on to ¼-inch audio tape or cassette, being closely matched to the image from a common start point, then dubbed on to the VCR when balance and sync are found to match well. Remember that the sync on such a 'wild' system will tend to drift as the tapes progress. If commentary needs to be very precise, it should be done 'live' as the video tape runs past. Music and commentary can still be passed through a mixer and equalizer and monitored as they are dubbed on to the tape.

If you wish to combine original with added sound on ½-inch cassette, you can use a variation of the editing technique. Play the video from VCR (A) into a recording VCR (B), while passing the audio through a mixer. There, you can add music or commentary as the audio is fed to VCR (B). The video will be second generation, but the original sound can be retained, and even enhanced if you pass it through an equalizer on the way.

On ¾-inch machines, the audio can be dubbed on to two tracks, which means that (apart from the possibility of stereo) commentary can have a track of its own. Partial erase is also possible.

Commentary In commentary, always try to add to what is being shown without duplicating it. Try to synchronize the words to exact cuts or to points in a shot without making too heavy an effect. Commentary is the art of minimal, accurate statement.

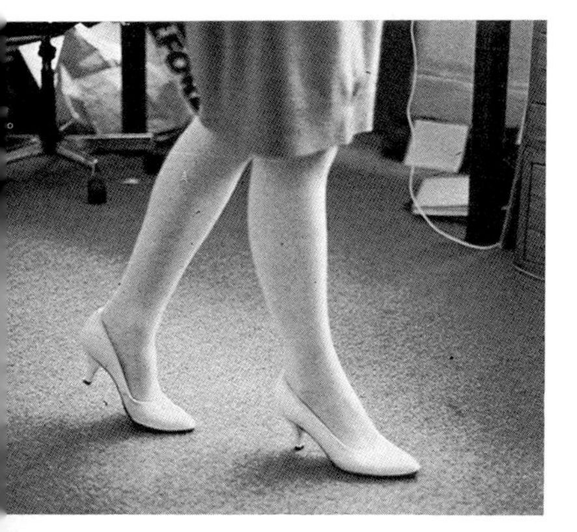

ight

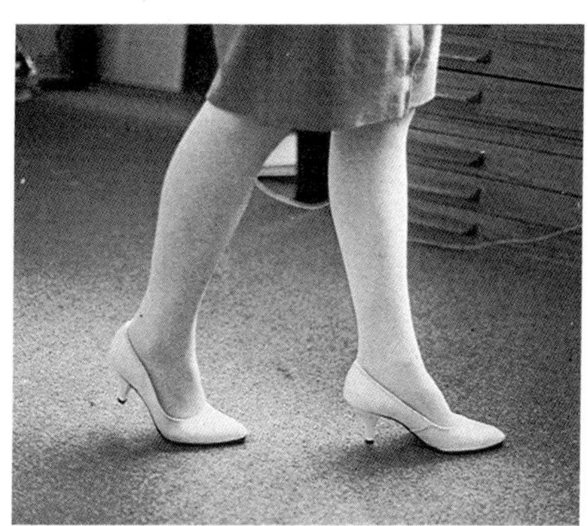

Wrong

Switching and special effects

Special Effects Generators (SEGs) vary greatly in flexibility and complexity and they are generally packaged to include switching systems for two or more cameras which must accept external sync from the SEG and perhaps a 'genlock' for connection to a second 'input' VCR. The range of special effects you can then achieve may include: fades, dissolves (or mixes), superimpositions, inlay, overlay, and wipes.

All switchers have separate faders for each camera. These act in the same way as volume controls on a sound mixer, and regulate the video gain of each input. For example, if camera 1 is selected as the output camera, the image from that camera can be faded up, or down to black, at will and the effect may be observed on the output monitor. Alternatively, as camera 1 is faded down, camera 2 may be gradually faded up. The effect here is a *dissolve*, or *mix* between one camera and another. The mix of the two inputs may be held at any given stage so as to produce a sustained *superimposition*. This can be used for a variety of effects including titling. For titling, the titles should be white on a black background, though other colours may be used in certain circumstances. Some sophisticated SEGs contain colour synthesizing circuits which can be used to manufacture any given colour electronically.

The input on one of the two channels could equally well be a video recorder, so that for example you could cut or mix from live action to tape, and back again. The flexibility of any switcher is circumscribed by the number of 'buses' it contains — buses are complete video and audio in-out circuits. Ideally, you should have one bus for each input source, though in practice it is possible to obtain quite adequate results from two buses only. The third bus may be used for special effects.

Wipes

A *wipe* differs from a mix in that the incoming image occupies an ever increasing area of the screen, and a hard line separates the incoming from the

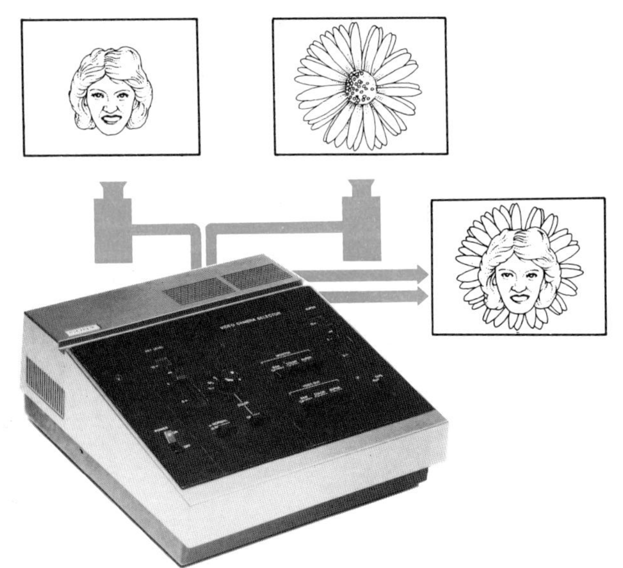

SEG A Special FX Generator can be used to switch between two or more inputs or, as here, to dissolve two images together. If a dissolve is sustained, it is a superimposition.

Quantel This tiny but highly sophisticated box of tricks enables images to be stretched, rippled, spun, reduced in size, and manipulated in a dazzling variety of ways (right).

outgoing image. The wipe may be a straightforward vertical or horizontal line. Alternatively, it may be a square, an iris, or any number of other variations. The direction and speed of the wipe can be controlled through the faders and through the controls on the SEG. If the wipe is left at a half-way position, for instance, the incoming shot may be referred to as an *insert*. For example, a split screen or a corner-insert is possible.

In this way separate shots from two cameras can be combined without mixing. It is not an effect which is particularly suited to realistic shooting, but it can be quite effective in some situations.

Keying

Keying is a system which permits any hard-edged portion of one input (such as a word caption) to entirely replace the other input on the screen: for instance, one camera could be on a caption card, while the other was on a face. Unlike a superimposition, this gives a hard white image to the caption, and this effect is important if clarity is to be retained. Alternatively, in more sophisticated versions *chroma key* can be used which replaces all the parts of one scene of a particular colour (usually blue) with another image. For instance, if a man is shot on one camera against a pure blue background, and another camera is pointed at a landscape shot, all the blue in camera 1 will be replaced by the landscape of camera 2. The result: man in landscape. This is known as 'Colour Separation Overlay', and hence the designer's phrase 'C.S.O. Blue'.

Second-generation special effects

Inserts and overlays such as the above techniques are highly sophisticated and correspondingly rather expensive, but they are very primitive when compared with the newest (and most expensive) boxes of tricks such as *Quantel,* in which video images can be stretched, twisted, spun, flung into space, or split into a dozen mosaics. All this can be pre-programmed into one microchip memory, rehearsed, and set. Then you just press a button, roll it, and astonish yourself.

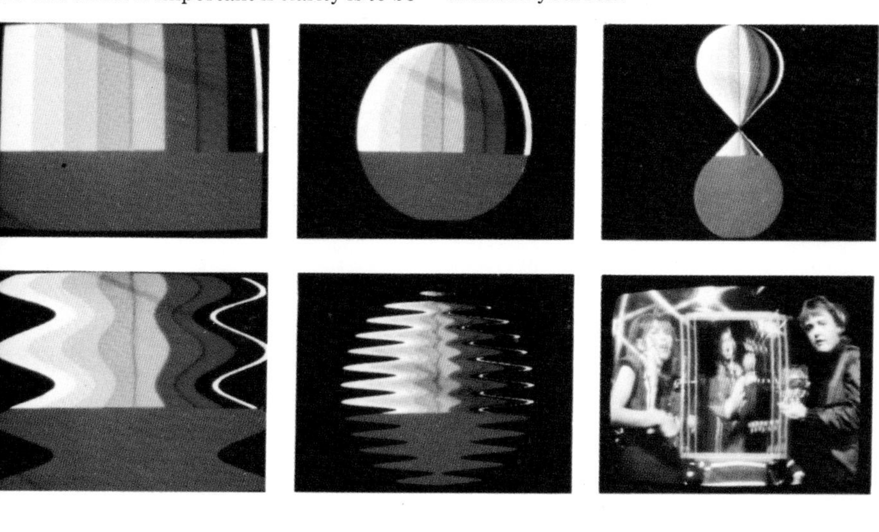

Film and tape transfer

Film to tape transfer

When a film is transferred on to tape, the set-up is known as a telecine-chain, and there are several ways in which this can be done at home. The simplest is to set up a video camera on a tripod just next to a projector. Then when the film is projected, the angle of view will not be greatly distorted, especially if a long lens is used in both cases. The sound (if any) should be fed to the VCR by a separate audio feed, by passing the camera's microphone entirely commentary or music may be added at this stage through an audio mixer.

Telecine attachments Most of the major manufacturers offer attachments which serve as an interface between a cine projector and a camera. They usually incorporate some form of mirror, so that the image is reversed in the same way that a

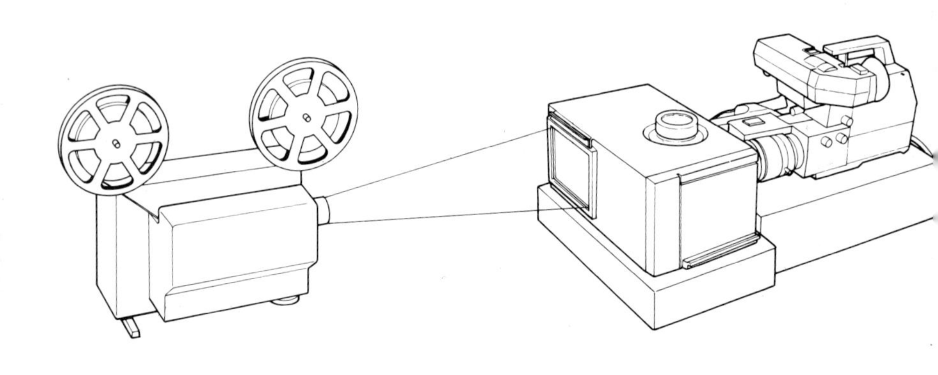

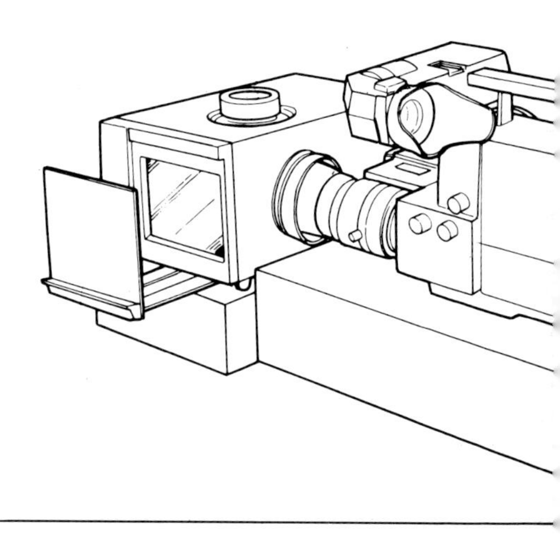

Film to tape There are considerable advantages to using a specially designed film to tape unit such as the Sony VCR-4, as opposed to the rudimentary process of recording the film image off a screen. With all such transfers, it is essential that the projector and the camera should be accurately aligned, to prevent 'keystoning'. It is also advisable to check on a monitor that the colour balance and flicker have been successfully controlled. Slides too can be transferred through such a system, so that the VCR can be used as a convenient photo album.

creen would reverse it, and a rear rojection screen on to which the camera an be focused. Several of them, such as the ony version, may also be used for ecording slides. It is important in all these et-ups that both projector and camera hould be exactly aligned, otherwise the nage will not be four square. The rojection of the film should be rehearsed nd the projector accurately focused before ny attempt is made to record the image. It useful to have a zoom lens on the rojector so that the image may be varied in ize without moving the projector.

licker and film speed One problem with mm projectors is that the normal pro-ction speeds of 8 mm films are 18 and 24 ames per second. These sometimes inter-re with the frame rate of video cameras, oth PAL and NTSC, in such a way that a icker is introduced into the image. This an be checked on a monitor or in an ectronic viewfinder, and if you have a ariable speed on the projector, this may be djusted, within certain limits, so that the icker is reduced or eliminated. The flicker a function of both the frame speed and the iple-bladed shutter that exists in 8 mm rojectors. A similar problem may exist ith 16 mm projectors which, though ormally shot at 24 or 25 frames per econd, have only a two-bladed shutter. hese are all problems that should be hearsed and checked for quality before an tual recording is made.

olour balance It may well be that the iginal film had a less satisfactory colour alance than you can obtain by the use of e white balance controls on the camera elf. Monitor the picture on a colour onitor, and adjust the colour balance ntrols on your camera before making the tual recording.

ape to tape transfer

ny VCR may be used to transfer its video d audio images on to another recorder. his may be done either through an 8-pin socket, if the machine is so equipped, or, more likely, through a direct line-to-line video and audio connection. It is also possible, though not advisable, to use the RF connection. This will involve tuning the slave recorder to the master recorder just as though the master were a TV station transmitting on its own frequency. This is not recommended for tape to tape copying since an extra electronic process is involved, which results in a small but appreciable degradation of the recorded signal on the slave tape. In any event the cabling between the two machines should be kept as short as possible.

The sound It is at this stage that you can introduce changes to the sound track while dubbing from one tape to another. To do this a sound mixer and possibly some form of equalizer may be introduced into the audio line input. Commentary and music may also be added via a microphone and/or tape or cassette deck. These too would be passed through the mixer before being fed to the slave VCR.

Multi-tape transfer If you wish to make more than one copy of a given tape the output from the master VCR or VTR should be fed through a video distribution amplifier (VDA) so that it can be amplified before being split. Typically, a small-scale VDA might have four outputs, each of which would feed a slave recorder, and in this way the total signal would remain at an optimum level for duplication. Do not forget the laws of copyright, especially if you intend selling the resultant tapes.

Quality and tape generation All tape copying involves loss of quality, and the smaller the gauge of tape the greater the acceptable loss in one-generation copying. On 1-inch helical scan tape, for instance, no loss is visible after one generation, whereas on ½-inch tape the loss of quality (visible principally as a rise in the noise level) is quite marked. For this reason, it is best to use only the finest quality tape for both the master recording and duplication.

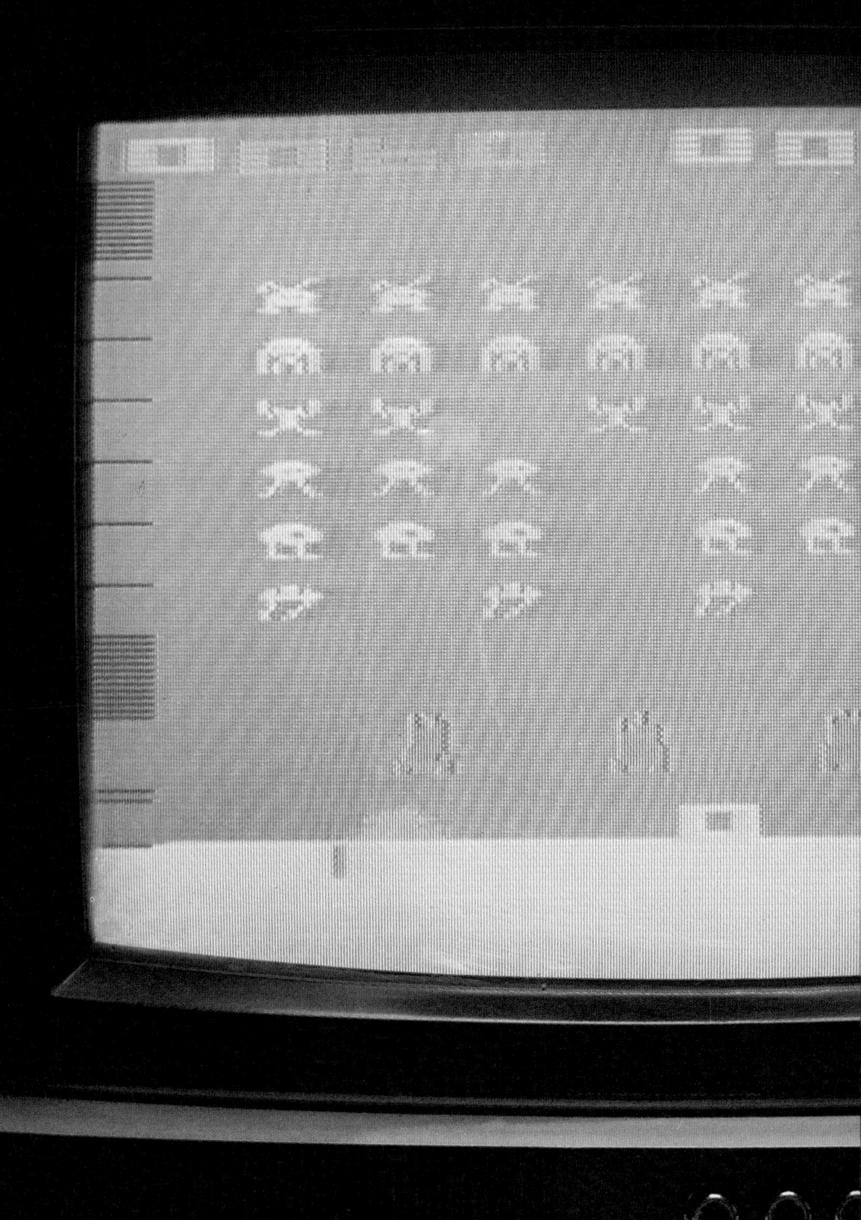

Adding to your system

Nowadays, a television is very much more than just a machine for watching the broadcasts that TV companies see fit for you to watch; and more, even, than a device for making your tapes visible. It can also be used as a display screen for computers or for viewdata, hooked up to the telephone, plugged into a satellite, linked to a video-disc replay unit, or used for games. It may even be replaced entirely by a wide screen for more expansive viewing. Each of these additions to the system represents a major enlargement of the possibilities that are open to you, both passively and creatively.

Wide screen

Projecting an image

All wide screen systems, whether front or back projection, use a very wide aperture lens to focus the high contrast output of one, two, or three tubes on to a screen. In a one-gun system, typically, a 38 cm (15 in) colour monitor is used as the basic light source. The image on the monitor is both reversed and inverted and the lens assembly which fronts the monitor then projects this very bright image on to a highly reflective screen. In a three-gun system, three monitors are used — red, green and blue. Because no shadow mask is required on these monitors, they can be exceptionally bright. Furthermore, the output of the three monitors is combined on arrival at the aluminized screen, so that the resultant image is anything up to four or five times brighter than the equivalent on
tube model. Three-gun projection TV
which certainly give the best and brighte
results of any available today, neverthele
have the disadvantage that th
convergence between the three monito
must be very accurately adjusted.

Although all wide screen TVs may b
divided between back projection and fro
projection sets, there is an almo
comparable division to be made betwe
one-piece and two-piece front projecti
equipment. One-piece units usually conta
a mirror in the form of a drawer at the ba
of the set: this is pulled out when the set is
be used. In a two-piece unit, whic
potentially provides a larger image, the
are more problems associated wi
convergence and with the placement of th

Projection machines A front projection screen (above) gives a slightly brighter image than a rear projection screen (right), though neither type is really suited to viewing in bright ambient light. The size of a front projection machine is minimized if, as here, the beams are focused through a mirror and reflected back on to the screen. However, this form of projection does not give as large an image as the two-unit systems.

projection unit. Furthermore, it is obviously essential that no one should walk between the projection unit and the screen during a programme.

Viewing a wide screen

Very high reflectivity can be obtained from a modern aluminized screen. However, this impressive increase in gain has only been obtained at the expense of a decrease in the angle of acceptance within which the viewer may sit. For example, a very bright image may be obtained by a viewer sitting directly next to the projection unit, whereas someone a metre (3 ft) away to his right would find himself confronted with a hopelessly dim image. In all cases, modern projection TVs require very low ambient lighting, and are not really suitable for viewing in daylight. For this reason, it is anticipated that in the very near future solid-state flat screens will replace the current somewhat primitive hybrids, which are in any case enormously bulky for the average living-room. It must be said, though, that in perfect viewing conditions and with a high-quality input, the results obtainable from wide screen viewing are very remarkable indeed. It is even more vital in view of the impressive video quality that the sound should have an equal brilliance and expanse. Ideally, the audio output from the set should be fed through an audio amplifier to stereo speakers placed equally on either side of the wide screen. The combined result should genuinely create the atmosphere of a cinema in the home.

Super-wide, ultra-large Matsushita display system Matsushita has developed an ultra-large screen which uses many thousands of coloured lights to provide very high-definition, very bright screens for large gatherings such as this pop concert in Japan. The breakthrough in wide screens that is confidently expected in the next few years will be the advent of solid-state flat screens that can be hung on the wall and which will require no projection system at all.

Games

Video games, whatever their nature, must be plugged into the aerial socket of your set, which is then tuned to receive the rf frequency transmitted by the game's modulator. Games may be conveniently divided into three types: simple 'dedicated' games; semi-programmable; and fully programmable.

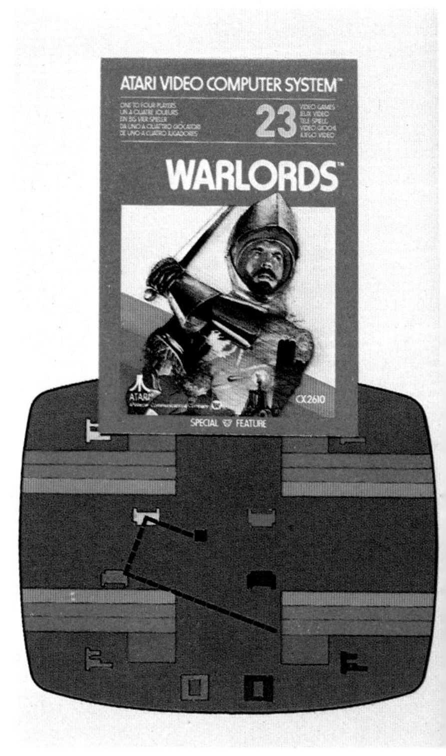

Dedicated games

These cheap and cheerful machines originally used transistors to play just one 'ball and paddle' game such as ping-pong. The later models use an integrated chip: this might, for instance, give tennis, soccer, squash, and a rifle target game on one chip, with joy sticks and a target rifle as possible accessories. More sophisticated developments include colour, variable speeds, and variable sizes, but all such dedicated units are incapable of expansion beyond their original pre-programmed games.

Semi-programmable games

Semi-programmable games are in essence a hybrid — they are an attempt to widen the possibilities of the dedicated game without the major expense of fully programmable games. Here, the custom-built integrated chip (IC) is housed in a small plug-in cartridge which may be replaced at any stage in the machine's life with additional cartridges that in turn contain a whole range of new games. However, the extra cartridges are comparatively expensive to produce and the range of software in these games is likely to be limited. In view of this it seems likely that semi-programmable games will in the long run be entirely replaced with a much more flexible fully programmable variety.

Fully programmable games

In a fully programmable game a central console is essentially a simple computer which reads and responds to the computer language on the plug-in cartridge. These cartridges are much cheaper to produce than the custom ICs used on semi programmable machines, and altogether vastly more flexibility is possible. Some o the more advanced machines in fact offe computer facilities, with keyboards, thu providing a bridge to the home use between games and the true home computer. A typical example in the middle range would be the Atari video compute system. In addition to the Combat an Space Invader games supplied with th basic unit, over thirty games are availabl to be plugged in to this machine. Thes include Air-Sea Battle, Basic Maths Basketball, Blackjack, Bowling, Brai Games, Break-Out, Chess, Circus, Code Breaker, and Golf. The basic unit in thi system costs in the region of £100 ($200

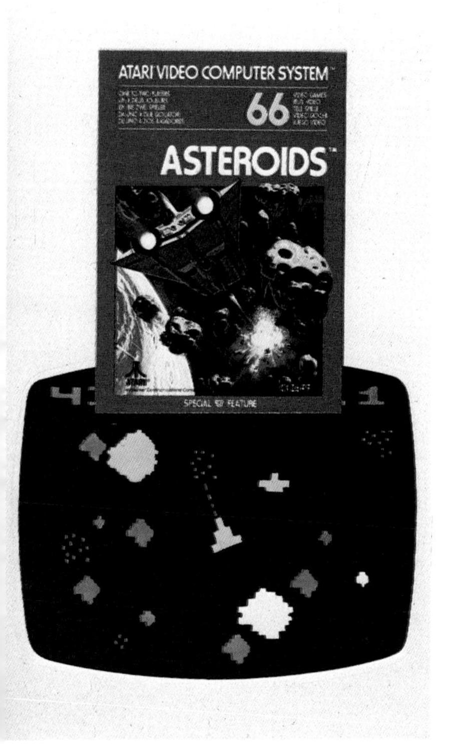

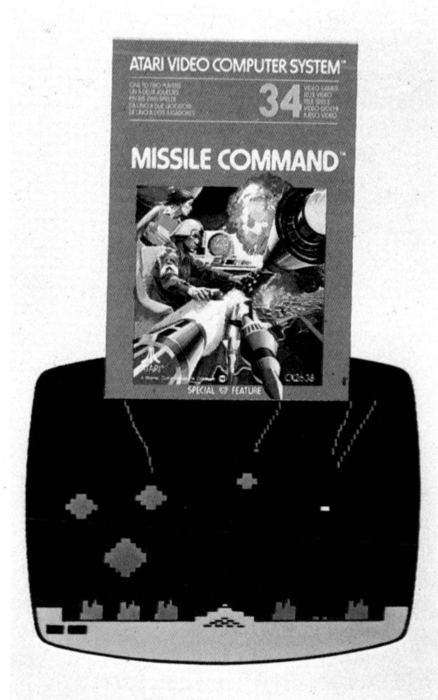

vhile the extra games range from £12.50 $25) to £33 ($65).

At the very top of the market, and indeed ’ay ahead of the field technologically, is the lattel Intellivision system. This is in fact uite a powerful computer, costing £200 $400) for the basic unit, and it offers not nly very advanced graphics, with three-imensional games and highly realistic novements that virtually amount to nimation, but also the facility of plugging n a keyboard (using BASIC language) so hat the control unit is turned into a owerful home computer. Intellivision will lso accept cassette programmes from rdinary audio cassettes that can be played nto the computer. It is not hard to see that he capacities of this remarkable system are nly beginning to be fully exploited.

The Atari video computer system covers a wide range of games to suit all interests and all ages. The three shown here are among the current favourites. Warlords has 28 game variations for up to 4 players, with 3 variations for young children; Asteroids has 66 game variations for 1 or 2 players, and features Hyperspace, Shields, and Flip; Missile Command has 34 game variations, 2 for young children. Warlords has paddle control, the other two games have joy stick control. All three feature on-screen scoring.

Computers

The home computer consists of several elements: it is a modular system which, ideally, can be expanded to include a very wide range of accessories. All home computers have in common a display on a video screen, which may be built in or may be your normal domestic receiver. They will also have a keyboard and some facility to accept extra programmes — a cassette recorder, for instance, or a plug-in cartridge. To clarify how it works, and what it can do for you, it is convenient to think of the home computer as consisting of three elements: 'hardware', 'firmware', and 'software'.

Hardware

This is essentially the Central Processing Unit, the 'number crunching' calculating side of the computer. Nowadays, this will consist of a large, fast microprocessor, probably on one chip. This will perform all the logical operations that are asked of it, but only by means of a form of dialogue through the firmware or software.

Firmware

This is the permanent operating system that is built into the computer's electro-mechanical structure, and takes the form of a 'Read-Only Memory' (ROM) that co-ordinates and organizes the operation of the Central Processing Unit. This memory cannot be altered during use, and is not affected by the removal of power from the computer. This is the crucial link between the crude computer and the fluid software. It may be thought of as equivalent to the structures within the brain which interpret the sounds and visions from the ears and eyes, and pass them on to the 'rational' faculties for a decision.

Software

Software includes the cassettes, tapes, or cartridge programmes that can be used by a computer. To encompass a large programme, many thousand pieces of information must be absorbed. One 'word' in computer language consists normally of eight 'bits', and is known as one 'byte'. A typical 'Random Access Memory' (RAM) on a home computer might need at least 8000 bytes (8 K.RAM), with the extremely desirable function that extra hardware memories (16 K, 32 K, 64 K, etc.) could be plugged in later. Small, cheap computers such as the Sinclair ZX 81 have a modest built-in memory 1 K, but compensate for this by efficient use of it and additional plug-in hardware.

The memories may be in the form of cassette, floppy disc, or solid state. All this software will vastly expand the capacities of any given computer, and may be combined with a printer for a more permanent record. The price of any computer is very often directly related to the size of its built-in RAM capacity.

What can they do?

Home computers can be used for a wide variety of domestic purposes including teaching, games, the control of domestic appliances (including video recorders), accounting — with a restricted access code if you wish to keep your account secret — and indeed as a do-it-yourself introduction to the larger world of computer programming. Many of the available computers offer software that enables you to make your own programmes with the minimum of pain and fuss. If you do intend to write your own programmes, and that is surely the object of the exercise, you should make sure that the system you are buying is designed for a computer language that is suitable to your needs. The most common language in use at the moment is BASIC and this is recommended for domestic use

Apple Here, an Apple computer has been linked to an Apple Writer word processing unit. When combined with a printer, the result is a useful word processing system.

Sinclair ZX81 This is perhaps the smallest, most economical home computer in the world, and though its capacities are limited in basic form, it will accept plug-in memories, a printer, and a cassette player for software. It has 8 K ROM capacity.

Points to look for

What is the capacity of the RAM?

What accessories will it take?

Do these include a printer, disc drive, floppy discs, acoustic coupler, a cassette deck, a voice synthesizer?

Is it black and white or colour?

What is the video resolution of the computer?

What range of software is provided that will be compatible with this computer?

What language is it designed to use?

Is a monitor included with the computer, or must it be connected to a separate TV?

Teletext/Viewdata

Teletext
Teletext is the generic name for all the existing systems which enable the user of a suitable receiver to receive up to 800 pages of computer information on any given channel. The information is inserted into the normal broadcast signal during the 12-line blanking period at the beginning of each frame (in fact only two of the lines are used at present in the UK). This digital information may sometimes be seen, if your receiver is incorrectly set up, as the tiny row of winking white lights across the very top of the screen. At a rate of nearly 7 million bits per second, these systems are able to transmit 800 pages of text every 30 seconds: each page can carry up to 24 rows of 40 characters each. The receiver must be equipped with a suitable decoder, either included with the set or added on. This will usually have a separate key-pad, which will enable a user to select any one of the pages from the Index. The decoder selects the page in question, stores it in its memory and displays it on the screen — the colours may be red, green, blue, cyan, yellow magenta, or white, and the background is normally black.

The possibilities of such a system are enormous. Each page is under permanent review, and can be updated by computer — for instance, a weather forecast or share prices will be absolutely up to the minute; train schedules can be cancelled or changed; theatre availability can be confirmed; and there is even a recipe of the day, based on the daily price of foods. All this depends on the willingness of the TV networks to provide the service, and at present only a few countries have it.
International standards The British system — the world's first — is standard on ITV

Viewdata When teletext is transmitted as part of normal TV broadcast services, there is no charge. However, in viewdata systems connected to the telephone a small charge may be made for each service — in the British Prestel system, for instance (right), 3 pence is charged for a weather forecast, and detailed forecasts are offered for a further small charge. Many thousand pages of such information are available at the touch of a button. This provides an invaluable service for commerce and industry (far right).

ınd BBC (called Oracle and Ceefax, ·espectively), and is transmitted ›ermanently on all three channels. The 'rench decided in favour of their own ystem, called Antiope. Like the British ·ystems, it can provide rather crude ;raphic letters or designs from a mosaic. 3ut the latest entrant, the Canadian system :nown as Telidon, uses an 'alpha-;eometric' system which permits much nore sophisticated graphics. All three ystems are capable of further refinement, .nd it is certain that this will take place very oon.

'iewdata

'iewdata is the collective name for systems 'hich use the domestic receiver to display ata from a central computer, which is onnected to the set either by cable or, most ramatically, through the ordinary telephone. The latter is already in operation in the UK, and it is the Post Office's Prestel. Prestel has a number of advantages over a broadcast-based teletext system: there is no limit to the number of pages that can be held by the central computer; the user can call back to the computer to actually buy goods through his key-pad, charging them either to a credit card or deducting the charge directly from his bank account; the computer may be linked directly to a home computer with restricted coded access provided for security; and there are even the possibilities of electronic mail and elections on the horizon. The disadvantage is the cost of placing the call, and the cost of some of the pages selected – this charge is placed directly on the ordinary phone bill, and the cost reflects the kind of services you have been requesting. Many are free, in which case only the phone call is charged.

Satellite and cable TV

In areas where reception is poor, which may well include inner cities in some countries, the solution is to be found in a cable link. Furthermore, this service may be used to extend the available programmes enormously, if the government permits (as in the USA). The cable companies are fed their various channels via a network of satellites, which beam literally hundreds of channels to earth-stations for distribution through cable. It is highly likely that in future, to cope with the huge bandwidths required for multi-channel broadcasting, optic fibr cable will be used rather than the curren coaxial high-loss cable. But severa domestic users have realized that they ca set up their own earth-stations, bypassin the cable companies entirely. The lega position is complex and far from clea basically the distributors claim that thei programmes are being 'stolen', but it ma be thought that this is like walking nake down the street and then accusing the tow of being peeping toms. In any event, hom earth-stations are now readily available i

the USA, and satellite-coverage will shortly exist in Europe (to the great alarm of national broadcasting organizations, who see their monopolies threatened).

Satellites transmit in the microwave band (3700—4200 MHz) from geo-stationary orbits over 32 000 kilometres (20 000 miles) above the earth, and a fairly large parabolic dish is needed to intercept their transmissions. Originally these were 3 metres (10 feet), but with the higher-power satellites now entering service, one-metre (3-foot) dishes will soon be common. They must be very precisely directed since microwaves are extremely directional. Then a low noise amplifier at the antenna will also be needed, and a receiver to convert the high-frequency microwave FM signal to a lower frequency AM signal that the TV can use. Some systems offer a remote control to swivel and tilt the dish from indoors. The prize for all this hard work is an embarrassment of programme choice and superb, studio-standard reception. Programme quality is sadly unaffected.

Teknik Earth Receiving Station This 1-metre (3-foot) dish is typical of currently available earth-stations for satellite reception. Since microwaves are very highly directional, the dish must be precisely aligned to the particular satellite for which it is intended. Other models may be remotely manoeuvred and in some cases this can be done by computer control.

Intelsat V Modern geo-stationary satellites transmit at considerable powers since the solar-powered panels can now be much larger than on previous satellites, and as a result their 'footprint' on the earth surface can cover several European countries at once. They are very precisely aligned, and transmit in the microwave band.

Future technology

Although the major video revolution has already occurred, and may be said to be well into the post-revolutionary phase, the next decade will undoubtedly see a number of developments that collectively could amount to a second revolution.

Cameras The present trend to ever smaller cameras will continue and, with the introduction of CCD chips, will accelerate. Initially, the new chips will probably run parallel to a new breed of smaller and more sensitive tubes, but it is doubtful if tubes are in the end immune to the onward march of solid-state technology. Shooting in ordinary room lighting will rapidly become normal practice. Black and white cameras will become rarities; and, most crucial of all, more and more portable recorders will become one-piece units (see pp. 74 – 5).

Tape and formats The microvision recorders have been made possible only by the introduction of metal and metal-evaporated tape, which give very high recording density and therefore permit the use of unprecedentedly small cassettes. Three incompatible microvision prototypes have been unveiled in recent years, all with tapes in the region of ¼ inch, plus Technicolor/Funai's ¼-inch system, and three ½-inch systems. The situation is absurd, and it is only to be hoped that a few of these perfectly plausible systems will fall by the wayside. However, the major Japanese manufacturers and Philips have arrived at a basic agreement for the new micro-cassette format, to be called 8 mm video. This could also be used as the basis for a small-scale domestic system. The most vulnerable of the ½-inch formats is perhaps V2000, which will have a hard time making an impact in the USA. What is certain is that the end to miniaturization has barely been glimpsed. The days of the heavy 'portable' are indeed already over.

Recorders It is possible that one-piece portables and normal domestic receivers will grow in parallel (though on different

The Sony Mavica is the first new breed of still video cameras. Each reusable recording disc takes 50 stills, which can be replayed or printed or recorded on tape.

The Sinclair flat-screen TV measures only 10 x 5 x 1.9 cm (4 x 2 x ¾in), with a revolutionary method of bending the electron path to achieve such compactness.

formats), in which case it becomes ever more vital that the provision for editing (a present very poor) on home-based VCRs should be radically improved so that the ful range of the portable's versatility can b exploited. With the newer tap formulations, the quality loss should soo become negligible. Other facilities to b introduced on ½-inch will include 'trick audio dubbing, improved cueing an counter systems, and stereo. X2 repla with intelligible sound will become in creasingly desirable, while noise reductio systems are rapidly becoming the norn already.

Receivers The arrival of stereo broad casting has already brought a whole nev breed of stereo receivers, which in any cas will have superior speakers. Tubes will b

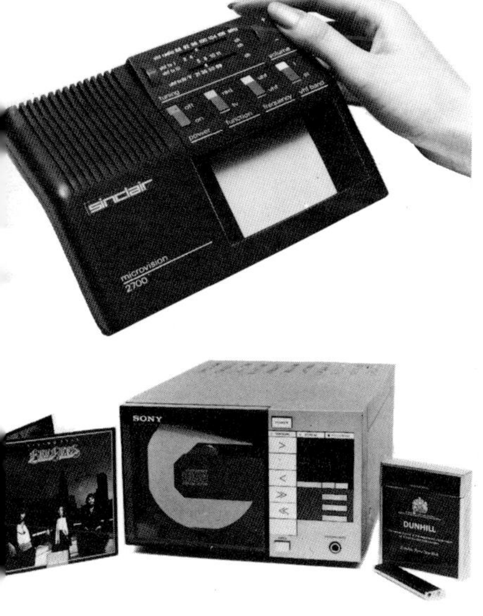

The Sony compact disc digital audio player uses laser-disc technology comparable to that of the Philips video-disc system, giving superb digital sound.

nore compact and brighter but will ventually be replaced by solid-state flat creens which will hang on the wall. These lectro-luminescent screens are under de-elopment and promise to be the biggest ingle advance in this area. Laser-projec-ion screens have also been mooted, giving he brightness to wide-screen projection ystems that they have lacked. Sony has een reported to be experimenting with oice-activated controls for receivers.

Wide-screen video will also spread to ommercial theatres using high-density TV HDTV) masters. This would contain at east twice as many lines as current ystems.

ideograms This is the generic name for ll pre-recorded programmes, whether disc r tape. The crucial question for the future is: will pre-recorded tapes, exorbitantly expensive at present, be able to compete with video discs, which should in theory be much cheaper and better quality? A high-speed duplicating system has been announced, but remains to be proved in practice. If the disc war is speedily resolved (unlikely) and quality is improved, it is very difficult to see how tape can compete in this area, particularly if video-disc derivatives replace the gramophone turntable in audio. In this connection, it is a tragedy that the new Sony/Philips audio laser player is incompatible with the Philips LaserVision video-disc system. If enough people have disc players, they will surely tend to rent or borrow the discs, and (illegally, of course) copy them on to tape, or (for the price of a blank tape) simply buy the cheap disc for themselves. In either case, the future for the pre-recorded tape looks perilous.

Plug-in accessories Since the most common form of plug-in accessories is some form of computer, whether game based or not, there is no limit to what may be routed through the TV screen. What is certain, however, is better graphics for computers and games, with increasing contact between the home computer and very large central computers and data banks. Such systems can already be used for computerized security and surveillance.

Instant still video The Sony Mavica is the first of a generation of still video cameras that, if refined, could well pose the kind of threat to film that video has represented to movie film. The present method uses a spinning disc to record the exposures, but in future the memory could well be solid-state. A printer is under development.

Finally, in the realm of science fiction, it has been seriously suggested that all video recording could be solid-state through the medium of holography, with laser projection of the image in three dimensions. This, however, is an area where no bets are being accepted.

Pre-recorded tapes

Pre-recorded tapes can be bought by any VCR owner in his chosen ½-inch format, although at the moment there is not a wide range available for V2000 users. In VHS or Beta format, however, virtually anything can be obtained. Feature films, including both the latest releases and the bluest pornography, are readily available, though many are pirated (see Videograms and the Law, opposite). But video cassettes are expensive, especially when compared to video discs or the cost of a blank tape, and you might prefer to confine your purchases to those tapes which you will want to watch repeatedly, or on which you could profitably use the freeze-frame facility — instructional tapes, coaching courses, educational programmes, do-it-yoursel lessons, even video instruction manuals.

The reproduction quality of pre-recorde tapes varies wildly: at best, it is excellent; a worst, in a third-generation pirated tape you should return it to the dealer forthwith Pre-recorded tapes remain an attractive bu expensive way of acquiring programmes.

Rental services and video clubs ar clearly more economical, and the modes week-end rental for a 2-hour feature i certainly less than the cost of taking even small family to the cinema. These faciliti are likely to grow rapidly in the future, an if laserdiscs (which are virtually immune t wear) take a hold it may be expected tha video-disc libraries will also spring up.

Videograms and the Law

The law in almost all countries has not kept pace with technology, and the situation is very unclear where videograms are concerned. A pre-recorded tape is usually covered by the copyright of the original programme-maker, unless this has expired.

If the tape is copyrighted, you may legally:

Watch it
Rent it to others
Resell it
Give it away
Show it to family or friends

It is illegal to:

Copy it
Charge an entrance fee for the viewing

The same applies in theory to all taping off air as well as to cable-vision, though the virtual impossibility of enforcing the law even in cases of major piracy, let alone the small-time 'thief', has brought it into some contempt. In particular, it is unclear whether it is illegal to buy a pirated, and therefore 'stolen', cassette.

Piracy Since pre-recorded cassettes are anything up to four times the price of blank ones the inducement to break the law has been considerable. The quality of pirated cassettes is often terrible, and there is no reliable way of identifying them except perhaps by shoddy packaging. The major manufacturers, however, especially in the USA, have found a system to defeat home copying.

Copyguard Copyguard, also known as Videoguard, Stop-Copy, etc. is an anti-piracy signal placed on the control track of pre-recorded tape. It weakens the vertical sync signal so that the tape can, in theory, be played, but cannot be copied on to another recorder without loss of vertical sync. Unfortunately, even playing such tapes on many receivers causes frame-roll, and not all receivers have accessible vertical-hold controls. To make matters worse, some recorders may be used quite successfully as record machines. Finally, devices are available which, placed between replay and record machines, defeat the Copyguard entirely. It is plainly illegal to *use* such devices but not, apparently, to sell them.

Video discs Video-disc manufacturers will be able to ignore the issue, since the discs should be so cheap that there will be no point in copying them on to expensive blank tape. This simple fact should, in a few years, eliminate the entire problem — and perhaps take pre-recorded tapes with it!

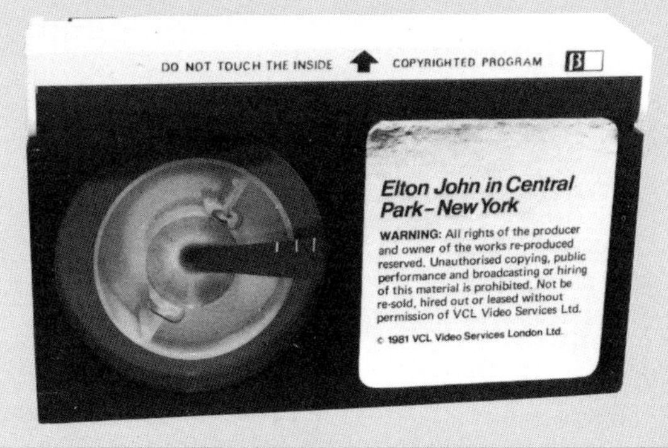

Building a library

For many videophiles, their tapes will be a mixture of pre-recorded tapes, tapes off air, and home tape movies. In all cases, it is good practice to have a sensible yet not too complex indexing system from the very start, even if at first you do not anticipate amassing a large collection. These things have a habit of growing, and can rapidly get to the point when you begin wiping important tapes by mistake. Pre-recorded tapes are very straightforward, and so, up to a point, are family tapes: they can be simply identified according to the subject, tape counter, and duration, and numbered for easy retrieval. Remember, though, that tape counters vary, and if a tape has been recorded on a portable it will almost certainly not correspond to a domestic recorder's counter at a later date. When recording off air, however, the problems are considerably more complex.

Recording off air

Before the question of indexing can even begin to arise, the recording itself must be guaranteed. If the timer is in use, always check before leaving the house that the recorder is switched to Timer and, if applicable, to Record. The tape should have been rewound, zeroed, then wound on to the recording position if you are not starting at the beginning of the tape. Make a note of the counter reading for the beginning of the recording. Allow plenty of leeway for off-air programmes, since they often begin, and therefore end, late.

Conversely, if you are recording a programme on a commercial channel while monitoring it yourself to edit out commercials, remember that less time wil

Cabinets and consoles Tapes can be housed in cabinets that range from 2-cassette size to open-out large-scale wardrobes. The cassettes themselves can be cased in matching 'books', too, if appearances are particularly crucial.

be needed on the tape than the total advertised duration. This consideration is particularly useful in the USA, where commercials may be 20 per cent of the total air-time.

Cataloguing and indexing

The counter The tape counters on all VHS and Beta machines do not operate in real time or in footage: in other words, '100' at the beginning of a 3-hour tape does not correspond in time to '100' at the end. (V2000 machines can offer a valuable real-time readout, however.) Therefore it is vital that in making all counter notes, the tape should have been accurately zeroed at the start, and that the end of the recording should have been noted. Time/counter calculators, at various tape speeds, have been marketed in the USA for both VHS and Betamax systems, and they have their uses in optimizing the use of blank tape. They are not, of course, applicable to European tape speeds, being purely mechanical card-calculators or charts.

Card indexing Make a separate card for each numbered tape, noting the counter numbers, duration, and title of each item, with recording speed if appropriate. On another card, list each title, with a cross-reference to the tape number. This may be one large card if you have fairly few tapes, or you could have a little box-file with a separate card for each item, filed alphabetically, for a larger library. Finally, on the stick-on labels that come with the blank tape, list the contents, with footages. This will need updating and replacement if the tape is used a lot, as will that on the spine of the cassette and cover.

The recording safety tab Every cassette has a safety tab (V2000 has two, one for each side), which can be removed to prevent erasure of a valuable recording. If there is a change of heart, the tab can be taped over with strong adhesive, and the recording can then take place.

Care and maintenance

Head cleaning

Cassette recorders All VCRs tend to accumulate deposits of dirt on the spinning video heads, the static heads, and the rollers. The dirt is an amalgam of oxide, dust, and grease, which is ventilated into the machine with cool air, and after about thirty hours of play this will produce noticeable degradation in the picture – drop-outs, streaking, and video noise. Quite a wide variety of so-called cleaning cassettes are available, but they should be chosen and used with great care since they are all, to a greater or lesser degree, abrasive, and in the process of cleaning the heads the eventual life is always shortened. Indeed, they may not be a good idea at all on older machines, where manual cleaning should be considered (see below). The cassette is inserted into the machine, and played for a few seconds only. Some cleaning cassettes are absorbent, and they can be soaked in a solvent (usually called TCTFE) which is highly effective at gently removing deposits.

Reel-to-reel: manual cleaning The manual method used for reel-to-reel recorders (VTRs) may also be used for VCRs, but

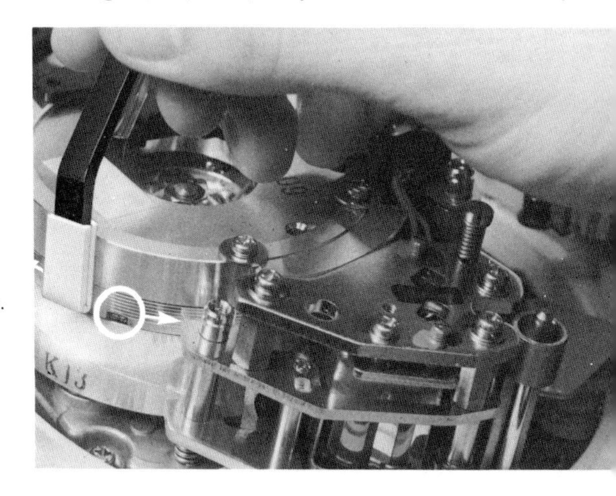

Head cleaning It is essential when cleaning video tapes that the swab should be moved horizontally in the line of the tape path. The swab should never be moved vertically up and down over the video heads or they may be permanently damaged. In general a cleaning cassette is a perfectly satisfactory solution for cassette recorders.

Demagnetizers After several hundred hours of use the heads may become permanently magnetized. Use a demagnetizer, but be sure not to scratch the heads by metal-to-head contact. The demagnetizer should be switched on, placed in close proximity to the head, then drawn very slowly away.

only if you are a skilled, meticulous worker. In particular, always disconnect the mains, be careful not to drop screws into the works, and if in any doubt, have the job done professionally. Suffice it to say that the top cover must be removed to gain access to the heads — to be more specific is impossible in view of the wide variety of machines. However, the following is a likely procedure; remove the Tracking knob; press Eject; unscrew all the Philips screws from the top cover, and carefully lift it clear. You should now have access to the heads, and from here on the principles are the same as for VTRs, in which the heads are always accessible. (When cleaning VTRs, however, the function lever should be placed in the REW or FF mode.)

Dip the swab into the cleaning solution, and very gently wipe it *horizontally only,* to and fro across the heads. This movement must only be in the same plane as the tape travel. The video erase, audio, and control track heads may be cleaned in the same way, as may the capstan and tape guides. If, in the case of a VCR, the top cover has been removed, take care not to drop any screws when replacing it.

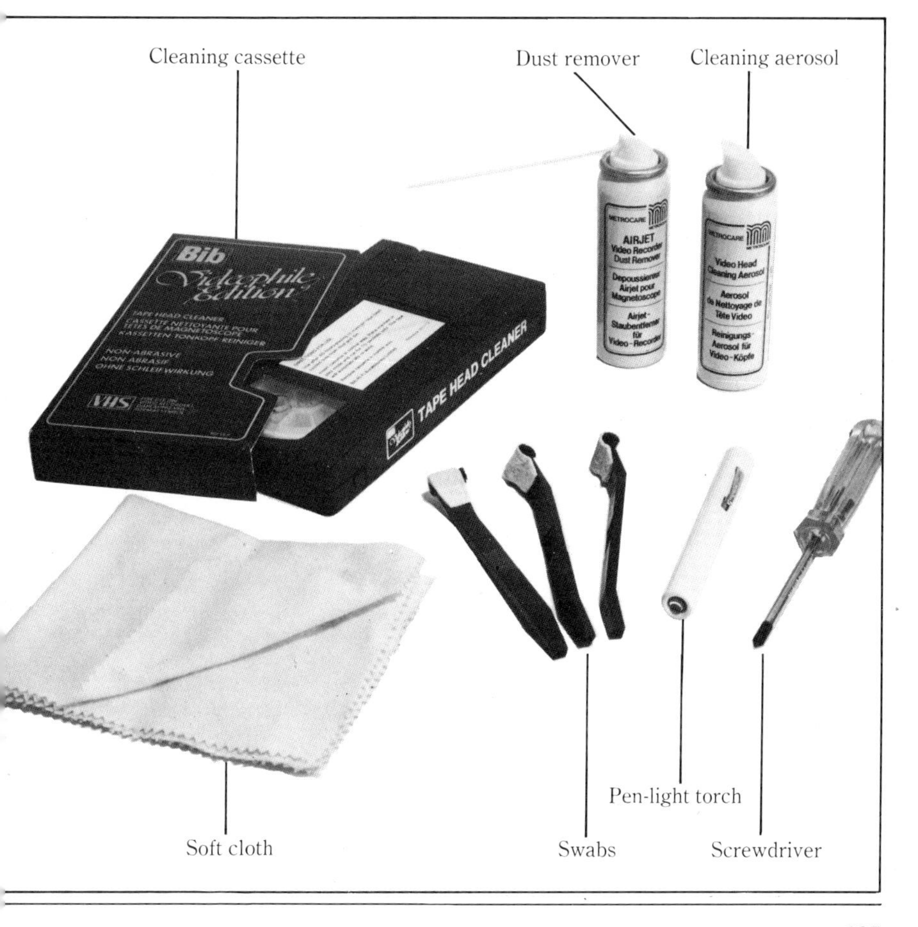

Though repair procedures are described below for ½-inch tape, they should be regarded as the very last resort: nothing is worth the possibility of damage to the heads. It is far better to avoid the necessity for repair altogether, and the first requirement is to purchase only top-brand cassettes. This is especially true if your machine offers slow motion and freeze-frame, which cause a lot of wear on the tape oxide. If the oxide separates, the tape will be noisy, and the same effect can be caused by allowing dust to get into the cassette: always keep cassettes in their cases, and always stand them upright to prevent misalignment of the tape. They should be preserved from the heat — the top of a hot amplifier or the back shelf of a car are lethal. Conversely, if you are moving from very cold to warm, humid conditions, the tape may develop condensation, with highly unpleasant consequences — let it warm up for an hour or so before use. Keep tapes well clear of powerful magnetic fields such as are to be found on the top of large speaker systems; try not to leave the tape on Pause for too long; and *never* touch the tape except in dire emergency: the grease from your fingers will in the end attract dust that could snarl up the tape.

If all these precautions fail, and the tape does break, it can be repaired, but *only with proper video splicing tape.* With a narrow Philips screwdriver, remove the screws on the underside of the cassette. Press the front panel release catch and open the front panel. Now carefully lift off the top panel, exposing the tape. Cut out all the damaged tape, and overlap the two ends in parallel. Hold them firmly together, and cut them with scissors, butt-joining them with the splicing tape; it must not go on the oxide side of the tape. Lastly, trim the splicing tape of all overlap, rewind it into the cassette, and, having made sure the tape is correctly threaded through the tape guides, replace the top lid.

The above method may also be used for ¾-inch cassettes and open-reel tape. In all cases, avoid touching the tape more than is absolutely necessary — cotton gloves would be ideal — and be sure that the two ends of tape meet precisely, without either overlap or daylight between them. The only certain way of obtaining this perfect match is to use a splicing block. Note that if the tape contains a recording, physical splicing will entail temporary loss of picture, since the flow of sync pulses will almost certainly have been gravely interrupted by the edit.

Care of equipment

Lenses They should never be cleaned with a cloth, and even lens tissues or special lens cloths should only be used for really stubborn smears that cannot be blown away with a blower or compressed air, nor brushed away with a squirrel's-hair brush. If you do use them, be careful not to grind dirt into the delicate coating on the lens. *Never* touch a lens, and use the lens cap when the camera is not in use.

Camera cases It is worth investing in a decent camera case, to preserve the camera from both shock and scratching. For real shock protection, use a heavy-duty aluminium case with a custom-cut foam interior.

Microphone care
Microphones should be handled gently, since severe shock, or even consistent rough handling, can damage the element. They should be preserved from excessive heat or humidity, and you should beware of leaving batteries for too long in an electret condenser mike.

Filters These always come in their own case (if new) which provide ample protection, but are fiddly if you are working rapidly. A filter box can be useful, into which all the filters can be slotted for speedy access. This would only apply if you were using a fairly large number of filters, which is rare in video work. Filters must be cleaned with the same meticulousness.

Tape splicing

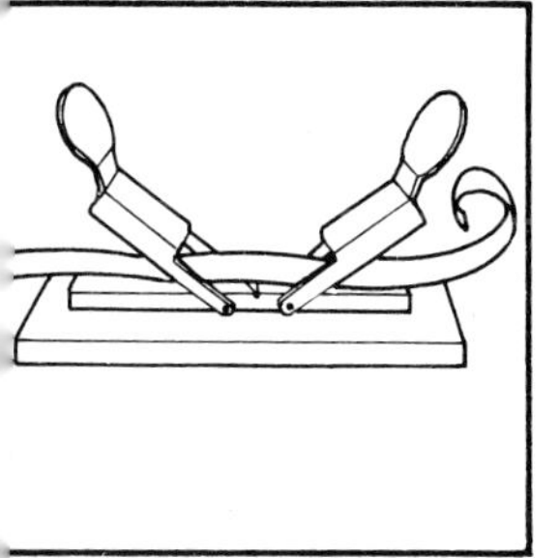

Remove the locking clamps
rom the splicer. Place a piece
f recording tape from the left
glossy side up) across the
plicer. Lower and lock the
eft clamp.

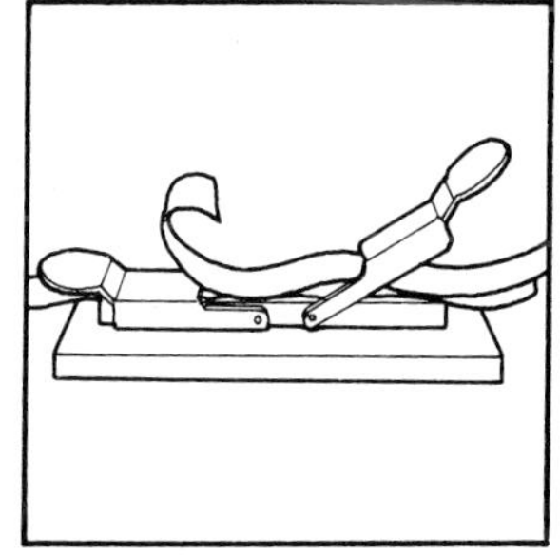

2 Lay the right-hand tape across the splicer so that the free end clears the diagonal slit. Lower and lock the right clamp.

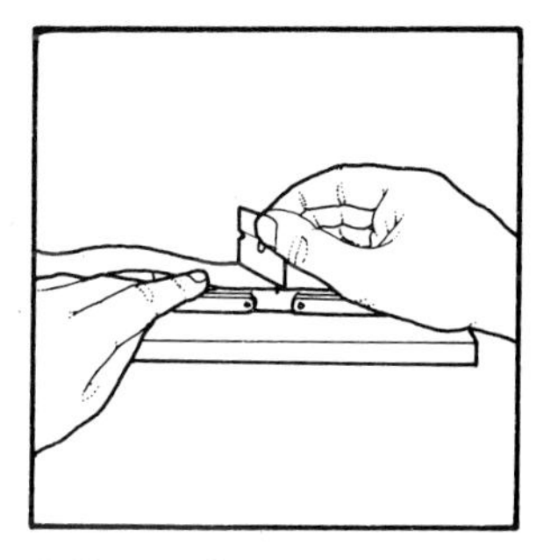

3 Place a finger on the tape to the left of the diagonal slit. Draw the cutter across the slit and remove surplus tape.

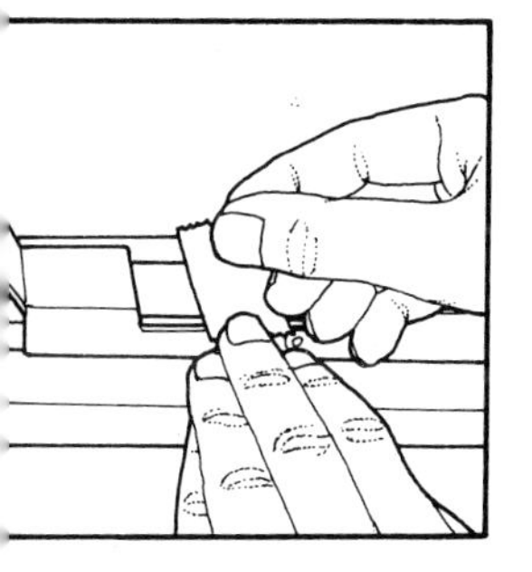

Place a short piece of
plicing tape across the cut
nds of the recording tape.
ress it down firmly.

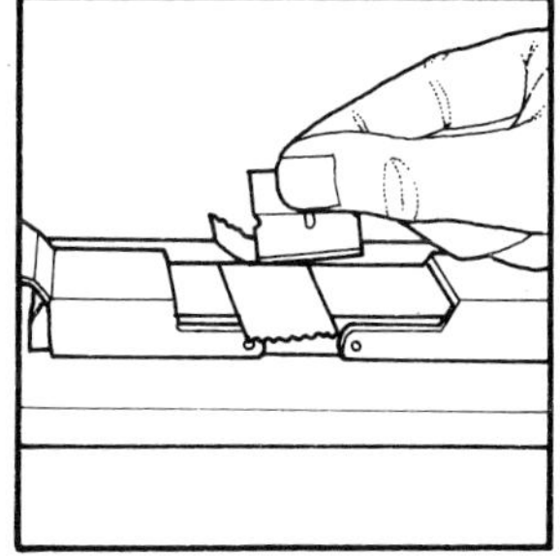

5 Cut the two lateral slits each side of the recording tape. Remove the surplus splicing tape. Lift the clamps and remove the jointed tape.

Plugs and cables

VIDEO PLUGS

UHF The basic European aerial socket and plug, used as the RF connector between VCR and receiver, with a 75-ohm coaxial cable. There is no screw thread on this fitment.

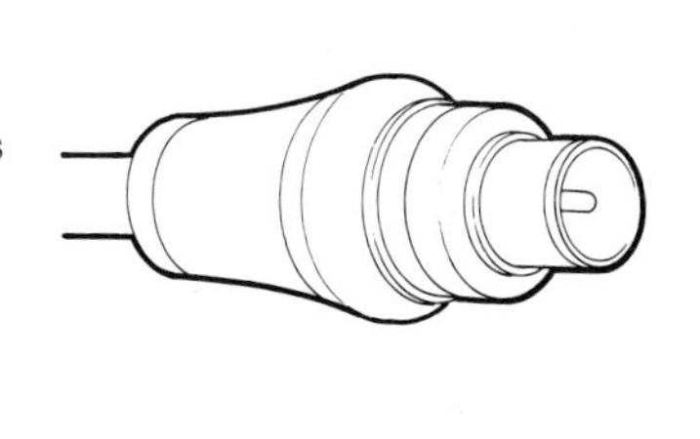

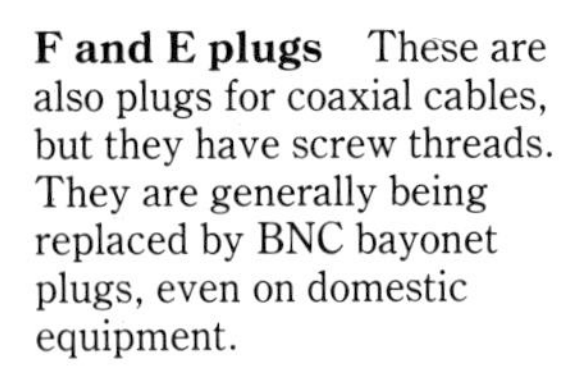

F and E plugs These are also plugs for coaxial cables, but they have screw threads. They are generally being replaced by BNC bayonet plugs, even on domestic equipment.

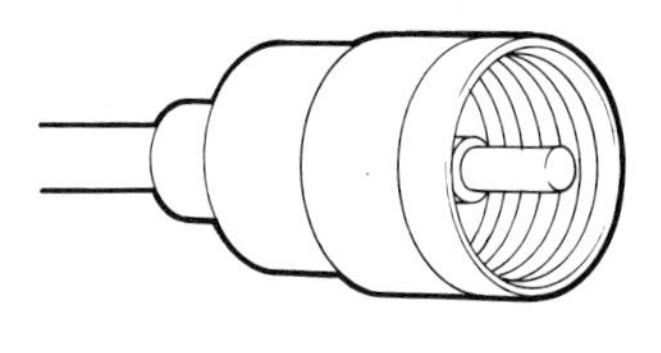

BNC BNC plugs are also used for coaxial cable, but have sturdy bayonet fittings. They are becoming standard as Video In/Out sockets, especially in Europe.

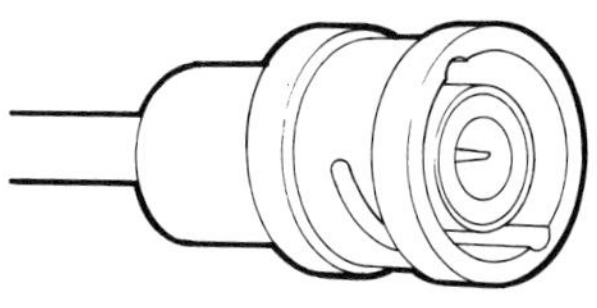

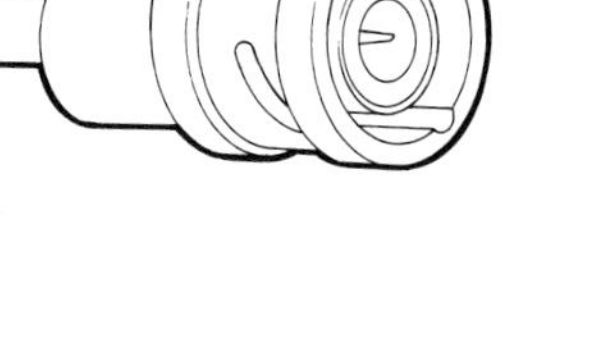

F pin connectors F plugs can sometimes have hexagonal as well as hurled ends for the screw mount. They too are designed for coaxial cable (RG — 59U, in the USA).

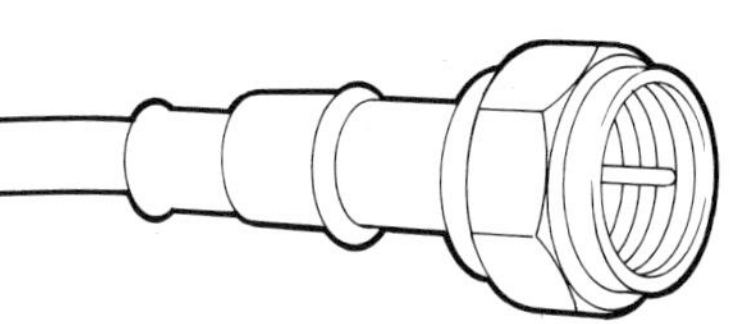

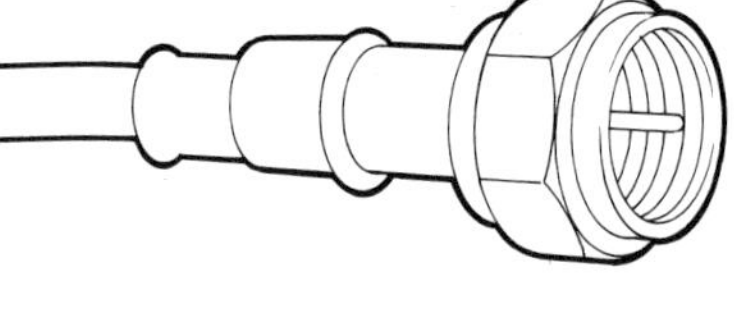

300-ohm twin feeder The twin-feeder cable, with a resistance of 300 ohms, standard for receivers in the USA and Japan, where the principal channels are in the VHF range.

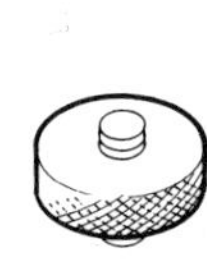

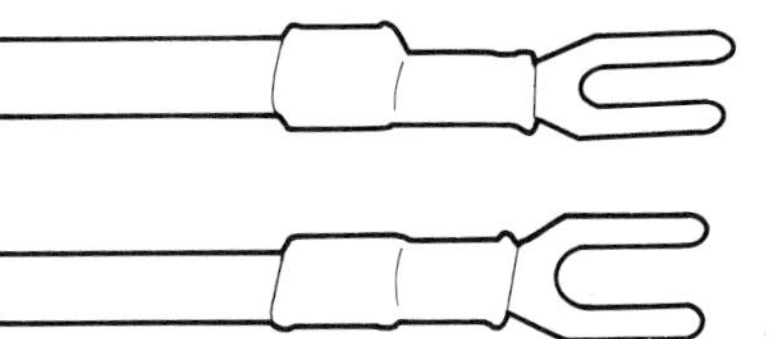

Converter To convert a 75-ohm coaxial feed to a 300-ohm twin feeder, a converter may be fitted.

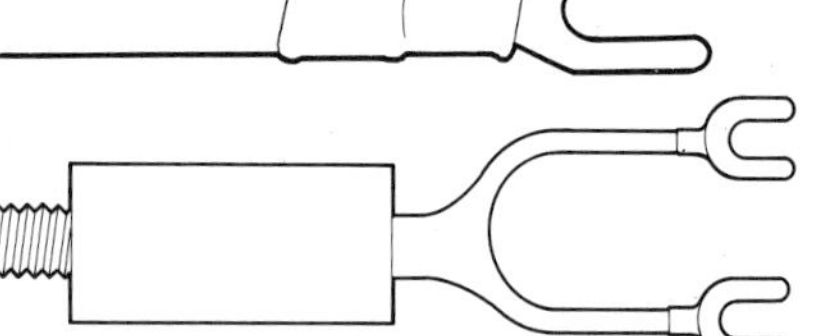

COMPOSITE PLUGS

8-pin This is the standard connector between VTRs and monitors. It carries all video and audio in/out connectors.

10-pin Multi-pin plugs – usually 10-, sometimes 14-pin – are nowadays often used to connect cameras to VCRs, whether portable or static. They lock with a screw thread. Though somewhat fragile and expensive, they are the ideal way of connecting a camera, since they incorporate all necessary functions in one cord.

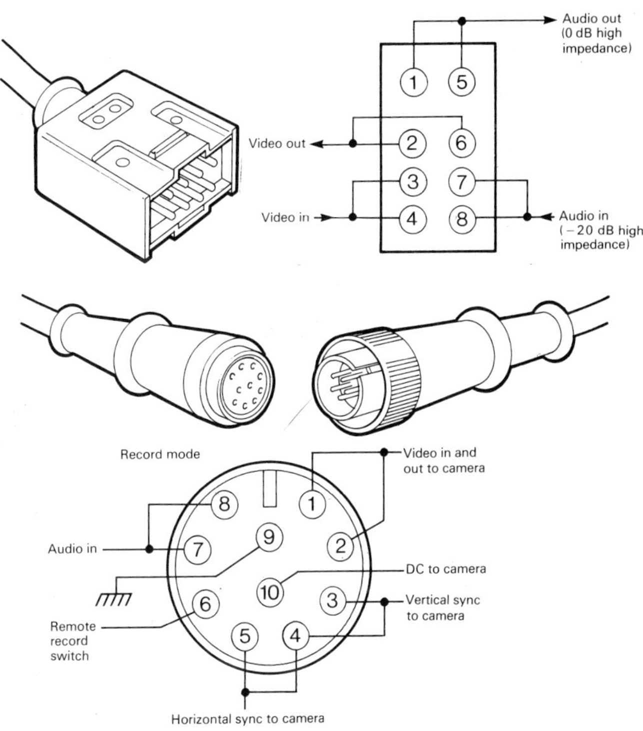

AUDIO PLUGS

5-pin DIN This is most commonly used as the Audio In/Out plug on the rear of a VCR. It is also used for video functions on Philips/Grundig.

RCA/Phono These are standard in hi-fi, and each carries one audio channel only, through thin coaxial cable. They may be needed for an Audio In socket on the rear of a VCR.

Jack/¼-inch Phono
Small jacks may be used on some machines (e.g. U-Matic) for connection to the Audio input of a monitor. Larger jacks are used for headphones and other audio connections.

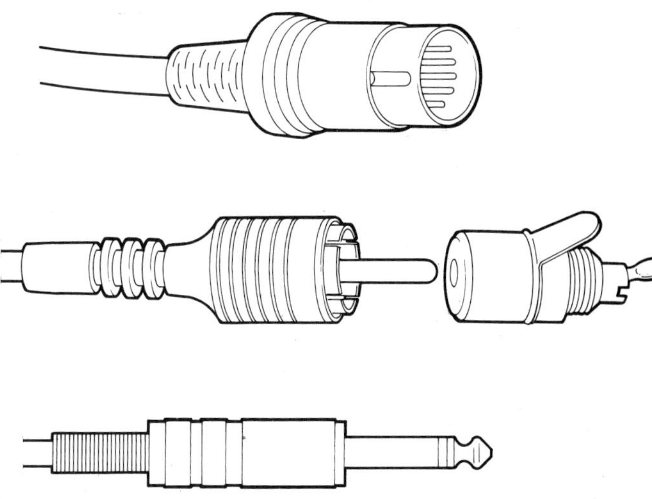

Connections: Playback & recording

Installing a VCR The aerial is plugged into the VCR. A coaxial lead runs from the RF Out socket on the VCR to the aerial socket on the receiver. Both receiver and VCR are connected to an AC power supply. NTSC receivers usually accept 300-ohm twin feeders.

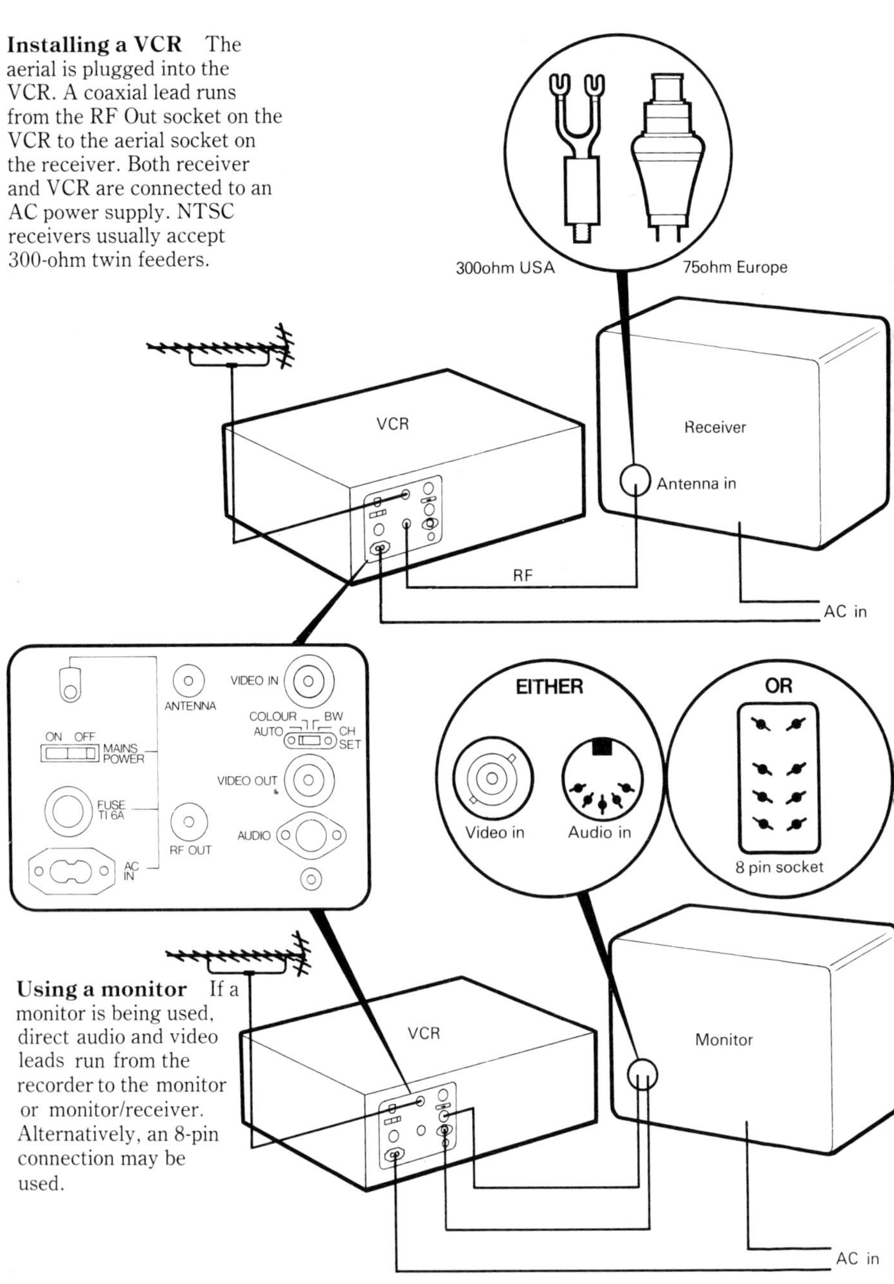

Using a monitor If a monitor is being used, direct audio and video leads run from the recorder to the monitor or monitor/receiver. Alternatively, an 8-pin connection may be used.

;amera recording For
:amera recording, the
implest connection is the
nulti-pin, which may be 10- or
.4-pin, according to make.
This unites all the functions,
ncluding audio and video
n/out, remote pause, and DC
)ower. Alternatively, these
unctions may be separately
vired into the appropriate
ockets. Sound, too, may be
ed into the Audio In socket,
vhich will normally override
he in-camera mike.

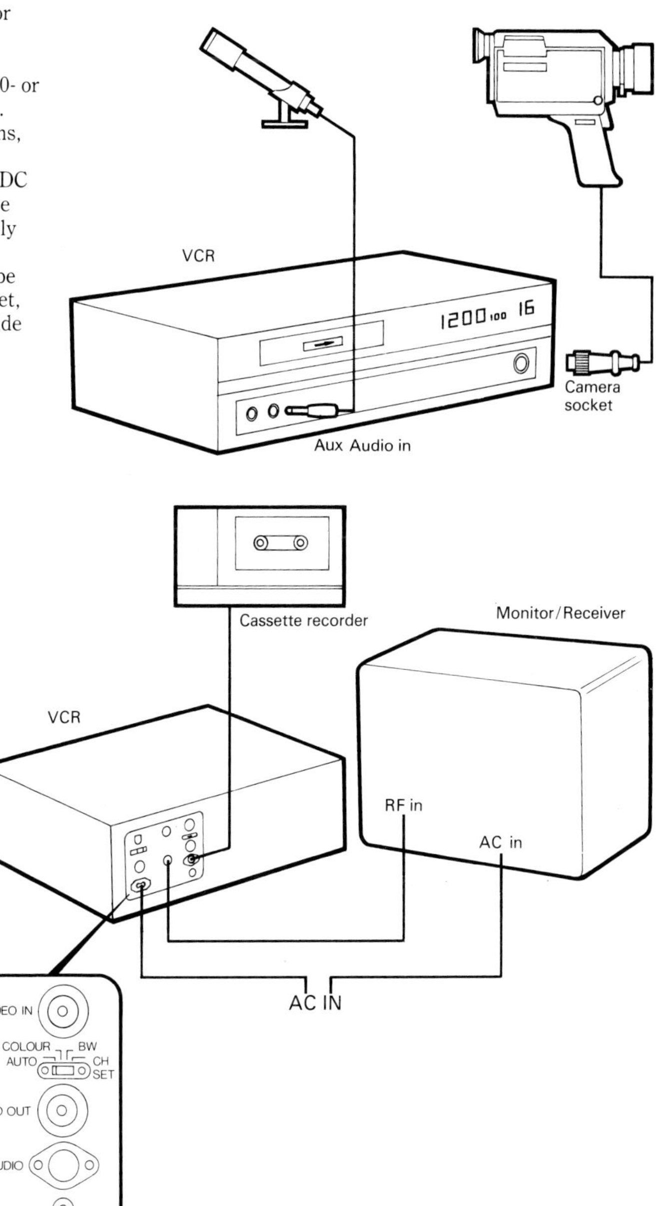

Copying & audio dubbing

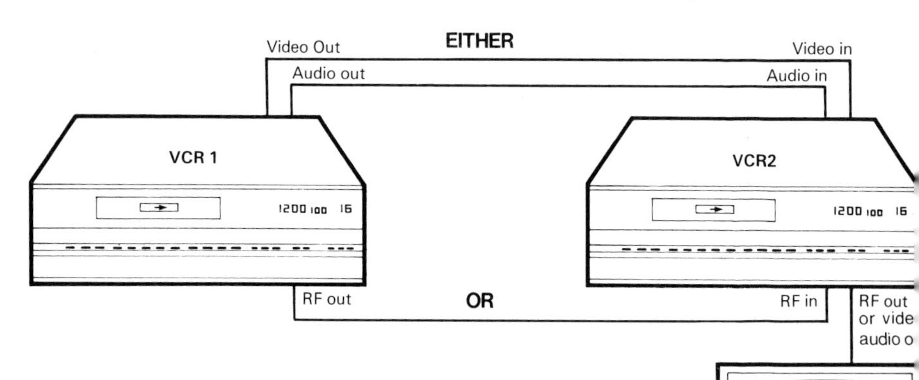

Copying from one VCR to another For straightforward copying from one VCR to another it is advisable to use the video and audio outputs rather than the rf connection. The latter introduces an extra complexity and therefore tends to result in some loss of quality, but if the rf connector is used the record machine must be tuned to the playback machine as though the playback machine were itself a broadcast channel.

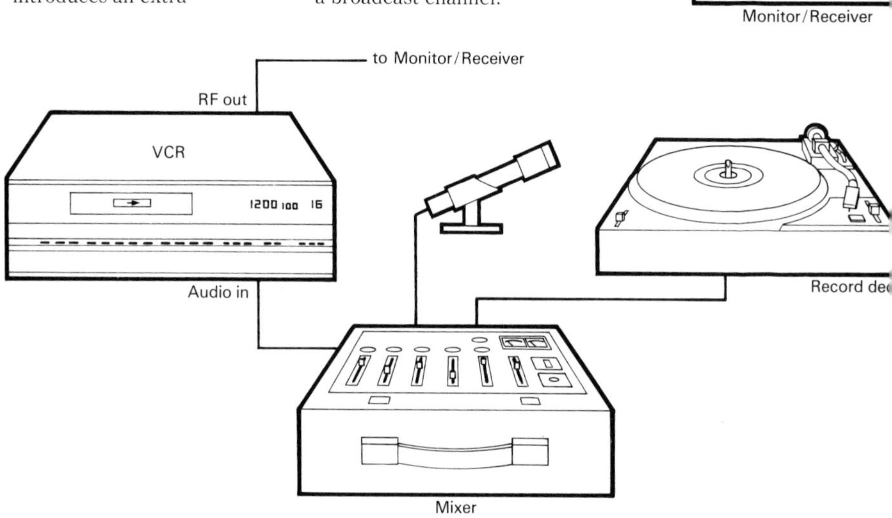

Audio dubbing When dubbing on to a VCR the audio signal which will replace the original track may be a single source, in which case it can go directly into the Audio In socket, or it may be composed of many sources, in which case it should be passed through a mixer. An equalizer can also be introduced to modify the tonal range of the sound track. On all current ½-inch VCRs audio dubbing involves the total erasure of the previous track.

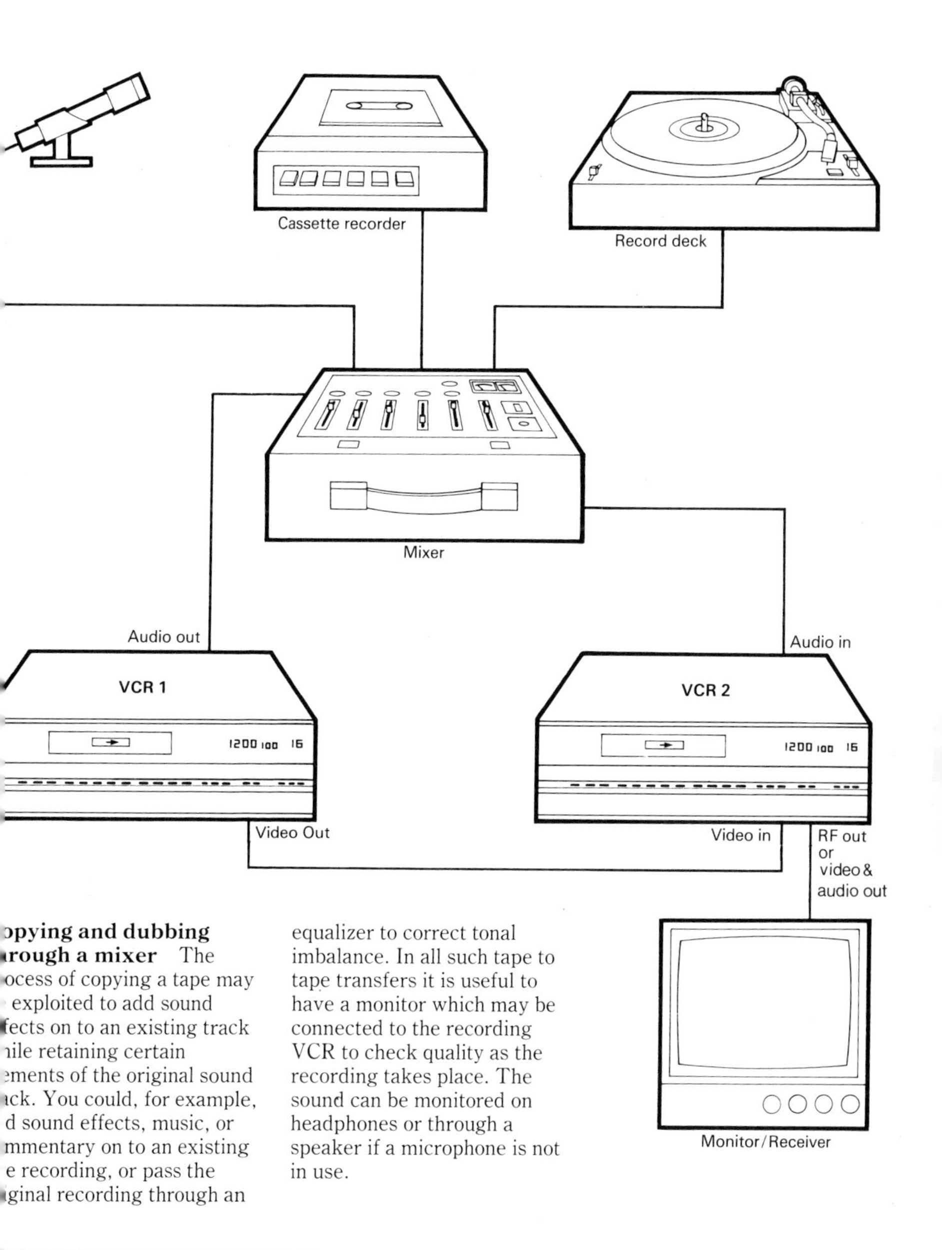

ɔpying and dubbing ɿrough a mixer The ocess of copying a tape may exploited to add sound fects on to an existing track ıile retaining certain ɜments of the original sound ıck. You could, for example, d sound effects, music, or mmentary on to an existing e recording, or pass the ıginal recording through an equalizer to correct tonal imbalance. In all such tape to tape transfers it is useful to have a monitor which may be connected to the recording VCR to check quality as the recording takes place. The sound can be monitored on headphones or through a speaker if a microphone is not in use.

Editing

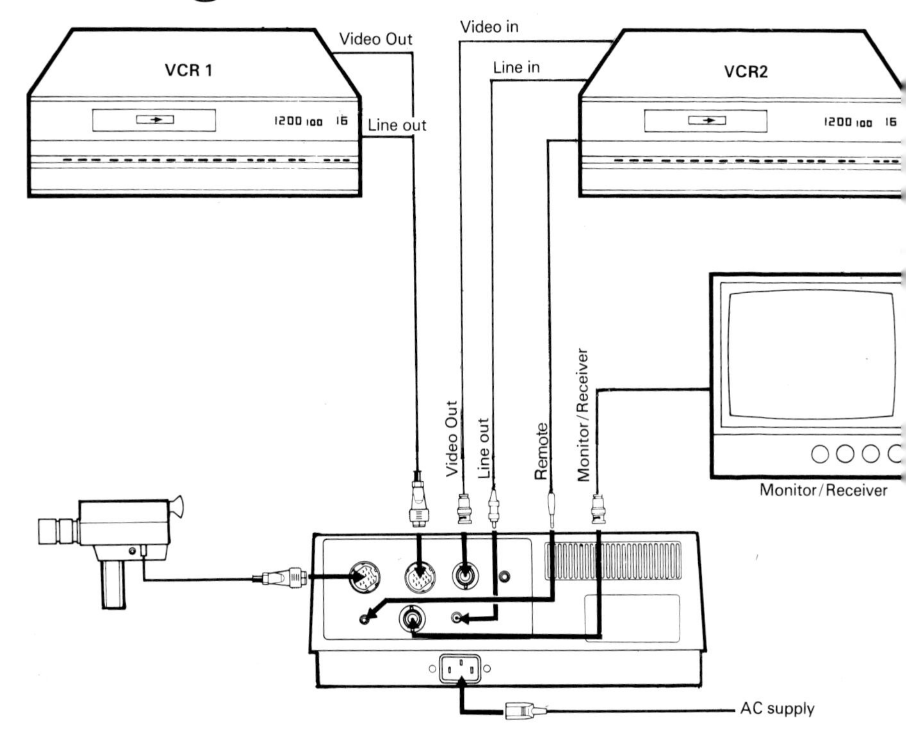

Editing controller An editing controller can be used to combine the output of a VCR and a camera. The resulting output may be monitored and fed to a second VCR.

?ortables & Tuner/Timer

ortable VCR and tuner/ mer A tuner/timer unit ·ovides all the in/out sockets at are available on a normal CR, and in addition has a 2-volt DC outlet to power, or ·charge, a portable recorder. he aerial should be plugged to the tuner/timer (as on a CR), and from there an RF video/audio feed can pass a receiver or monitor, spectively. The RF feed is ore likely to be 75-ohm axial in the European untries, while USA ceivers tend to accept 00-ohm twin feeders, for hich a converter may be quired in some cases.

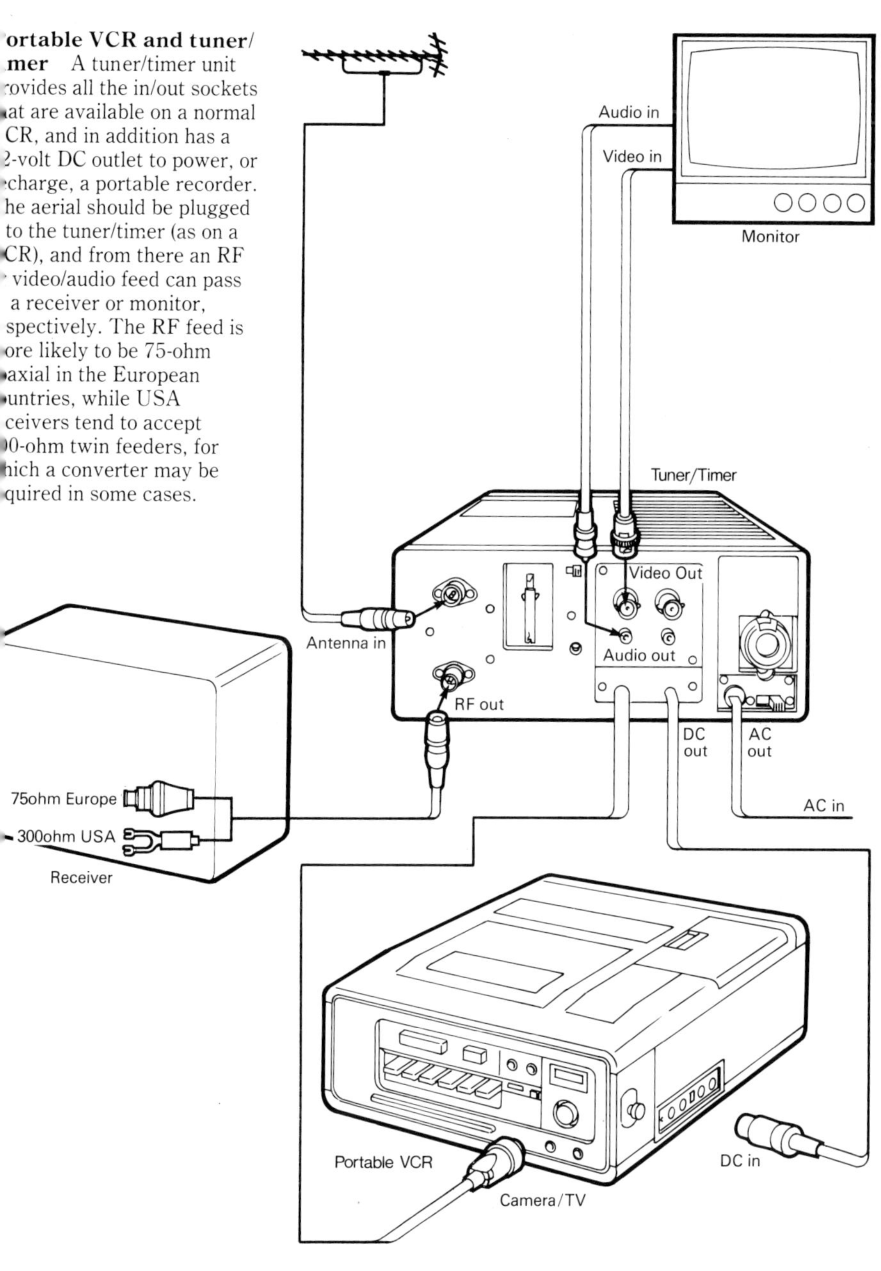

Tables: International standards

The world's TV systems vary in four fundamental respects: line voltage; AC frequency (and therefore frame rate); the number of lines per frame; and the choice of colour encoding system. Added to this, domestic recorders in Europe run at different speeds from US/Japanese models, and the tapes are therefore not compatible. In fact, no 50 Hz tape is compatible with a 60 Hz machine, and vice versa. Portab recorders may be used anywhere since they run off DC, but a transforme may be needed for the AC adaptor if foreig voltages do not match. SECAM may b viewed on a PAL receiver in black an white only, and vice versa. Within the limit of PAL and SECAM there are minc variations in certain countries.

	UK/Europe	**USA/Japan**
Power supply	210–40 V	110–20 V
Frequency	50 Hz	60 Hz
TV standards		
System Scan lines	PAL (France: SECAM) 625	NTSC 525
Field frequency	50 Hz	60 Hz
Bandwidth	5.5 MHz	4 MHz
Line frequency	15.625 kHz	15.75 kHz
Picture frequency	1/25 sec	1/30 sec
Colour subcarrier frequency	4.43 MHz	3.58 MHz
Video standards		
Frequency band	UHF (channels 21–68)	VHF (channels 1–13) UHF (channels 21–68)

Note UK transmissions on 405-line VHF still take place in black and white.

Tape times and speeds

	Track width (μm)	UK/Europe Speed	UK/Europe Time	USA/Japan Speed	USA/Japan Time
VHS	49	2.34 cm/sec (0.92 ips)	3 h, 4 h	SP LP SLP	2 h 4 h 6 h
Betamax	33	1.873 cm/sec (0.74 ips)	3¼ h	(X1, obsolete) X2 X3	 3 h 20 min 5 h
V 2000	23	2.44 cm/sec (0.96 ips)	2 x 4 h	Not yet launched	

International TV standards

PAL

Argentina
Australia
Austria
Belgium
Brazil
Bulgaria
Canary Islands
Cyprus
Czechoslovakia
Denmark
Egypt
Finland
Germany
Ghana
Gibraltar
Greece
Guadeloupe
Hungary
Iceland
India
Indonesia
Iraq
Israel
Italy
Jamaica
Kenya
Kuwait
Lebanon
Liberia
Malta
Mauritius
Netherlands
Nigeria
Norway
Poland
Rhodesia
Romania
Sierra Leone
Singapore
Spain
Sweden
Switzerland
Syria
Turkey
United Kingdom
USSR
Venezuela

SECAM

Algeria
Belgium
France
Luxembourg
Monaco
Morocco
Tunisia

NTSC

Bermuda
Canada
Chile
Colombia
Costa Rica
Cuba
Dominican Republic
Ecuador
El Salvador
Guatemala
Haiti
Hawaii
Honduras
Iran
Japan
Korea
Libya
Mexico
Nicaragua
Panama
Peru
Phillippines
Portugal
Saudi Arabia
Thailand
Trinidad & Tobago
Uruguay
USA

Focal length/angle of view

⅔-inch vidicon tube

The angle of view for any given lens is determined by the focal length and by the size of the tube. The longer the focal length, the narrower the angle of view; and the larger the tube, the wider the angle of view for a given focal length. The focal length and angle of view are shown here for ⅔-inch and 1-inch tubes. Most domestic cameras have ⅔-inch tubes.

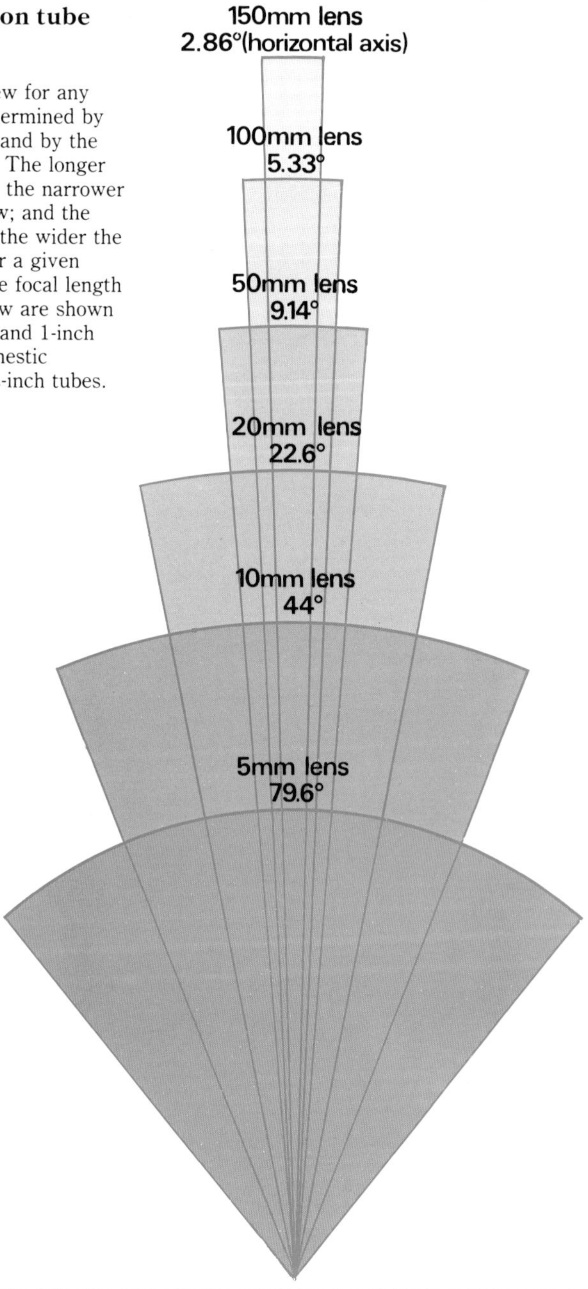

-inch vidicon tube

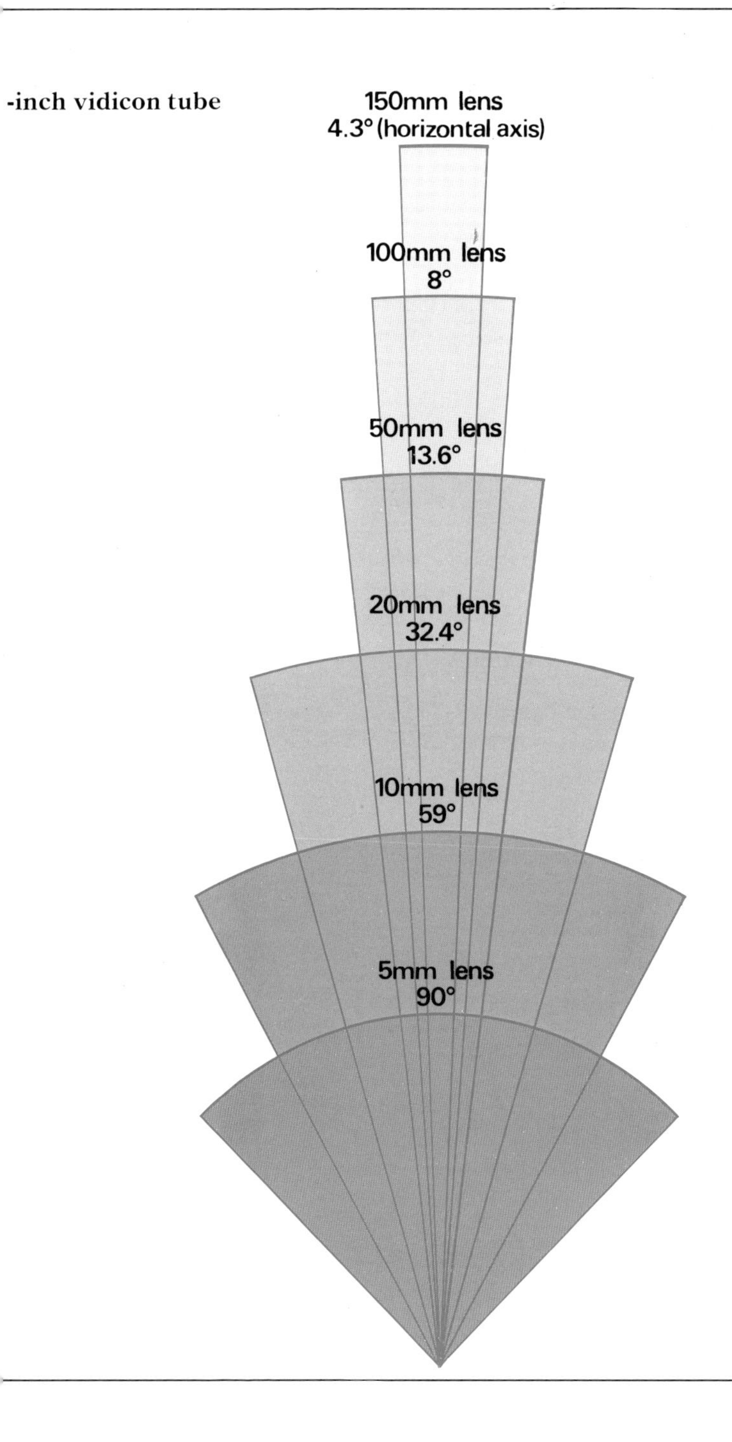

Glossary of technical terms

AGC *see* Automatic Gain Control.

Alternating current or line voltage This may be at a frequency of 50 Hz (Europe) or 60 Hz (USA, Japan, and certain other countries).

Aperture Adjustable opening, known as the iris, which controls the amount of light reaching the vidicon tube. The aperture is calibrated in f-stops.

Aperture grille The masking screen on Sony Trinitron receivers and monitors. It serves the same function as a shadow mask.

Assembly editing A method of electronic editing in which shots are rearranged one after the other to form a coherent sequence.

Attenuator A device for reducing the strength of any electrical signal.

Audio A general term for the sound portion of a composite sound/video signal.

Audio head A magnetic recording head that records or replays sound.

Audio-in The jack that delivers an audio signal to a recorder or mixer.

Audio mixer A circuit that permits several sound inputs to be mixed on to a composite track. Their relative levels may be adjusted in the process.

Audio-out The audio output jack or socket.

Automatic Gain Control (AGC) An electronic circuit that automatically controls audio or video input levels during recording.

Auxiliary-in (Aux) An audio line input.

Auxiliary-out An audio line output.

Azimuth The angle of a given recording head in relation to the video or audio track.

Barn doors Metal flaps fitted in front of a lamp. They can be adjusted to give selective illumination.

Betamax The Sony ½-inch video cassette format, also known as Beta format.

Black level That portion of a video signal which determines pure black in the video image.

Blanking That period of time during the TV scanning of the raster when the beam is shut off as it returns to scan the next line on either camera tube or receiver.

Blues A common term for blue light filters.

Bounce Light reflected off wall or ceiling.

Bus One complete channel of a video or audio system. Frequently used of switchers and Special Effects Generators.

Cannon connector A high-quality secure audio jack also known as an XLR plug.

Capstan The roller in the VTR that governs the speed of the tape transport.

Capstan servo A method of controlling the speed of one recorder by linking the capstan speed to that of a master machine – used extensively in electronic editing.

Cardioid A heart-shaped microphone response.

CCU Camera Control Unit.

Charge-Coupled Device (CCD) A solid-state electronic silicon chip which performs similar functions to the vidicon tube but which is much smaller.

Chroma The hue or saturation of colour in a video signal.

Chroma key The electronic replacement of one colour in a given scene by another video input – the colour is usually blue.

C-mount A standard screw thread for 16 mm cameras, also found on video cameras with interchangeable lenses.

Coaxial cable A single-ground one-conductor cable frequently used for video connections. It has a resistance of 75 ohms.

olour burst A very ccurately phased burst of igh frequency at the eginning of each scanning ne. This determines the olour of the signal.

omposite sync The omplete sync containing both orizontal and vertical sync ignals.

ontrast ratio The range f brightness between the ghtest and darkest objects in given scene.

ontrol track The track long the length of tape which ontains speed control pulses.

ontrol track head The tationary head which lays the ontrol track during ecording.

opyguard One of several atent systems to prevent a re-recorded tape being opied.

ue An electronic signal laced on a tape to indicate an diting point or the beginning f a recording.

b *see* Decibel.

C Direct current. In atteries for use on portables is is commonly 12 volts.

C restoration A circuit, ometimes known as black vel clamp, which ensures a ll tonal range.

Decibel (dB) A logarithmic unit which expresses ratios of powers, voltages, and currents. The scale is logarithmic. It is commonly used for signal-to-noise ratios and for the evaluation of sound volume.

Depth of field The range of distances within which a subject is in acceptably sharp focus at any given aperture and focal length.

Dichroic mirrors Mirrors commonly used in cameras which allow some colours to pass, while others are reflected.

Dipole The simplest form of primitive aerial.

Dropout A defect of tape or signal that causes momentary interruption to audio or video.

Earth-station A dish for reception of satellite communication.

EFP *see* Electronic Field Production.

EIAJ Electronic Industries Association of Japan. They established the standard ½-inch helical scan reel-to-reel format in both colour and black and white.

Eight-pin connector A standard connecting jack between VTRs and monitors providing full in-out audio-video connections.

Electron gun The device inside a camera or receiver which fires electrons at the surface of the cathode ray tube.

Electronic Field Production The use of small, high-quality recording equipment for purposes other than news gathering.

Electronic viewfinder A camera viewfinder in which the image is generated by a cathode ray tube rather than optically.

Encoding Electronic circuitry which combines three colour signals into one composite video signal.

ENG Electronic News Gathering.

Erase head The head on a recorder (either static or rotating) which erases a previous signal on a tape during recording.

Field Half of a complete TV picture. Two fields when interlaced combine to make one frame.

Flyback The period during scanning when the electron beam returns rapidly to the beginning of the next line.

Flying erase head An erase head which is incorporated in the rotating disc of a recorder. Essential for perfect electronic editing.

Focal length The distance between the optical centre of a lens and the surface of the tube when the lens is set at infinity.

Foot-candles The illumination from one candle power falling on one square foot pure white surface at a distance of one foot.

Frame A complete TV picture, being comprised of two interlaced fields. The frame is either 625 lines (Europe) or 525 lines (USA/Japan) scanned respectively in 1/25 sec or 1/30 sec.

Frame rate The frequency at which these frames appear.

Frequency The number of times an electrical signal vibrates per second expressed in Hertz (Hz).

Fresnel A lens of stepped construction used in lighting to minimize physical weight and dimensions.

Front porch Period of time in the video signal which precedes the line sync pulse.

F-stop Number which indicates the relative aperture of a lens at different iris settings. The higher the f-number the smaller the iris setting.

Gain The degree of amplification of an electrical signal.

Gel Gelatin. Commonly used for orange filters on windows or blue filters on lights.

Generation Duplicating for recording from an original. The fidelity of any recording is described in times of first, second, or third generation, etc.

Genlock The locking or enslaving of one or more recording systems to the sync of a master recorder or Special Effects Generator.

Guard bands The gaps between video tracks on a tape which prevent 'cross-talk'.

Helical scan The recording system common to all except 2-inch Quad machines in which a rotating drum records a long diagonal series of tracks from the video heads on a laterally moving tape.

Hertz (Hz) The frequency per second of any electrical signal.

High-band A video recording system with very high-frequency response and consequently excellent quality.

Horizontal resolution The number of vertical lines that can be observed by camera or receiver in a horizontal direction on a test chart.

Horizontal sync The sync pulses that control the line-by-line scanning of the target.

Image enhancer An accessory for sharpening the video image.

Insert The replacement of part of one video image by another.

Insert edit The introduction by electronic editing of one scene into the middle of an existing recording.

Iris The diaphragm in the lens which controls the intensity of light reaching the tube.

Kelvin (°K) Unit of colour temperature of light.

Keying The matteing of one video image over another.

Key light The light which principally illuminates a given scene.

Kilohertz (kHz) A thousand cycles.

Lag Image retention on a camera tube when shooting at low levels of illumination.

Lavalier microphone A 'personal' microphone worn around the neck.

Line frequency The number of horizontal lines scanned in one second: 15.62 kHz in UK and Europe, 15.75 kHz in USA.

Low-band A low-frequency colour recording technique commonly used on ½-inch machines.

Lumen A standard unit of luminous flux.

Lux One lumen per square metre (1 foot-candle equals 10.76 lux).

Macro lens A close-up lens capable of very high magnification.

Matrix Electronic circuit that combines several electronic signals.

Matte box A device on the front of the camera to contain filters or other special effects devices.

Megahertz (MHz) A million Hertz.

Mistracking Incorrect tape-to-head contact or tape-path contact causing picture distortion as bursts of noise on replay.

Mixer A device for combining several audio or video inputs.

Modulation The process of adding video and audio signals to a pre-determined carrier frequency.

Neutral density filter A filter which reduces the brightness of a scene without affecting its colour balance.

Ni-Cad Nickel cadmium rechargeable batteries.

Norelco The name under which the Philips organization trades in the USA.

NTSC National Television System Committee of the Federal Communications Commission. Commonly used to describe the USA/Japanese colour system.

Octopus cable A multi-plug cable with a number of jacks at one or both ends for interfacing video equipment.

Oscilloscope Cathode ray tube connected to electronic test device for aligning video equipment.

Oxide The magnetic particles that record sound and vision on conventional tape. Now being replaced by metal and metal-evaporated formulations.

PAL Phase Alternation Line. The European standard colour system except for France.

Pan The horizontal (panoramic) movement of a camera.

Picture-search The rapid scanning in vision only of a recorded tape.

Plumbicon tube A high-quality lead-oxide tube much used in professional broadcasting.

Pre-roll The process of running two tapes in sync in preparation for an electronic edit.

Quadruplex (Quad) A video recording system on 2-inch tape using four rotating video heads at right angles to the direction of tape travel.

Quartz lighting High-intensity lighting using quartz halogen bulbs.

Raster The pattern formed by the scanning spot of a TV system.

RF Radio Frequency.

RF adaptor A modulator for converting video and audio signals into radio frequency for replay on a conventional receiver.

Rotary erase head *see* Flying erase head.

Saticon tube An arsenic tellurium tube offering improved lag performance over conventional vidicon tubes.

Saturation The intensity of colour in an image.

SECAM Séquentiel Couleur à Mémoire. French colour TV system also adopted in Russia.

SEG *see* Special Effects Generator.

Shadow mask Screen inside conventional TV tubes through which electrons are passed to hit correctly coloured phosphors.

Shuttle-search *see* Picture-search.

Signal-to-noise ratio (S/N) The ratio between the video or audio signal and noise or interference. The higher the signal-to-noise ratio the better the quality.

Skew Tape tension. Incorrect skew results in distortion at the top of the picture.

Special Effects Generator (SEG) Unit in video production to mix, switch, or process video signals.

Spun glass Material clipped on the front of a lamp to diffuse the light.

Stripe filter A single-camera tube that can produce three-colour output.

Subcarrier The frequency on which colour information is modulated in a colour TV system: 4.43 MHz in UK/Europe, 3.58 MHz in USA/Japan.

Switcher A device for cutting from one video input to another.

Sync Synchronization. The vertical and horizontal pulses that co-ordinate the TV scanning system.

Tally light The light on a camera which indicates that it is in use at a given moment.

Target The face of a camera pick-up tube.

Tearing A distortion caused when horizontal sync is lost or distorted.

Telecine (film chain) The total system for transferring film on to video tape or on to a live-output video system.

Time-base corrector A device that corrects mechanical and electronic errors in a video system for purposes of transmission.

Time code A frame-by-frame time reference recorded on the spare track of a video tape.

UHF Ultra-High Frequency (300 to 3000 MHz). Also used to refer to coaxial cable connectors.

U-Matic Sony trade name referring to ¾-inch video cassette format.

V2000 (Video 2000) Philips ½-inch video cassette system.

Vertical sync The sync pulse which controls the field-by-field scanning of the target area.

VHF Very High Frequency. Commonly referred to as 30 to 300 MHz.

VHS Video Home System, the ½-inch cassette format developed by JVC.

Video Picture information. Also generic term for all matters televisual.

Video disc Replay system for pre-recorded video information on high-speed rotating disc. May be scanned electro-mechanically or optically.

Vidicon tube The most common pick-up tube used in TV cameras.

VU meter Volume Unit meter for measuring audio levels.

White balance The system for calibrating colour balance on a domestic colour camera.

Wipe The term in special effects when one image replaces another on the screen with a hard-edged boundary between the two.

Y The symbol for the luminous portion of a colour video signal.

Zoom lens A lens of variable focal length and therefore variable angle of view.

Bibliography

Audio and Video Recording, *David Kirk,* Faber and Faber

Beginner's Guide to Television, *Gordon King,* Newnes Technical Books

The Book of Movie Photography, *David Cheshire,* Ebury Press

The Complete Guide to Home Video, *Martin & Greenfield,* Harmony Books

The Complete Home Video Recorder Book, *Len Buckwalter,* Bantam Books

The Focal Encyclopedia of Film and Television Techniques, Focal Press

From Television to Home Computer, *ed. Angus Robertson,* Blandford Press

The Home Video Handbook, *Charles Bensinger,* Video-Info Publications

Sound with Vision: Sound Techniques for Television and Film, *Glyn Alkin,* Newnes Technical Books

The Technique of Lighting for Television and Motion Pictures, *Gerald Millerson,* Focal Press

The Techniques of Film Editing, *Karel Reisz and Gavin Millar,* Focal Press

Using Videotape, *Joseph Robinson and P. H. Beards,* Focal Press

Video Cassette Recorders, *Gerald McGinty,* McGraw-Hill

The Video Guide, *Charles Bensinger,* Video-Info Publications

The Video Primer, *Richard Robinson,* Quick Fox

Video Production Techniques, *ed. Hannen Foss,* Kluwer

Videotape Recording: Theory and Practice, *Joseph Robinson,* Focal Press

Index

Numbers in italics refer to illustrations and captions

Acknowledgements

We gratefully acknowledge the co-operation and assistance of the following for information, photographs, and loan of equipment:
JVC (UK) Ltd
Sony (UK) Ltd
Grundig International Ltd
National Panasonic (UK) Ltd
Matsushita Electric Industrial Co, Ltd
Technicolor Ltd
Hitachi Ltd
Prestel
Bib Audio/Video Products Ltd
Network Marketing Ltd
Infopress Ltd
Megasat Ltd
Sinclair/Daniel J. Edelman Ltd
Atari/Jaffe Young Advertising
Ray Hodges Associates
Jaybeam Ltd
Antiference Ltd
Bell & Howell A-V Ltd
Azat (London) Ltd
Keith Johnson Photographic Ltd
Keith Ewart of Ewart Television Ltd, London
Good Relations Group Ltd

Photographs on the following pages were specially taken for the book by
David Cheshire 26-7; 43; 45; 46-7; 79 (left); 80; 87 (six, bottom); 88; 89(Macro); 90-1; 92-3; 94-5; 96-7; 98-9; 100-1; 102-3; 104-5; 106-7; 110-11; 116-17; 125; 131; 132; 139 (top); 143; 145 (five); 146-7; 160-1; 162-3; 164-5; 167 (Diffusion filter, Graduated filter); 171; 175 (fiv
Stephanos Attalides 22; 120-1
© BBC 115
Michael Busselle 138; 140-1; 166
J. Allan Cash 126-7
Michael Freeman jacket (UK edn.);8-9; 36-7; 76-7; 108-9; 128-9; 178-9
Elizabeth Hollingsworth 139 (top); 145 (Romantic); 167 (Star filter, Multi-prism filter]
Bob Lamb 50; 87 (six, top); 89 (top) ; 118 – 19 124; 139 (bottom); 142; 172-3; 175 (bottom rig
193; 195; 197
Roger Phillips jacket (US edn.);6-7
François Prins 122-3
Mike Rose 69 (bottom right)
Anthony Wellar 20

We should also like to thank John Symonds fo technical advice and assistance.